THE TWISTED HISTORY OF THE GOP

Mike Luckovich

ECW

Two-time Pulitzer Prize–winning cartoonist

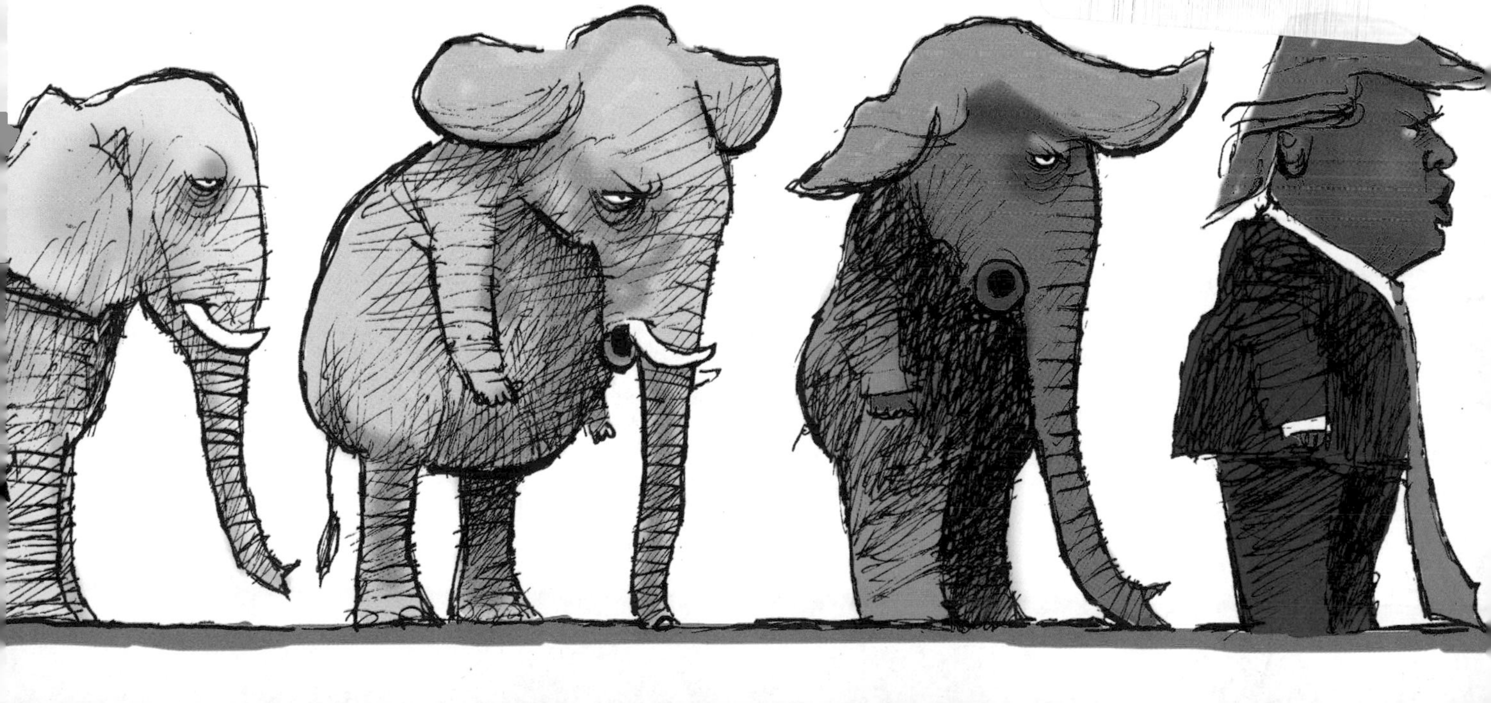

Published by ECW Press
665 Gerrard Street East
Toronto, Ontario, Canada M4M 1Y2
416-694-3348 / info@ecwpress.com

LIBRARY AND ARCHIVES CANADA CATALOGUING IN PUBLICATION

Title: The twisted history of the GOP / Mike Luckovich.

Names: Luckovich, Mike, 1960- author, artist.

Identifiers: Canadiana (print) 20220213410 | Canadiana (ebook) 20220213445

ISBN 978-1-77041-687-1 (softcover)
ISBN 978-1-77852-044-0 (ePub)
ISBN 978-1-77852-045-7 (PDF)
ISBN 978-1-77852-046-4 (Kindle)

Subjects: LCSH: Republican Party (U.S. : 1854-)—Caricatures and cartoons. | LCSH: Conservatives—United States—Caricatures and cartoons. | LCSH: American wit and humor, Pictorial. | LCSH: United States—Politics and government—1993-2001—Caricatures and cartoons. Classification: LCC E885 .L83 2022 | DDC 973.92902/07—dc23

PRINTING: FRIESENS 5 4 3 2 1
PRINTED AND BOUND IN CANADA

MIX
Paper from responsible sources
FSC® C016245

Table of Contents

Once upon a time, the Republican Party was a responsible member of our two-party system. But as America grew more diverse, Republicans began to see a future that wasn't bright for them. Instead of making itself into a 21st-century party that would attract more voters, the Republican Party doubled down on holding on to their dwindling white voter base by using Fox News and right-wing media to keep those voters scared and angry. Lately, Republicans have become even more brazen, promoting Trump's big lie that the 2020 election was stolen and using that as a pretext for rigging future elections in various states. Instead of offering solutions, they gave up governing and are only about rewarding their wealthy donors with tax cuts. The Republican Party has become a deformed image of itself, promoting lies and stupidity to their radicalized base, hoping to maintain power.

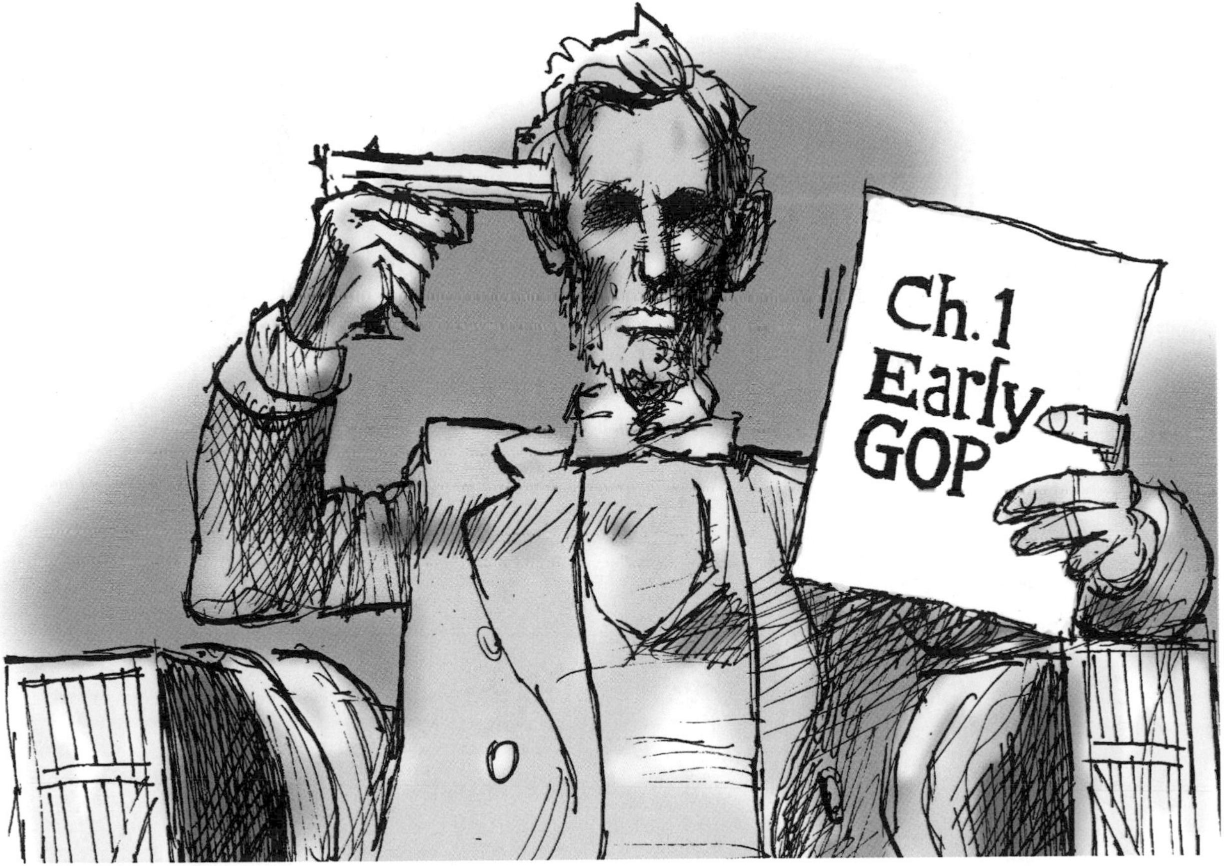
Ch. 1
Early
GOP

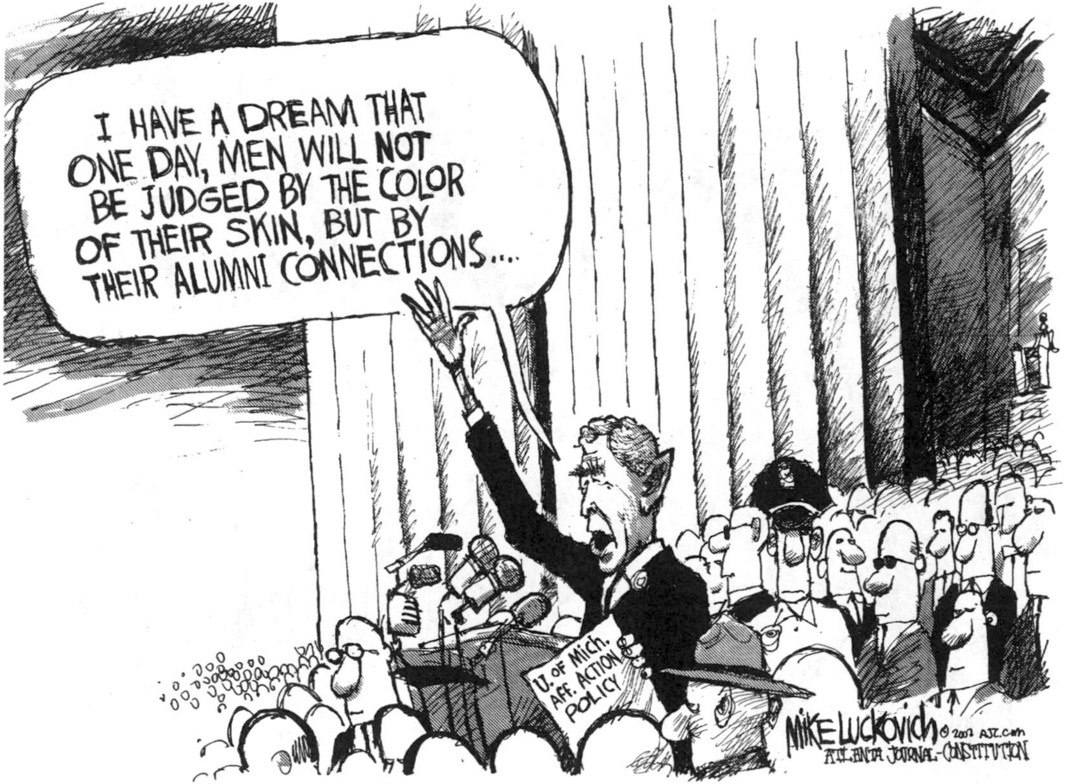
I HAVE A DREAM THAT ONE DAY, MEN WILL NOT BE JUDGED BY THE COLOR OF THEIR SKIN, BUT BY THEIR ALUMNI CONNECTIONS....
U. OF Mich. AFF. ACTION POLICY
MIKE LUCKOVICH © 2003 AJC.com
ATLANTA JOURNAL-CONSTITUTION

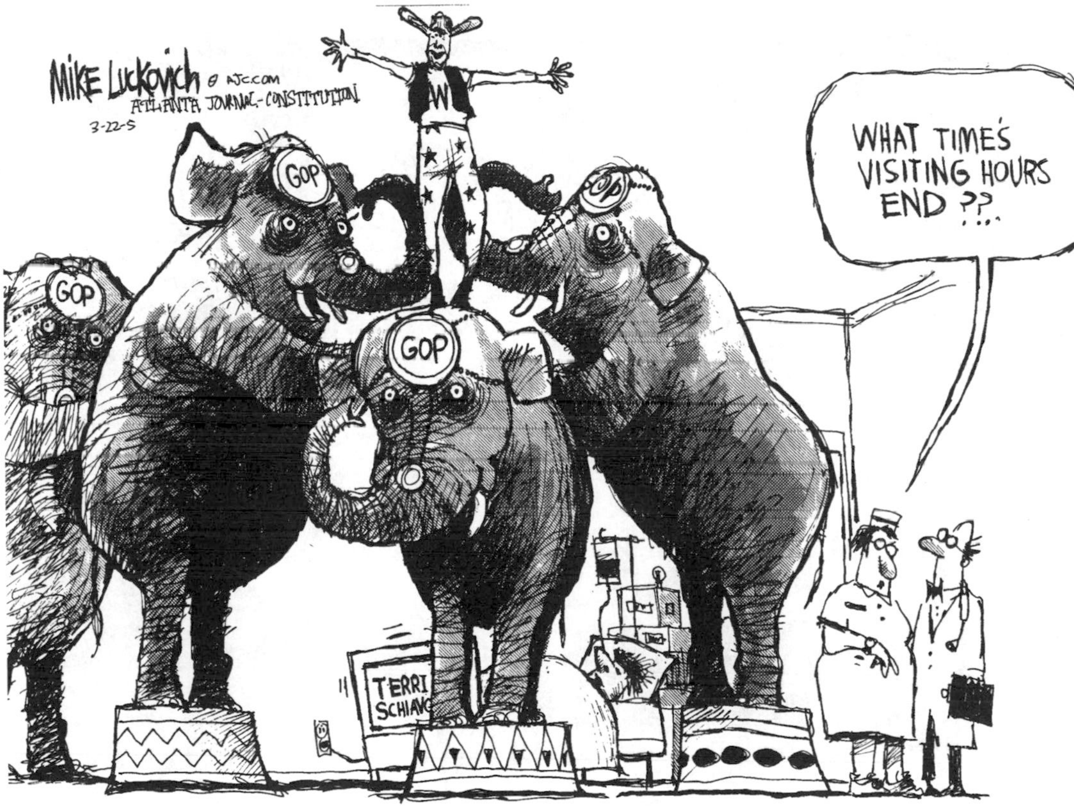
MIKE LUCKOVICH © AJC.COM
ATLANTA JOURNAL-CONSTITUTION
3-22-5
GOP
GOP
GOP
W
TERRI SCHIAVO
WHAT TIME'S VISITING HOURS END ??...

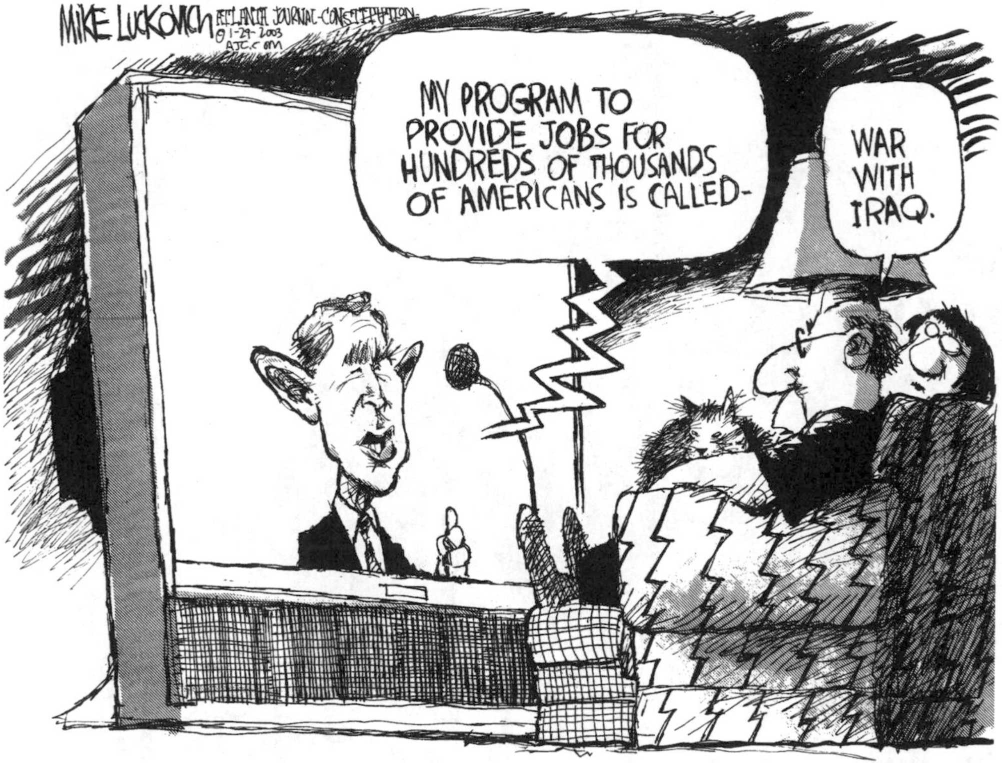
MIKE LUCKOVICH ATLANTA JOURNAL-CONSTITUTION ©1-29-2003 AJC.COM
MY PROGRAM TO PROVIDE JOBS FOR HUNDREDS OF THOUSANDS OF AMERICANS IS CALLED-
WAR WITH IRAQ.

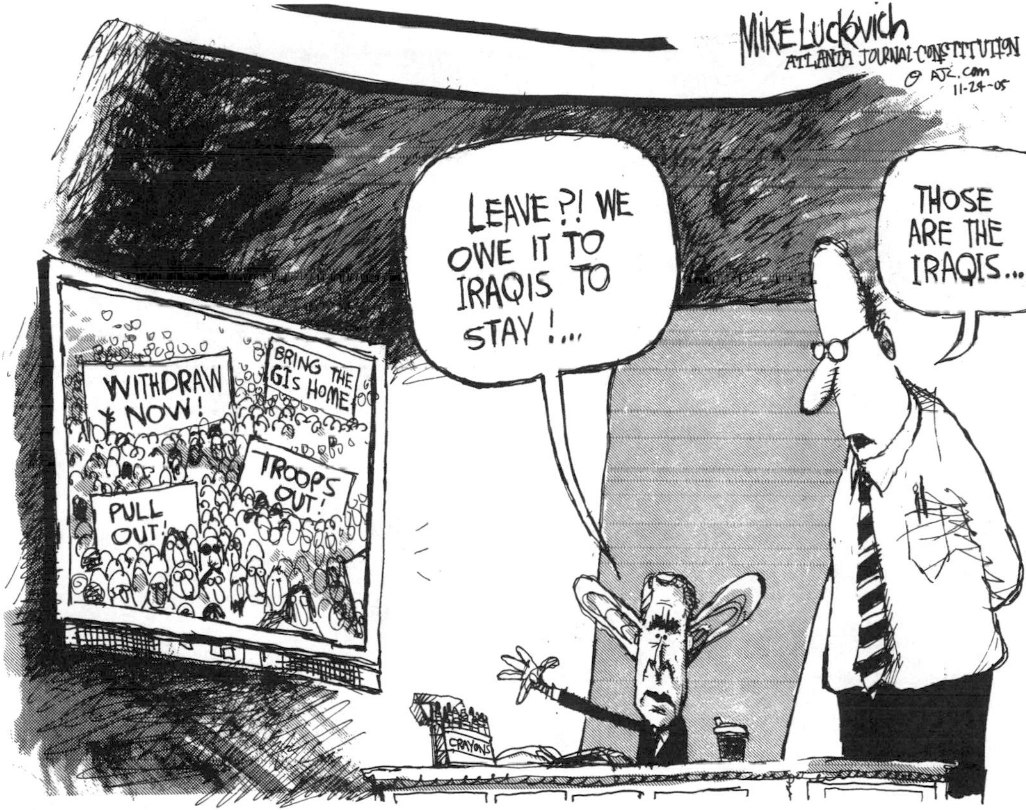
MIKE LUCKOVICH
ATLANTA JOURNAL-CONSTITUTION
© AJC.com
11-24-05
WITHDRAW NOW!
BRING THE GIs HOME
TROOPS OUT!
PULL OUT!
CRAYONS
LEAVE?! WE OWE IT TO IRAQIS TO STAY!...
THOSE ARE THE IRAQIS....

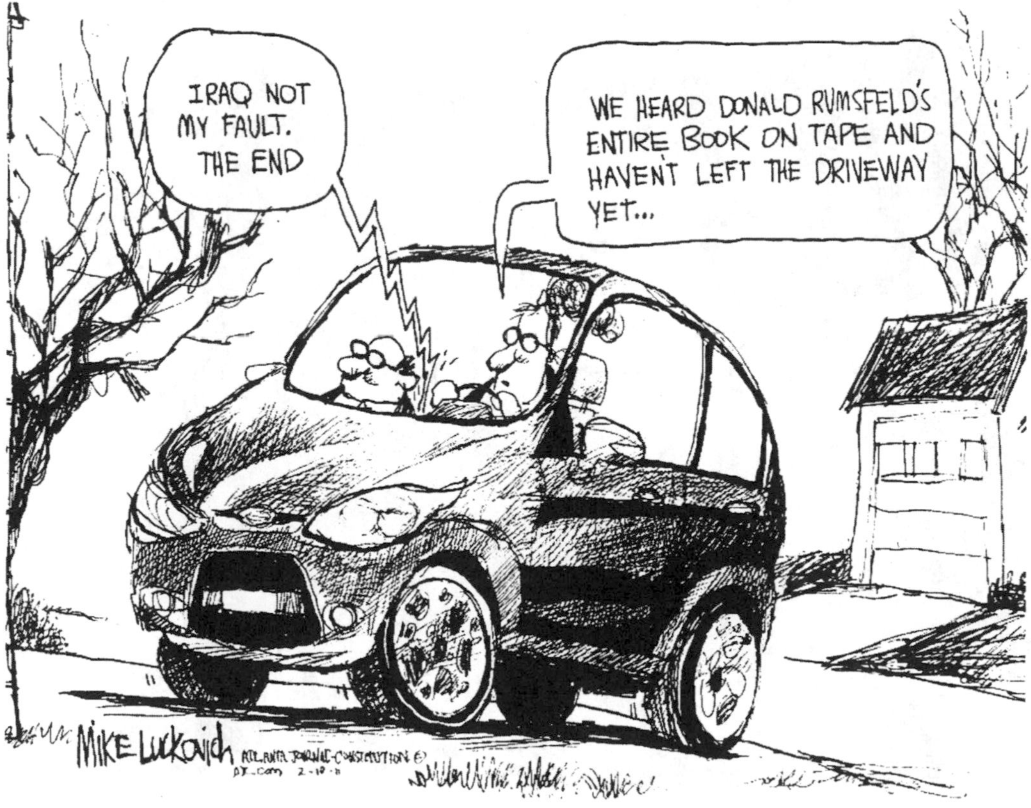
IRAQ NOT MY FAULT. THE END
WE HEARD DONALD RUMSFELD'S ENTIRE BOOK ON TAPE AND HAVEN'T LEFT THE DRIVEWAY YET...
MIKE LUCKOVICH

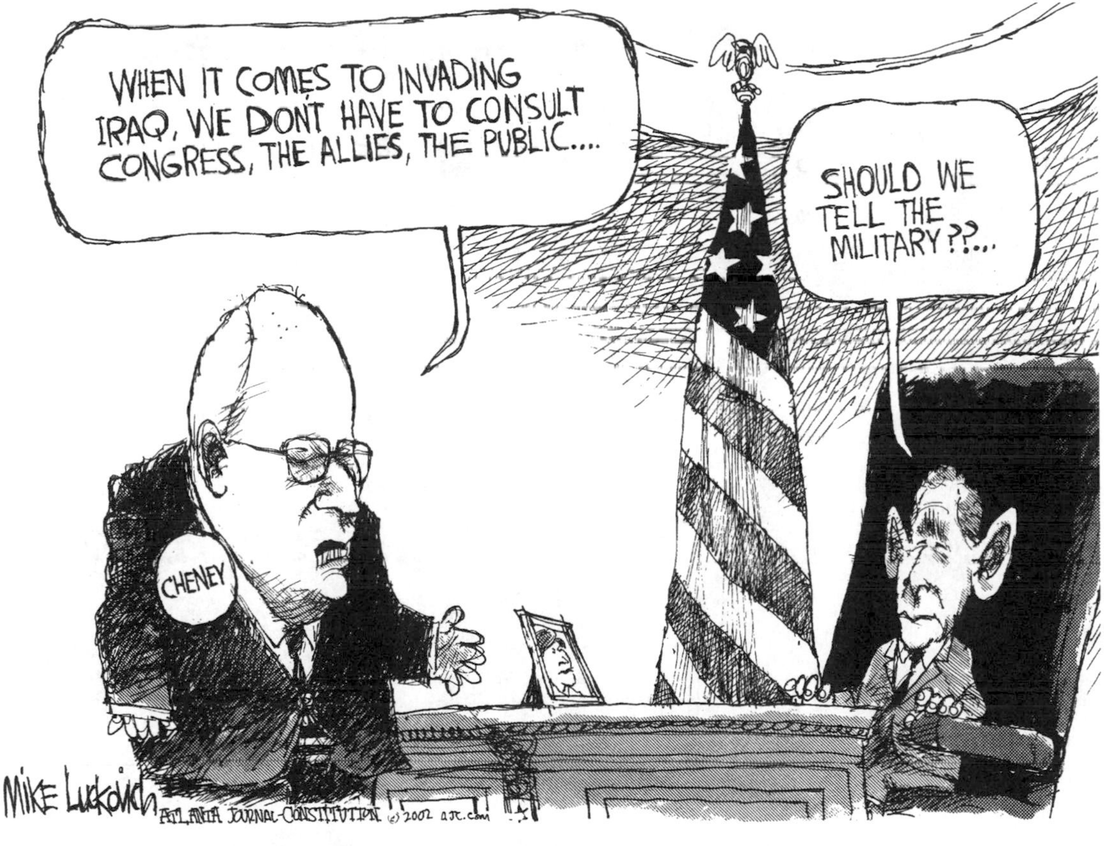
WHEN IT COMES TO INVADING IRAQ, WE DON'T HAVE TO CONSULT CONGRESS, THE ALLIES, THE PUBLIC....
SHOULD WE TELL THE MILITARY??...
CHENEY
MIKE LUCKOVICH ATLANTA JOURNAL-CONSTITUTION (c) 2002 ajc.com

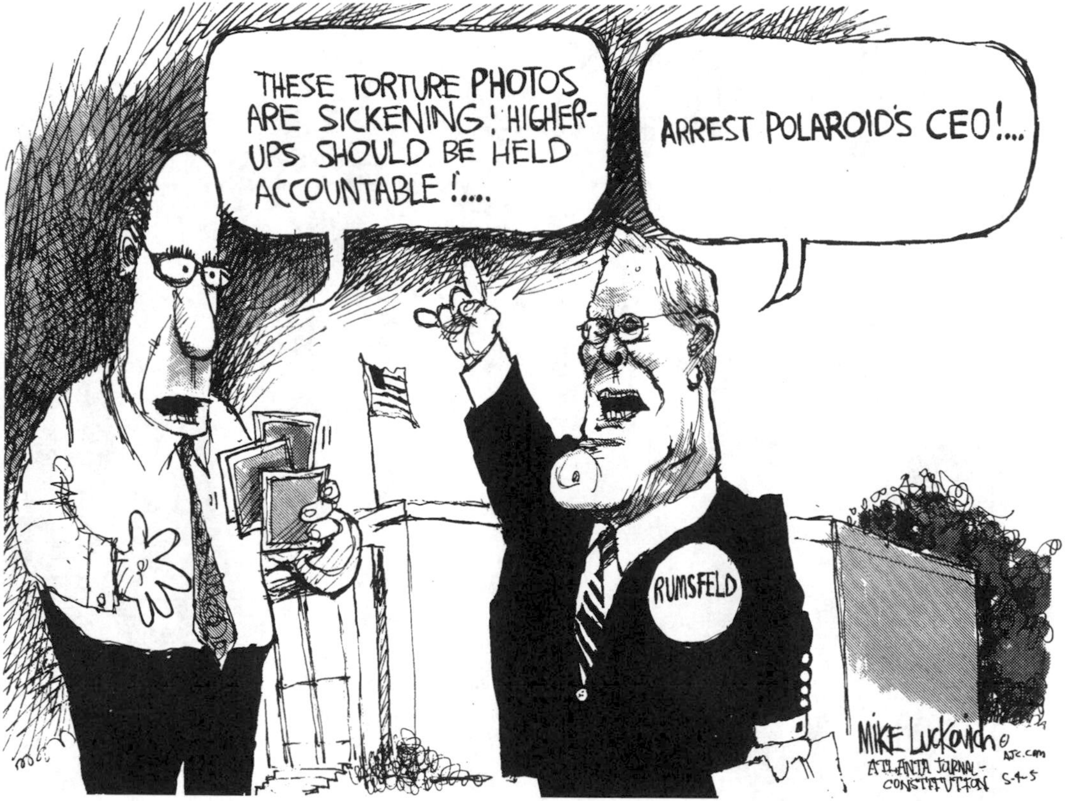
THESE TORTURE PHOTOS ARE SICKENING! HIGHER-UPS SHOULD BE HELD ACCOUNTABLE !....
ARREST POLAROID'S CEO!...
RUMSFELD
MIKE Luckovich
AJC.com
ATLANTA JOURNAL-CONSTITUTION
5-4-5

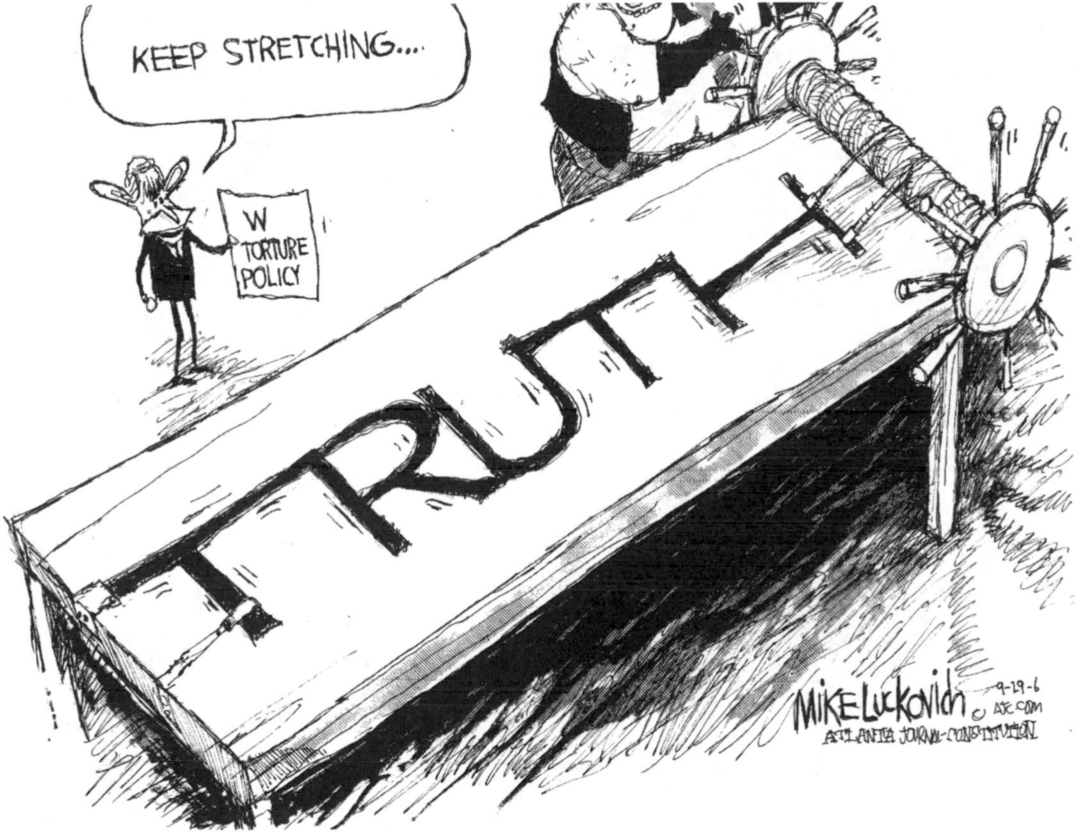
KEEP STRETCHING....
W
TORTURE
POLICY
TRUTH
MIKE LUCKOVICH
9-29-6
© AJC.COM
ATLANTA JOURNAL-CONSTITUTION

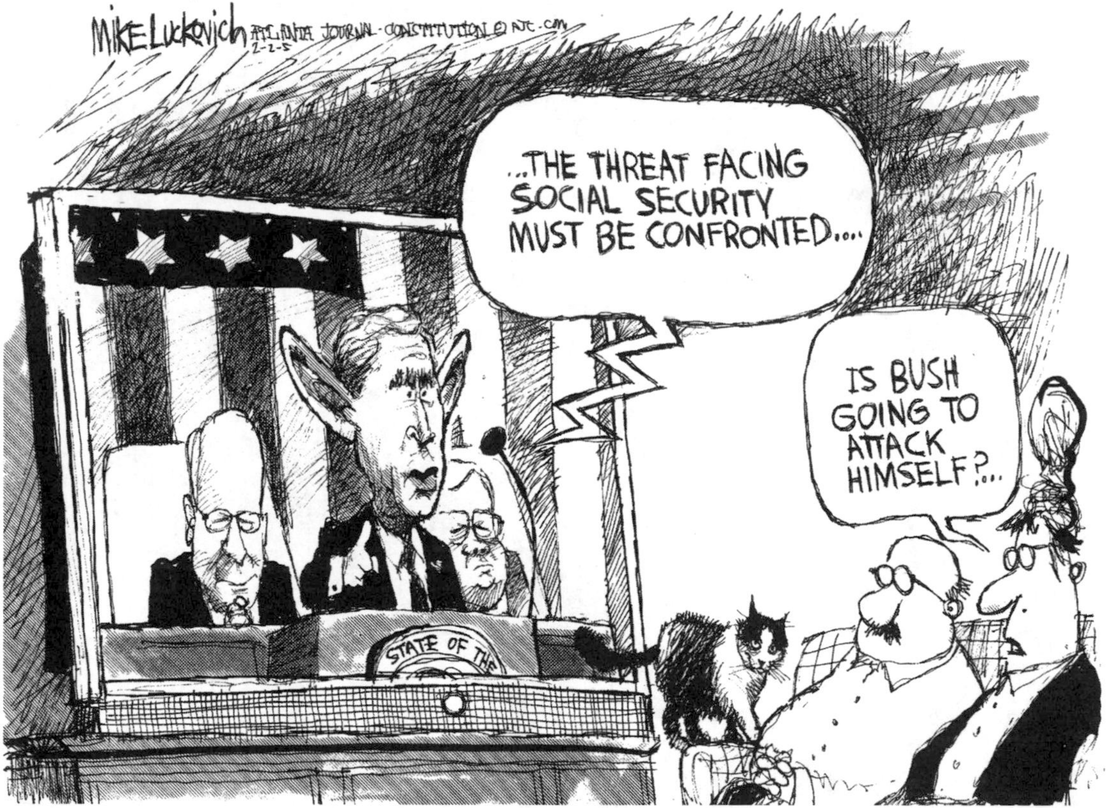
MIKE LUCKOVICH
...THE THREAT FACING SOCIAL SECURITY MUST BE CONFRONTED....
IS BUSH GOING TO ATTACK HIMSELF?...
STATE OF THE

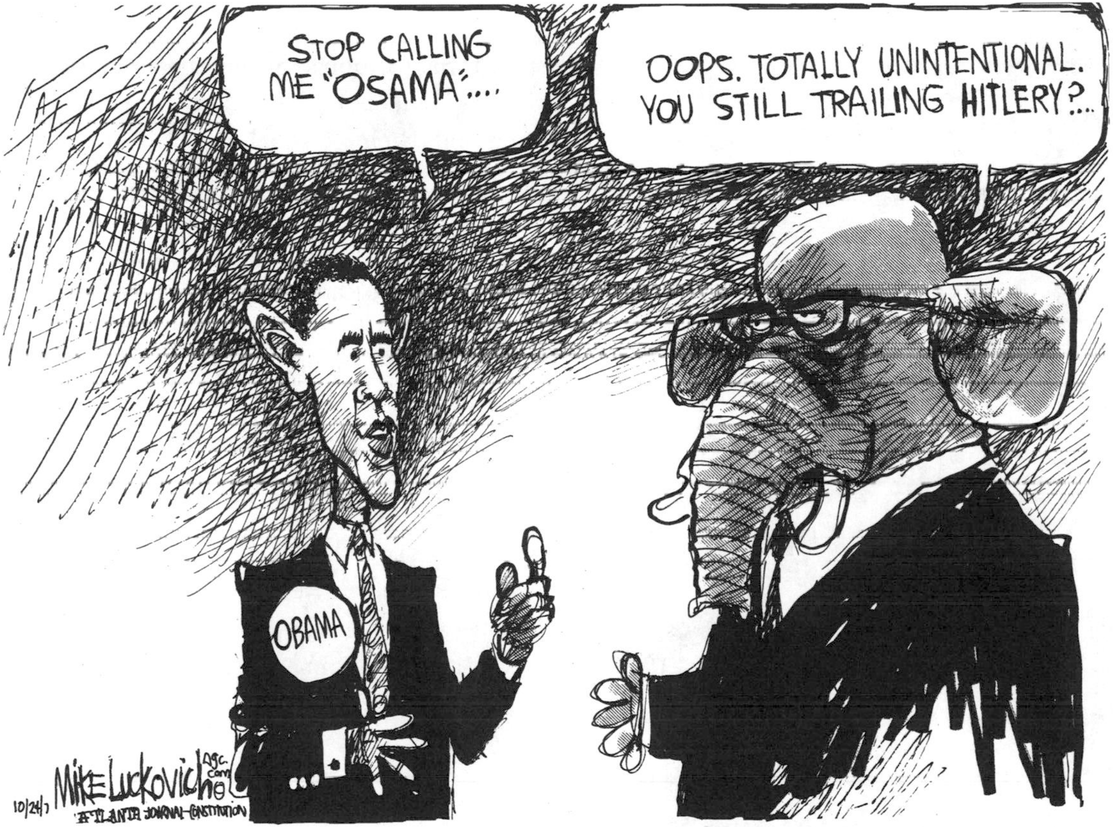
STOP CALLING ME "OSAMA"....
OOPS. TOTALLY UNINTENTIONAL. YOU STILL TRAILING HITLERY?...
OBAMA
MIKE LUCKOVICH
10/24/7
ATLANTA JOURNAL-CONSTITUTION

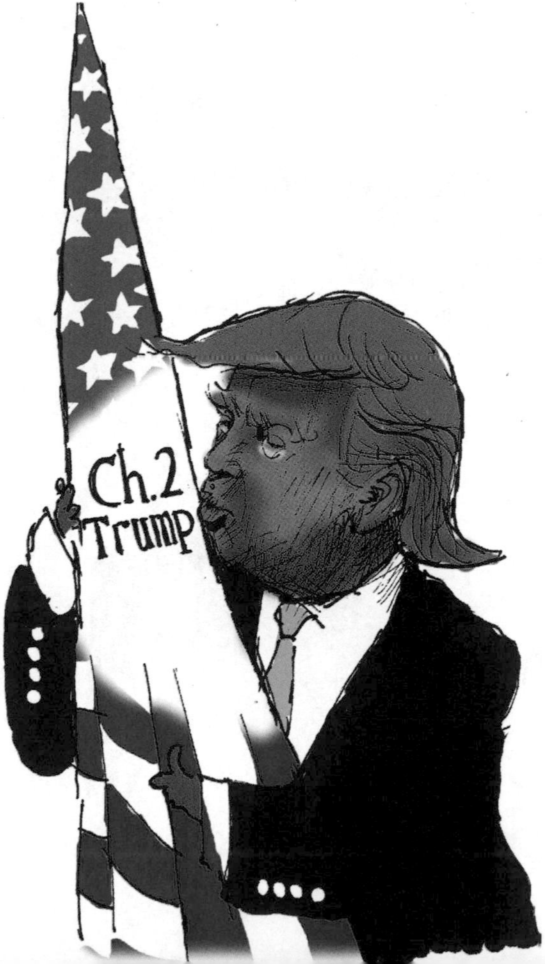
Ch.2
Trump

As an editorial cartoonist during the Trump presidency, I was forced to focus on his daily crazy nonsense. It was very stressful waking up each day and wondering what he was up to. Every six months during his presidency, my wife and I escaped to Paris to get some relief. I'd wonder what Parisians thought of us during those visits, knowing that America had elected a nut. I made sure to wear an Obama ball cap to signal we hadn't voted for the orange fool. I thought that after Biden's election America would start to regain respect in the world, but sadly things seem to have gotten worse. Trump's gone, but Trumpism lives. The big lie that the election was stolen continues. On January 6, 2021, a mob of fascist Trump-loving goons stormed the U.S. Capitol, seeking to overturn his defeat. Republicans are still in the thrall of this mentally ill doofus. I'm so embarrassed for my country that the next time we go back to Paris, so they won't suspect we're Americans, I'm wearing a beret and carrying a baguette.

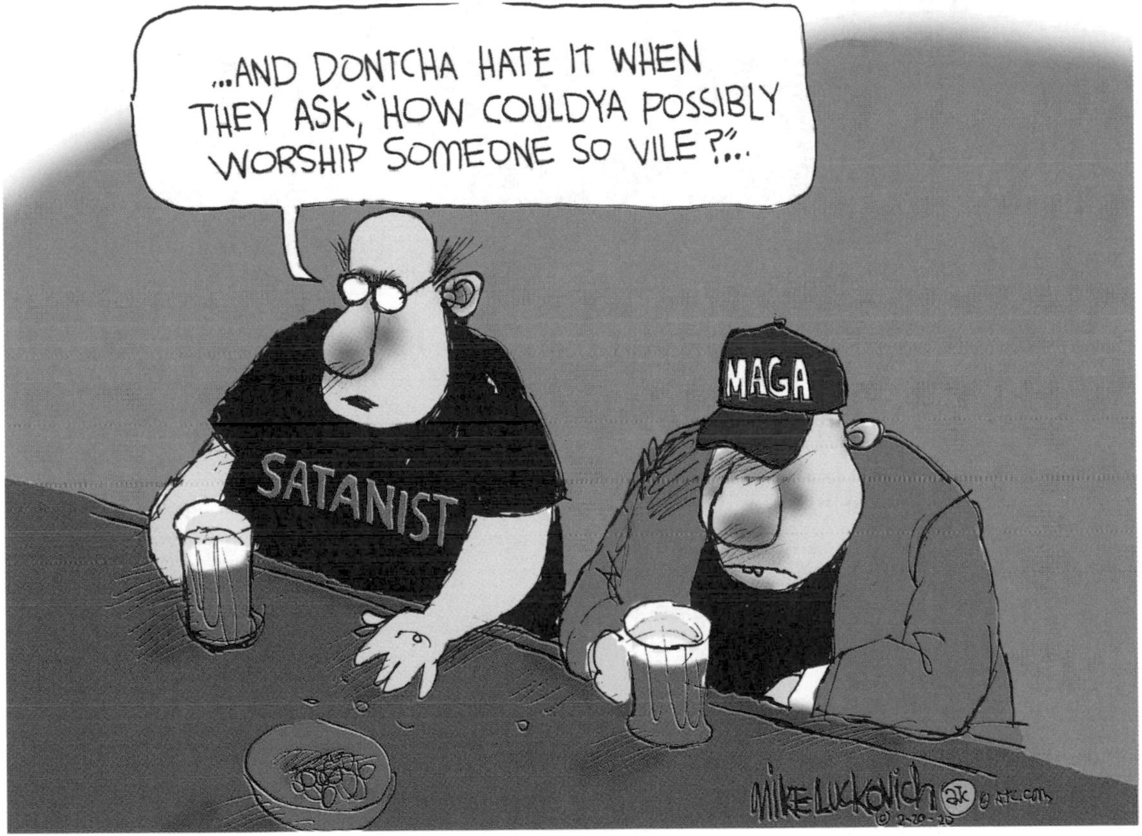
...AND DONTCHA HATE IT WHEN THEY ASK, "HOW COULDYA POSSIBLY WORSHIP SOMEONE SO VILE?"...
SATANIST
MAGA
MIKE LUCKOVICH

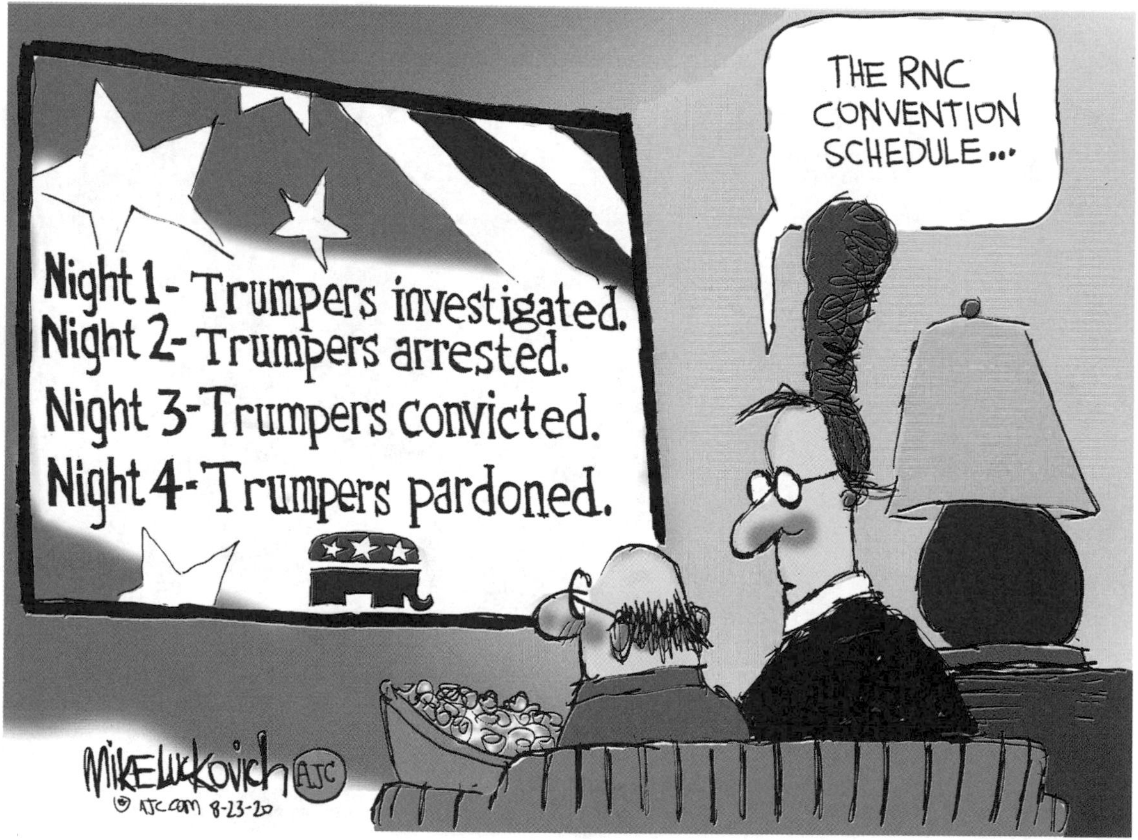
Night 1- Trumpers investigated.
Night 2- Trumpers arrested.
Night 3-Trumpers convicted.
Night 4-Trumpers pardoned.
THE RNC CONVENTION SCHEDULE...
MIKELUCKOVICH AJC
© AJC.COM 8-23-20

REMEMBER, IF I LOSE, THIS RACE IS RIGGED!..
USA
MIKELUCKOVICH
AJC.com 8-9-16 ©

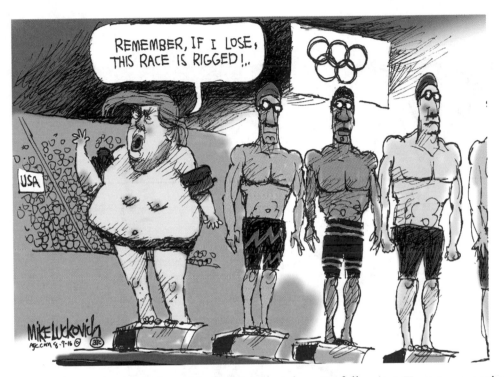

During the 2016 Summer Olympics, with the presidential race in full swing, Trump was saying that if he lost the election against Hillary, it would be because it was rigged. So, I did this cartoon. Back in 2016, he was claiming that the election had been stolen even before it happened. It boggles my mind that he followed his same shallow playbook to claim a rigged election once again in 2020 and that so many gullible Americans continue to believe his bullshit.

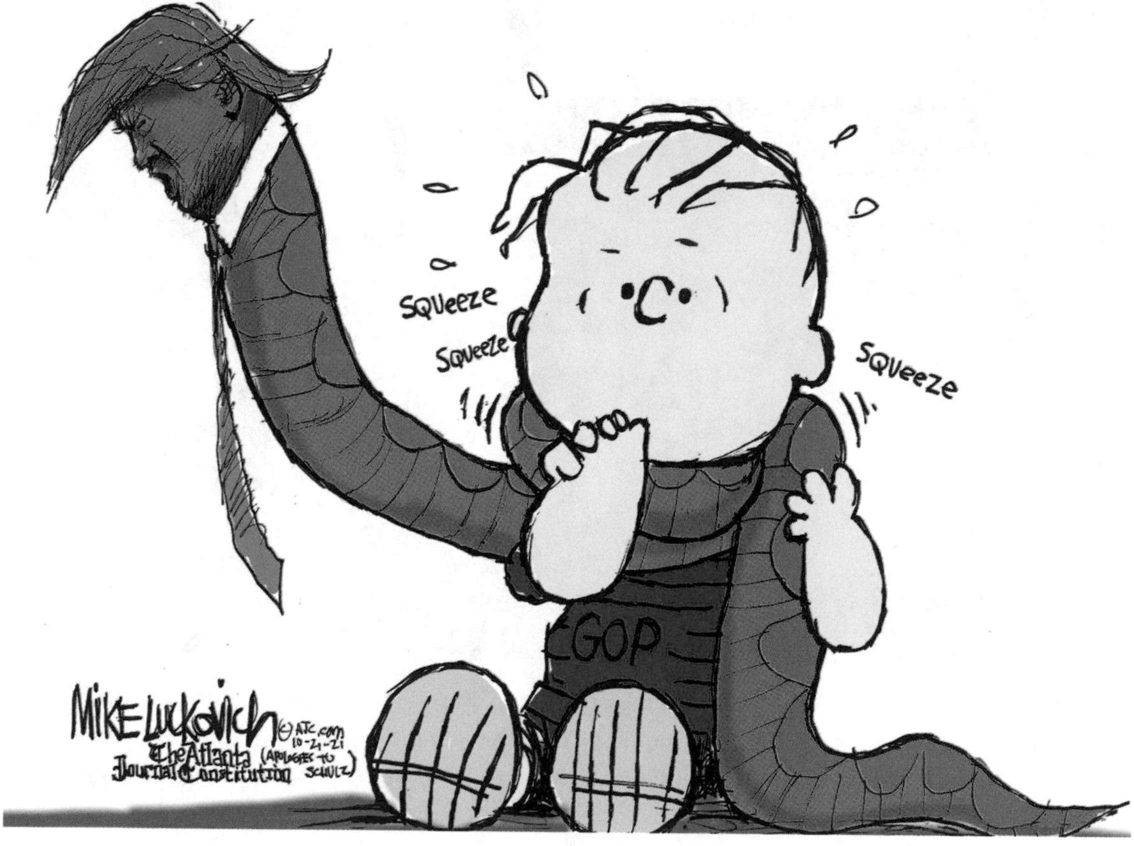
SQUEEZE
SQUEEZE
SQUEEZE
GOP
MIKE LUCKOVICH ©AJC.com 10-21-21
The Atlanta Journal Constitution
(APOLOGIES TO SCHULZ)

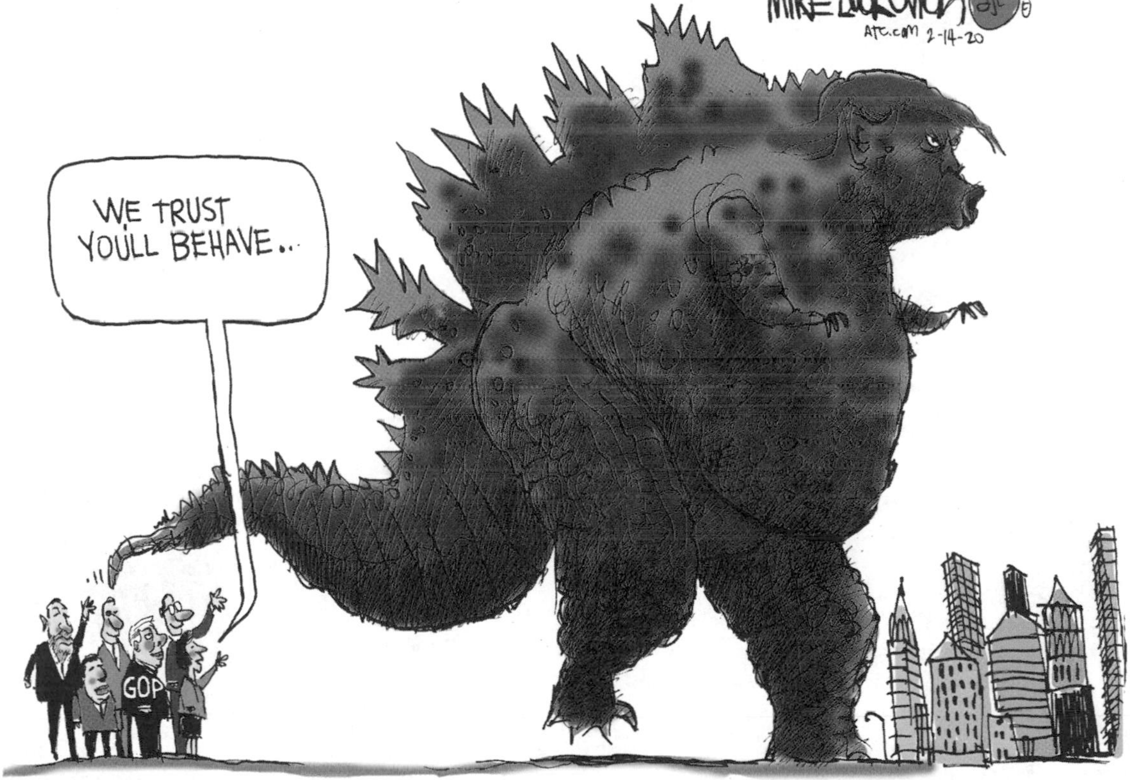
MIKE LUCKOVICH AJC
AJC.COM 2-14-20
WE TRUST YOU'LL BEHAVE...
GOP

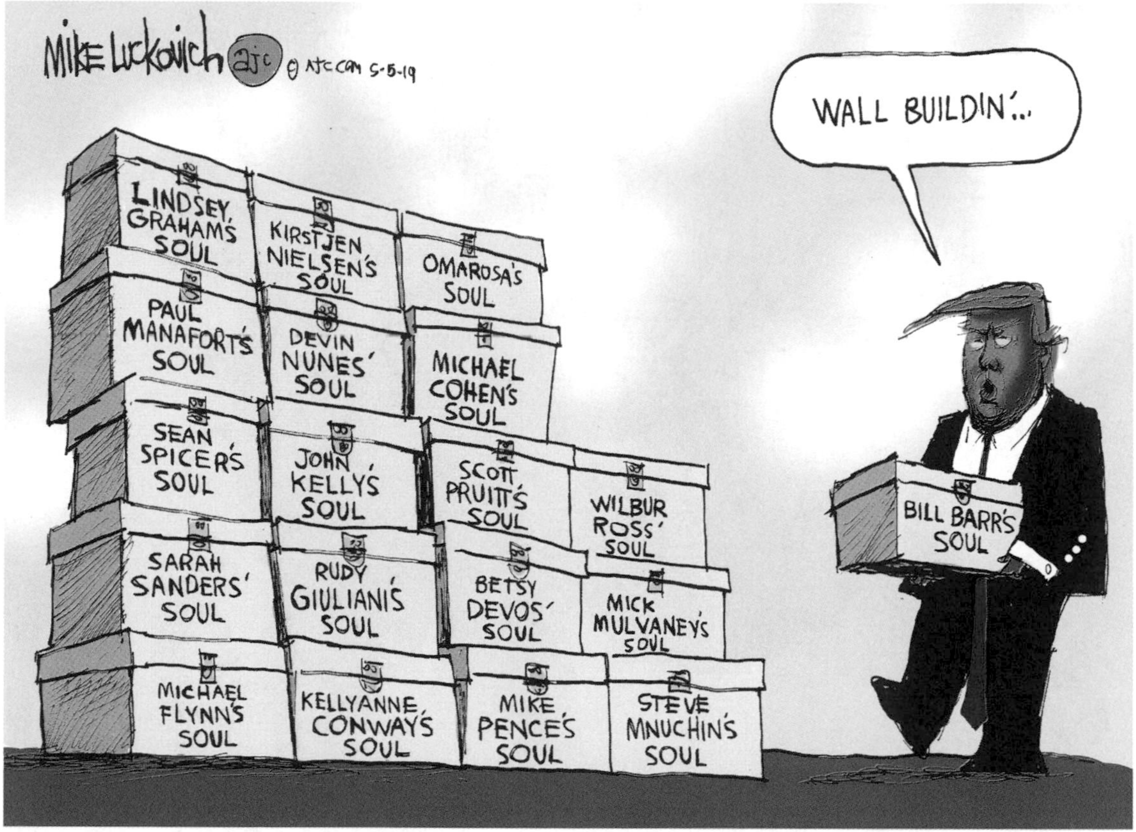
MIKE LUCKOVICH ajc © AJC.COM 5-5-19
WALL BUILDIN'...
LINDSEY GRAHAM'S SOUL
KIRSTJEN NIELSEN'S SOUL
OMAROSA'S SOUL
PAUL MANAFORT'S SOUL
DEVIN NUNES' SOUL
MICHAEL COHEN'S SOUL
SEAN SPICER'S SOUL
JOHN KELLY'S SOUL
SCOTT PRUITT'S SOUL
WILBUR ROSS' SOUL
SARAH SANDERS' SOUL
RUDY GIULIANI'S SOUL
BETSY DEVOS' SOUL
MICK MULVANEY'S SOUL
MICHAEL FLYNN'S SOUL
KELLYANNE CONWAY'S SOUL
MIKE PENCE'S SOUL
STEVE MNUCHIN'S SOUL
BILL BARR'S SOUL

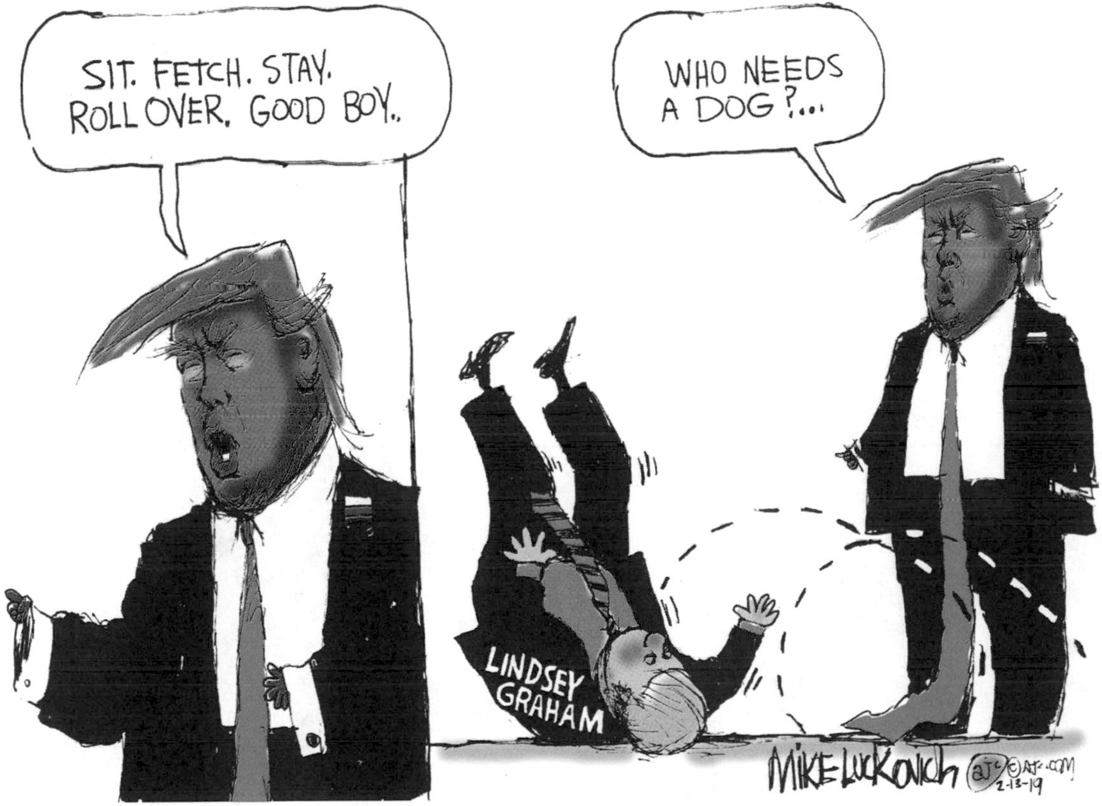
SIT. FETCH. STAY.
ROLL OVER. GOOD BOY..
WHO NEEDS
A DOG?....
LINDSEY
GRAHAM
MIKE LUCKOVICH
2-13-19

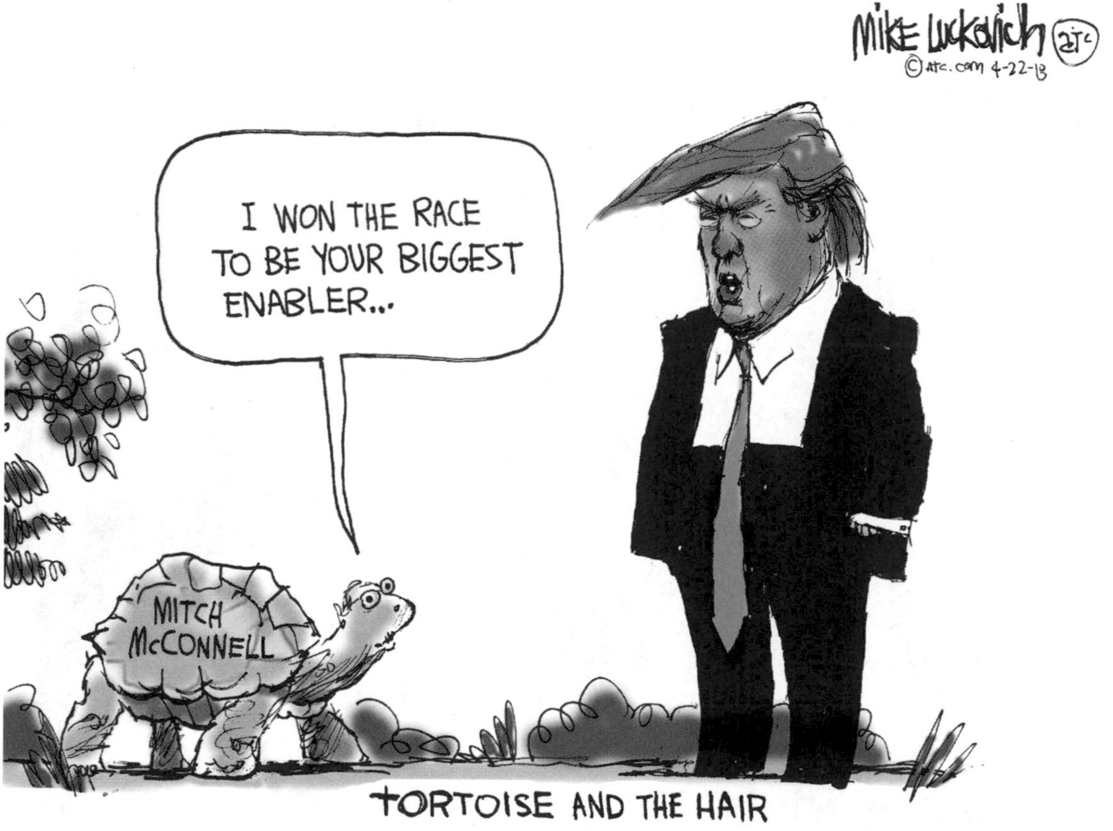
MIKE LUCKOVICH
©AJC.com 4-22-18
I WON THE RACE TO BE YOUR BIGGEST ENABLER...
MITCH McCONNELL
TORTOISE AND THE HAIR

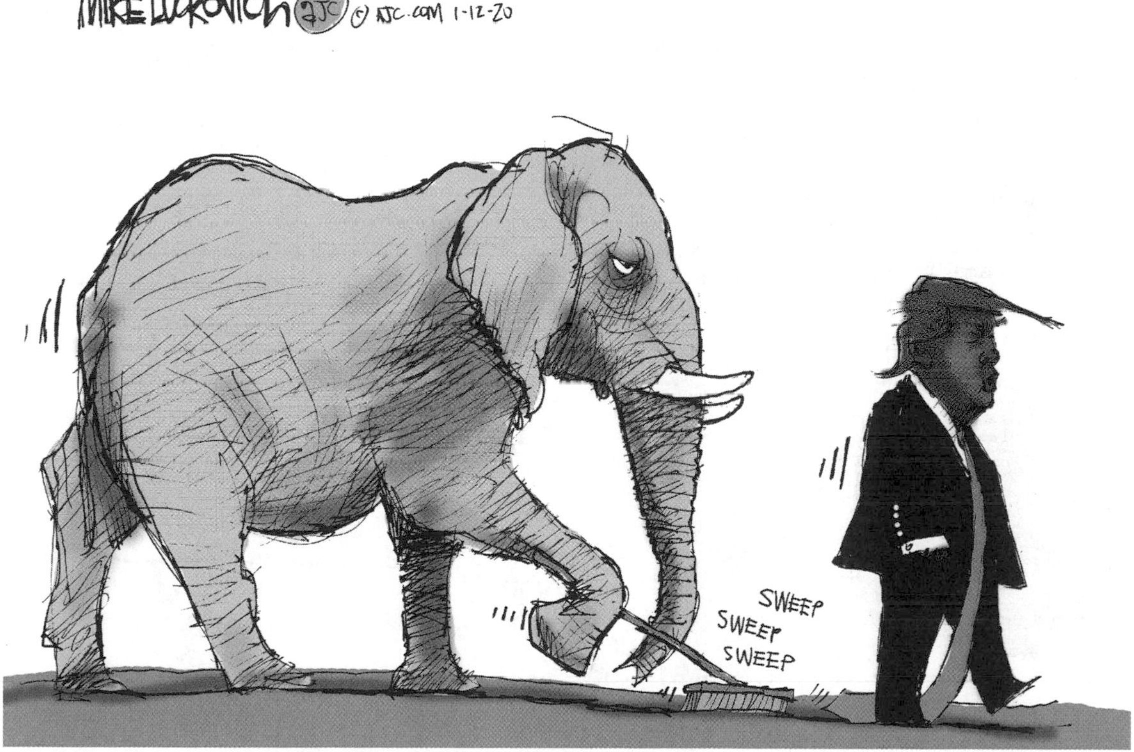
MIKE LUCKOVICH AJC © AJC.COM 1-12-20
SWEEP
SWEEP
SWEEP

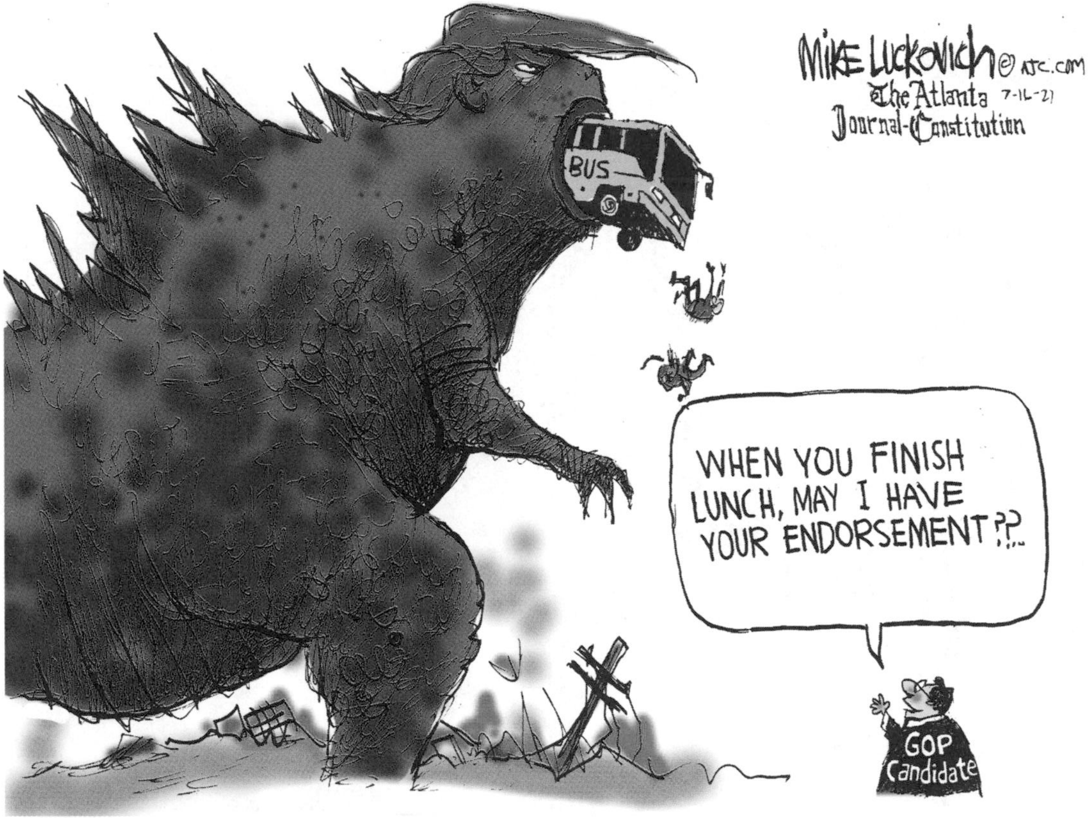
MIKE LUCKOVICH © AJC.COM
The Atlanta Journal-Constitution 7-16-21
BUS
WHEN YOU FINISH LUNCH, MAY I HAVE YOUR ENDORSEMENT?!?..
GOP Candidate

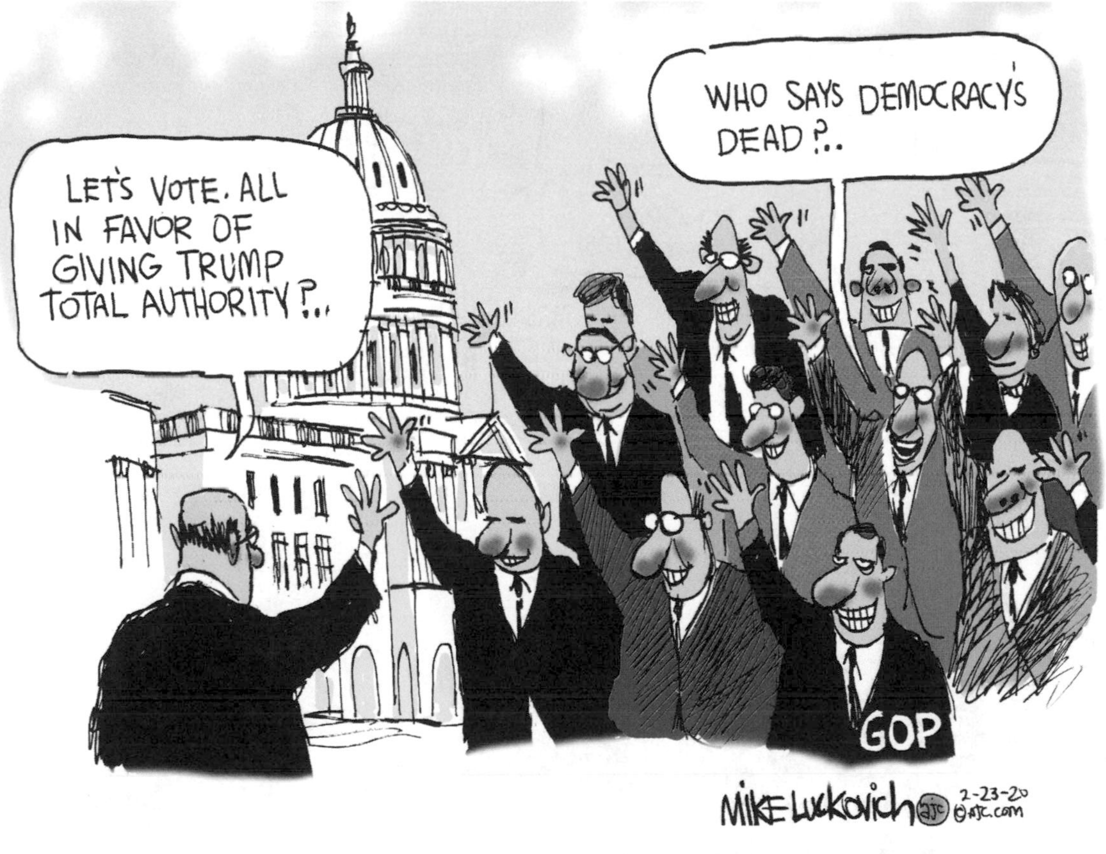
LET'S VOTE. ALL IN FAVOR OF GIVING TRUMP TOTAL AUTHORITY?..
WHO SAYS DEMOCRACY'S DEAD?..
GOP
MIKE LUCKOVICH ajc 2-23-20 ©ajc.com

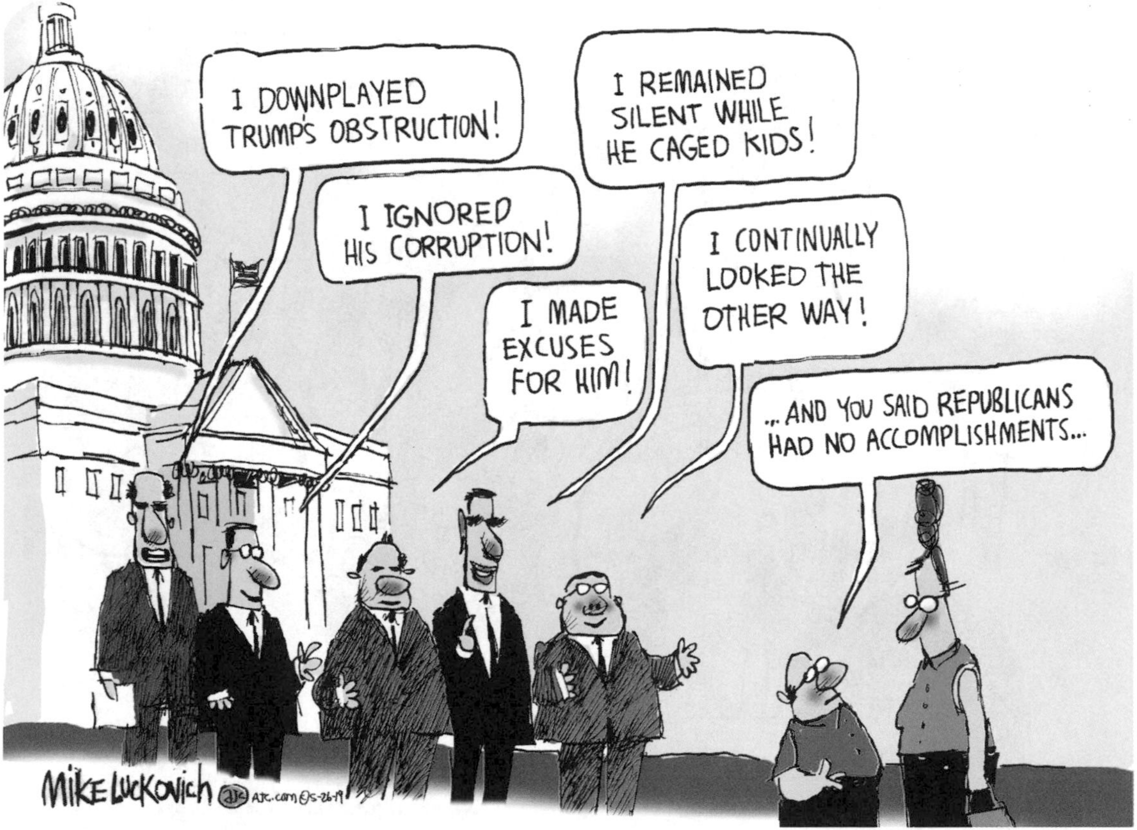
I DOWNPLAYED TRUMP'S OBSTRUCTION!
I IGNORED HIS CORRUPTION!
I MADE EXCUSES FOR HIM!
I REMAINED SILENT WHILE HE CAGED KIDS!
I CONTINUALLY LOOKED THE OTHER WAY!
...AND YOU SAID REPUBLICANS HAD NO ACCOMPLISHMENTS...
MIKE LUCKOVICH AJC.com ©5-26-19

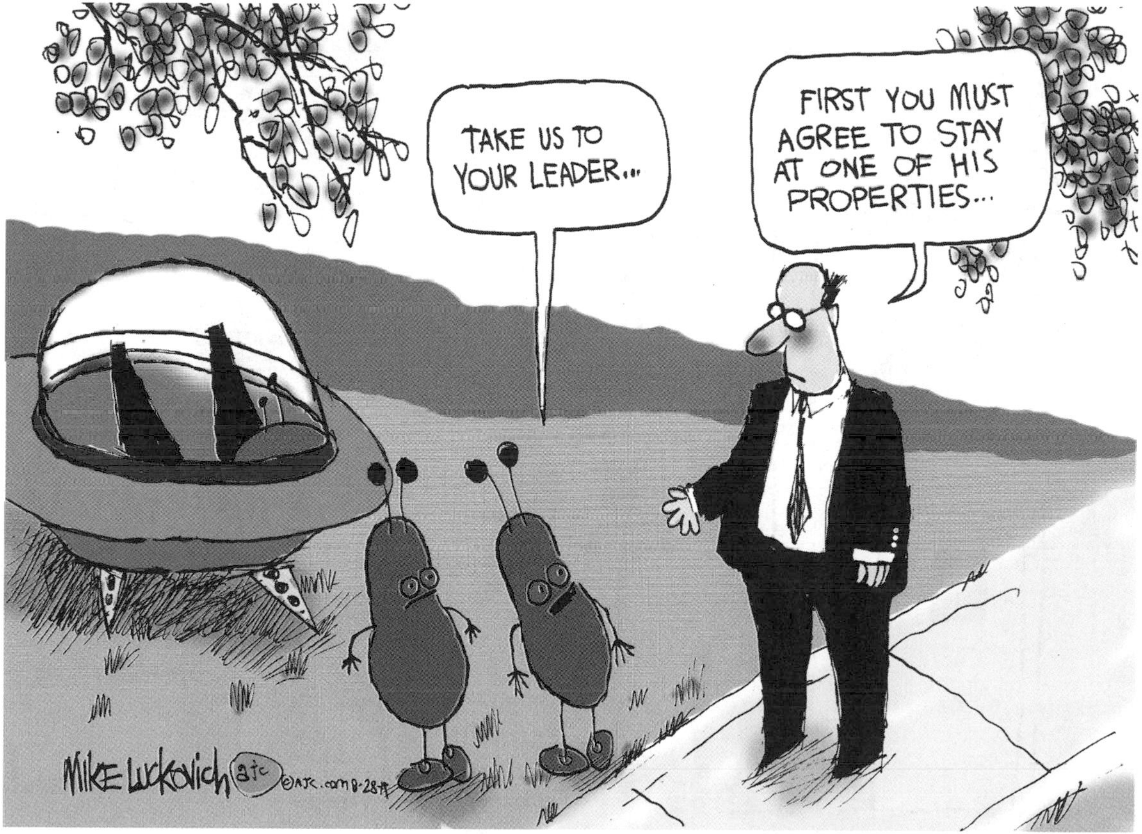
TAKE US TO YOUR LEADER...
FIRST YOU MUST AGREE TO STAY AT ONE OF HIS PROPERTIES...
MIKE LUCKOVICH

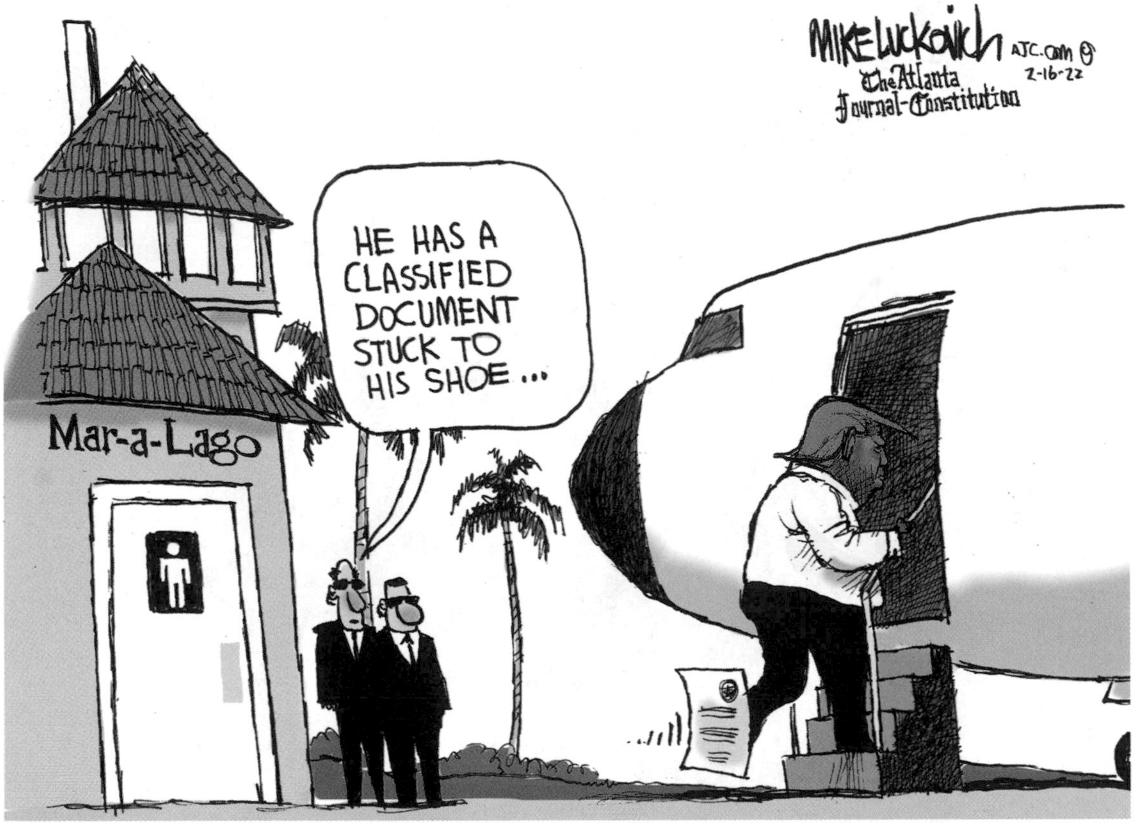
MIKE LUCKOVICH AJC.com ©
The Atlanta Journal-Constitution
2-16-22
HE HAS A CLASSIFIED DOCUMENT STUCK TO HIS SHOE...
Mar-a-Lago

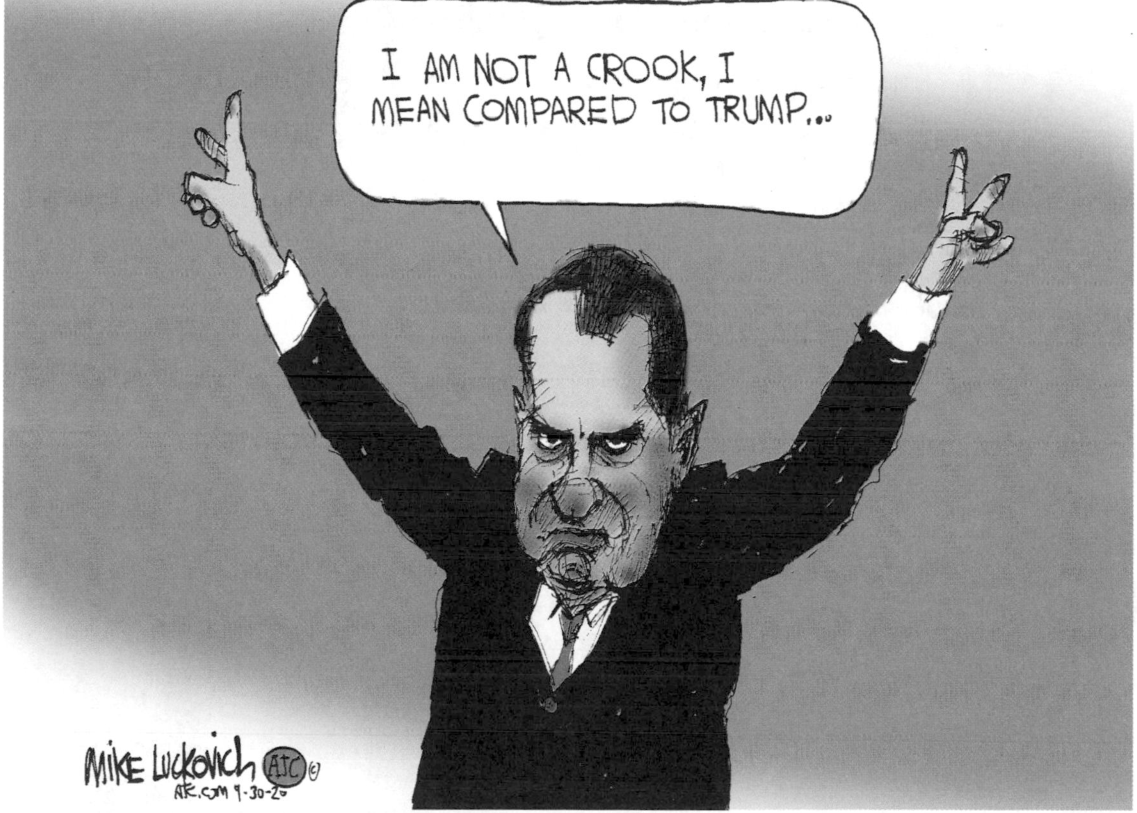
I AM NOT A CROOK, I MEAN COMPARED TO TRUMP...
MIKE LUCKOVICH AJC ©
AJC.COM 9-30-20

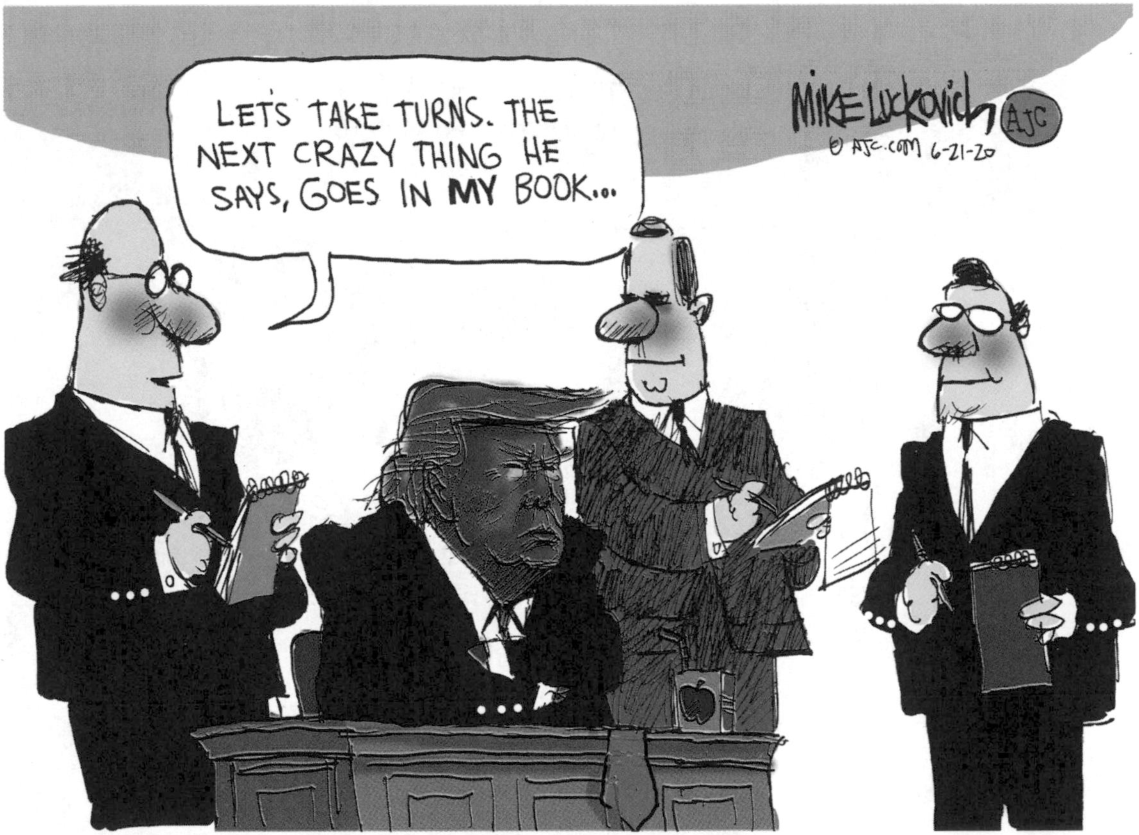
LET'S TAKE TURNS. THE NEXT CRAZY THING HE SAYS, GOES IN **MY** BOOK...
MIKE LUCKOVICH
AJC
© AJC.com 6-21-20

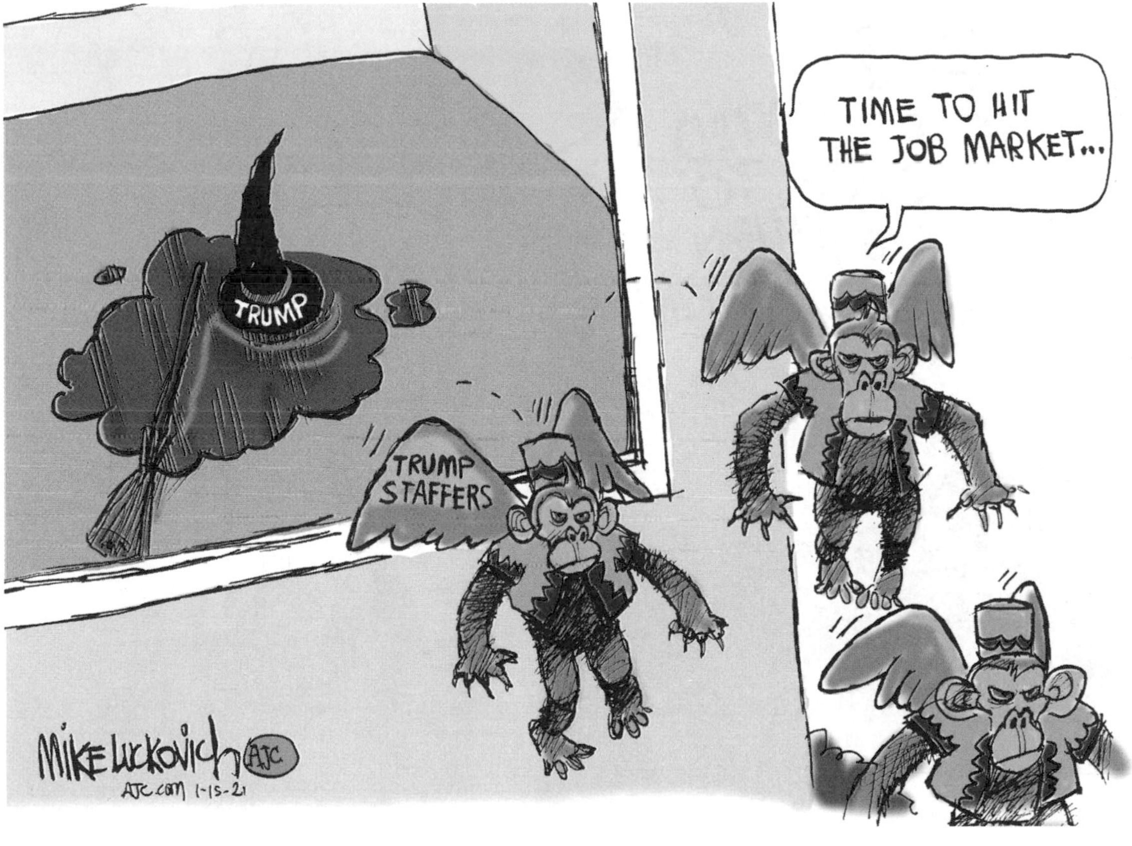
TIME TO HIT THE JOB MARKET...
TRUMP
TRUMP STAFFERS
MIKE LUCKOVICH AJC
AJC.com 1-15-21

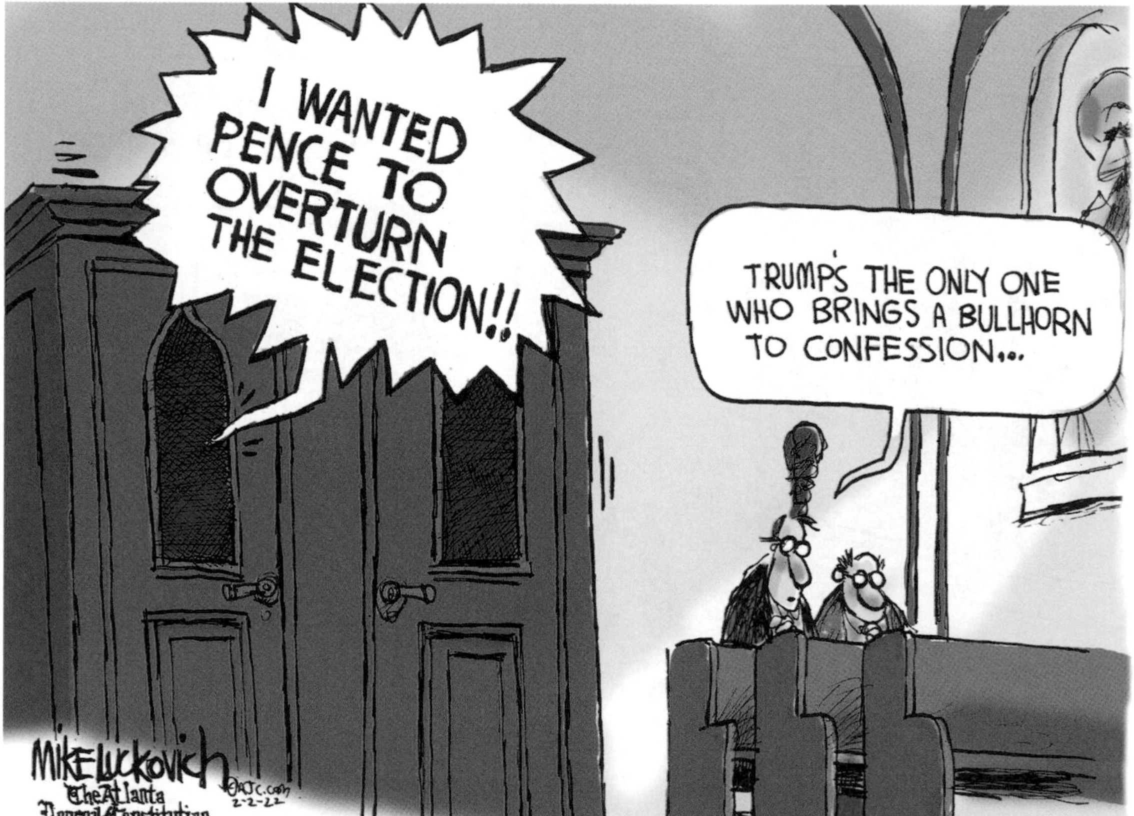
I WANTED PENCE TO OVERTURN THE ELECTION!!
TRUMP'S THE ONLY ONE WHO BRINGS A BULLHORN TO CONFESSION...
MIKE LUCKOVICH
The Atlanta Journal-Constitution
2-2-22

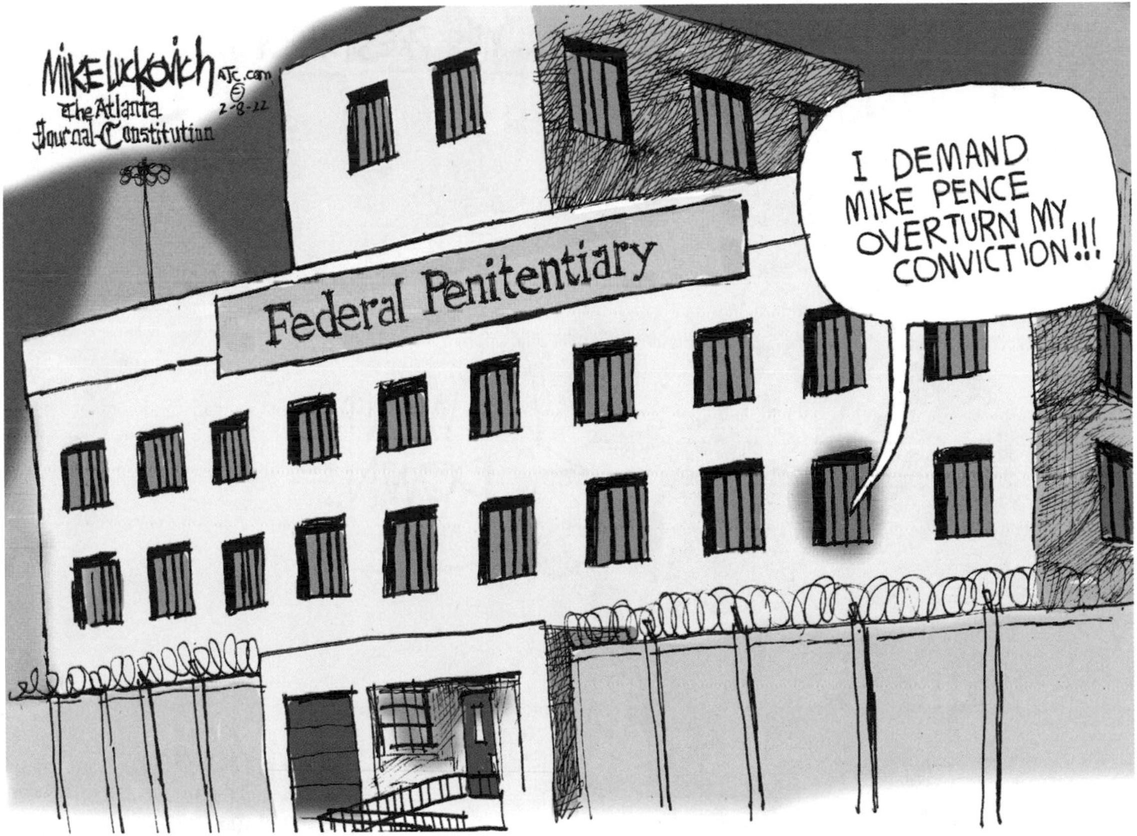
MIKE LUCKOVICH AJC.com © 2-8-22
The Atlanta Journal-Constitution
Federal Penitentiary
I DEMAND MIKE PENCE OVERTURN MY CONVICTION!!!

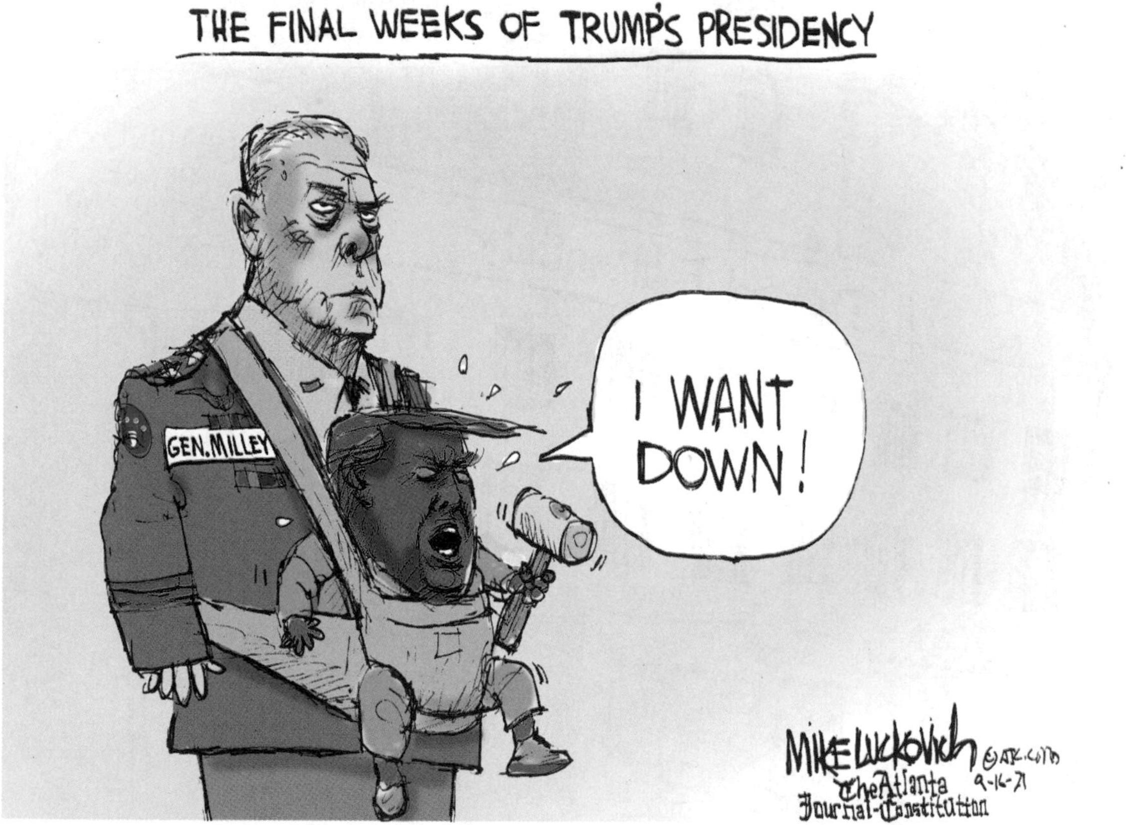
THE FINAL WEEKS OF TRUMP'S PRESIDENCY
GEN. MILLEY
I WANT DOWN!
MIKE LUCKOVICH
The Atlanta Journal-Constitution

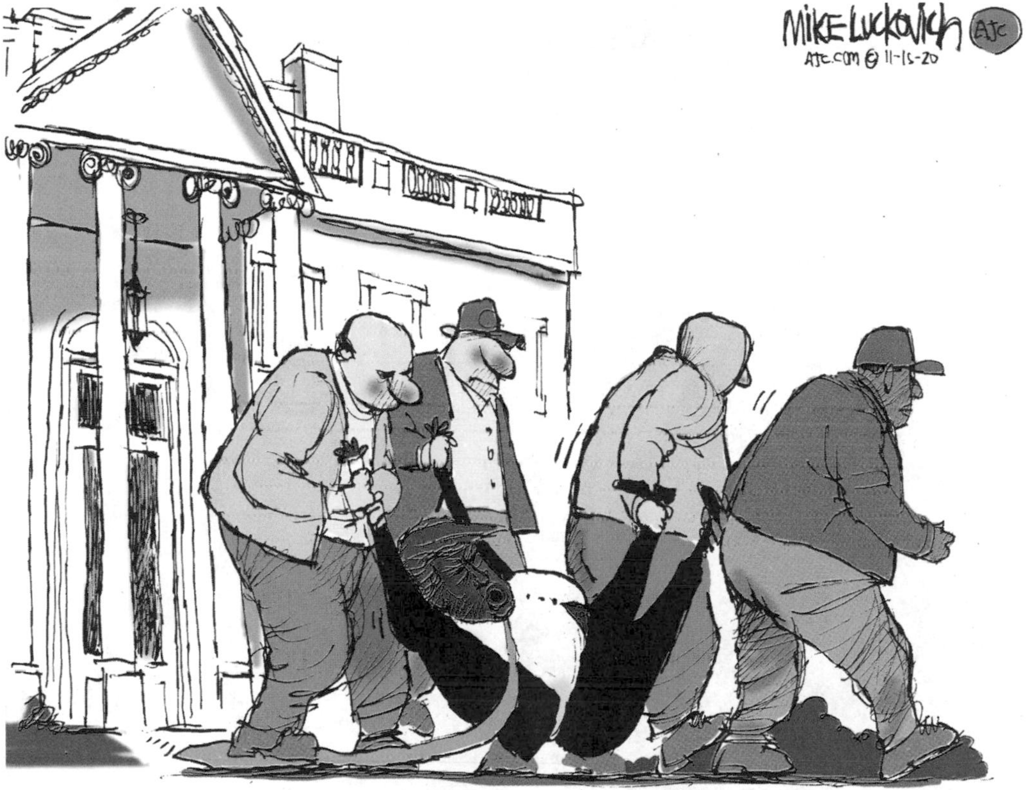
MIKE LUCKOVICH AJC
AJC.COM © 11-15-20

TRANSITION TEAM

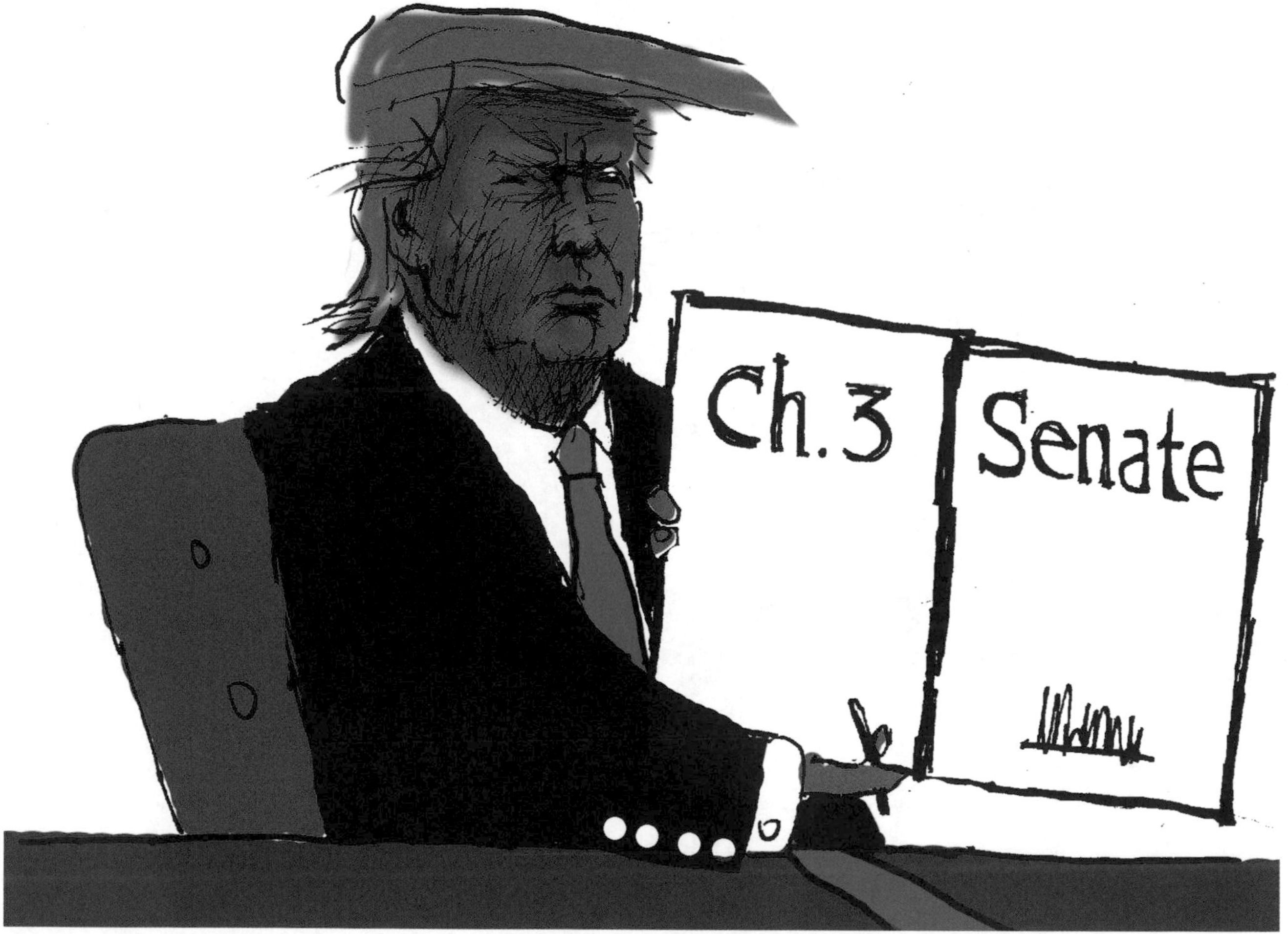
Ch. 3
Senate

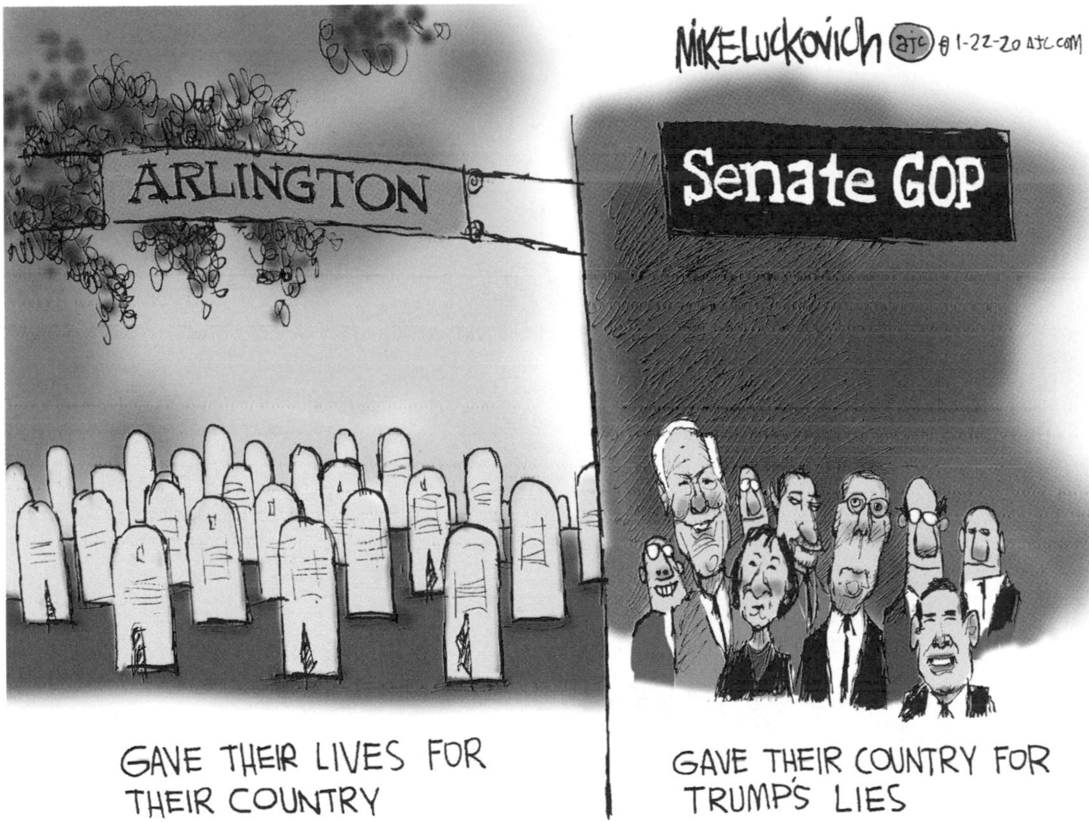
ARLINGTON
MIKELUCKOVICH AJC 1-22-20 AJC.COM
Senate GOP
GAVE THEIR LIVES FOR THEIR COUNTRY
GAVE THEIR COUNTRY FOR TRUMP'S LIES

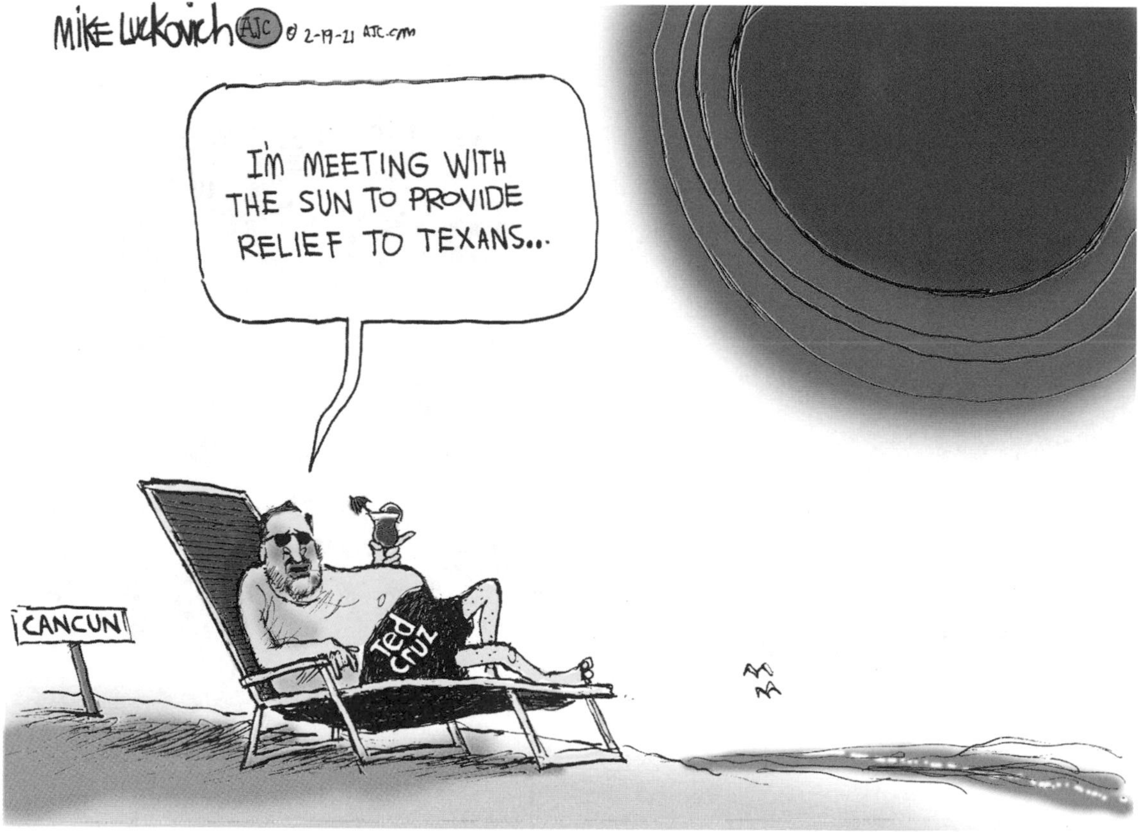
MIKE LUCKOVICH AJC © 2-19-21 AJC.com
I'M MEETING WITH THE SUN TO PROVIDE RELIEF TO TEXANS...
CANCUN
Ted Cruz

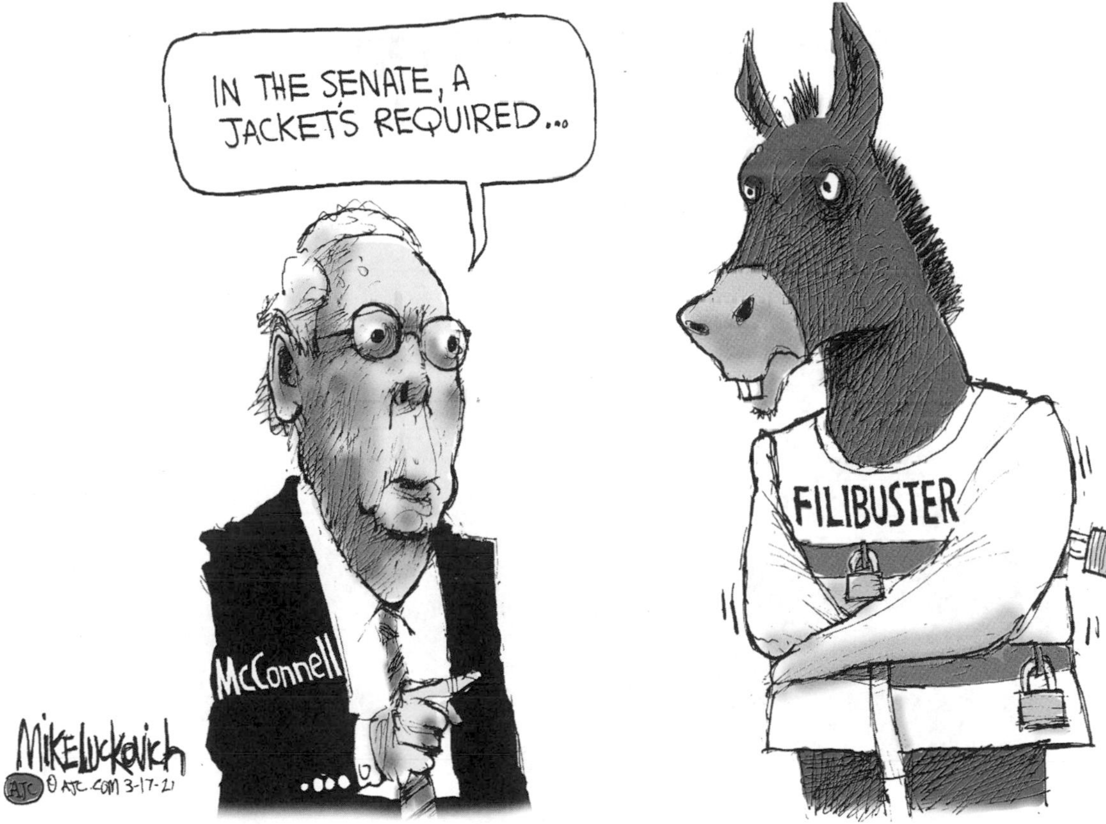
IN THE SENATE, A JACKET'S REQUIRED...
McConnell
FILIBUSTER
MIKE LUCKOVICH
AJC © AJC.COM 3-17-21

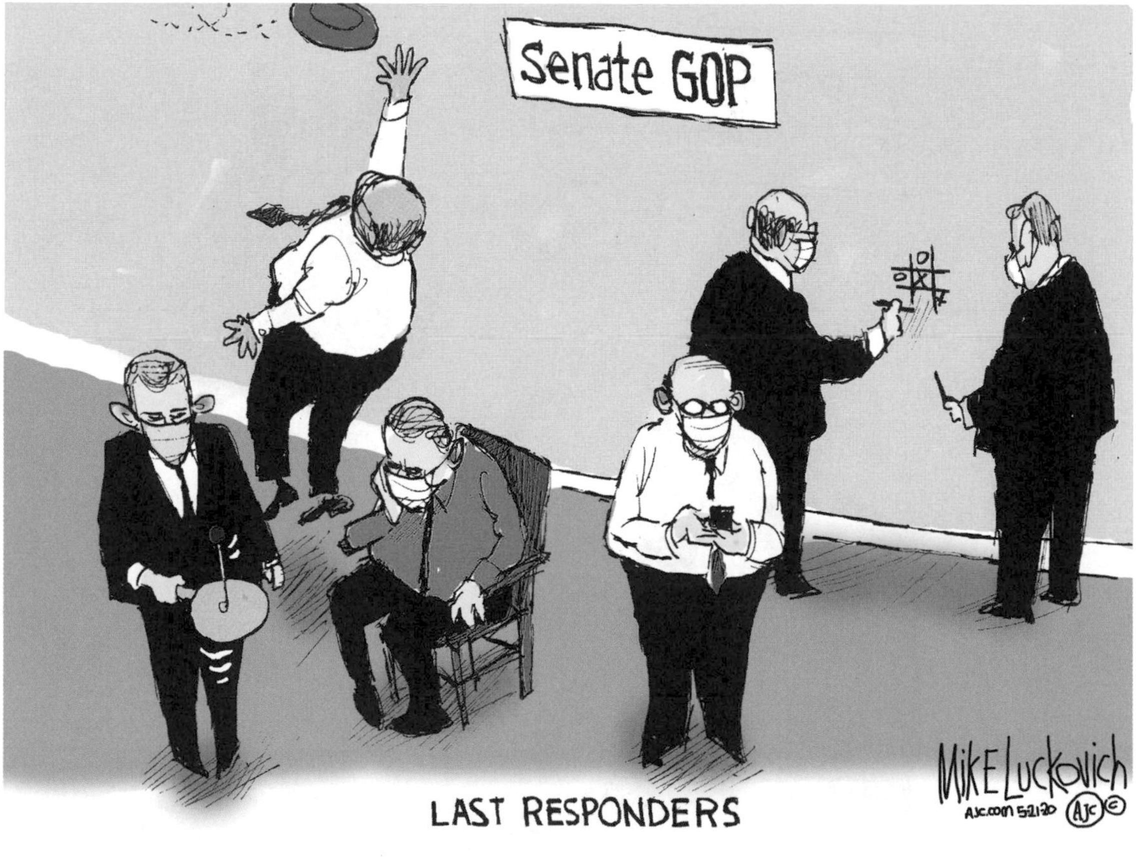
Senate GOP
LAST RESPONDERS
MikE Luckovich

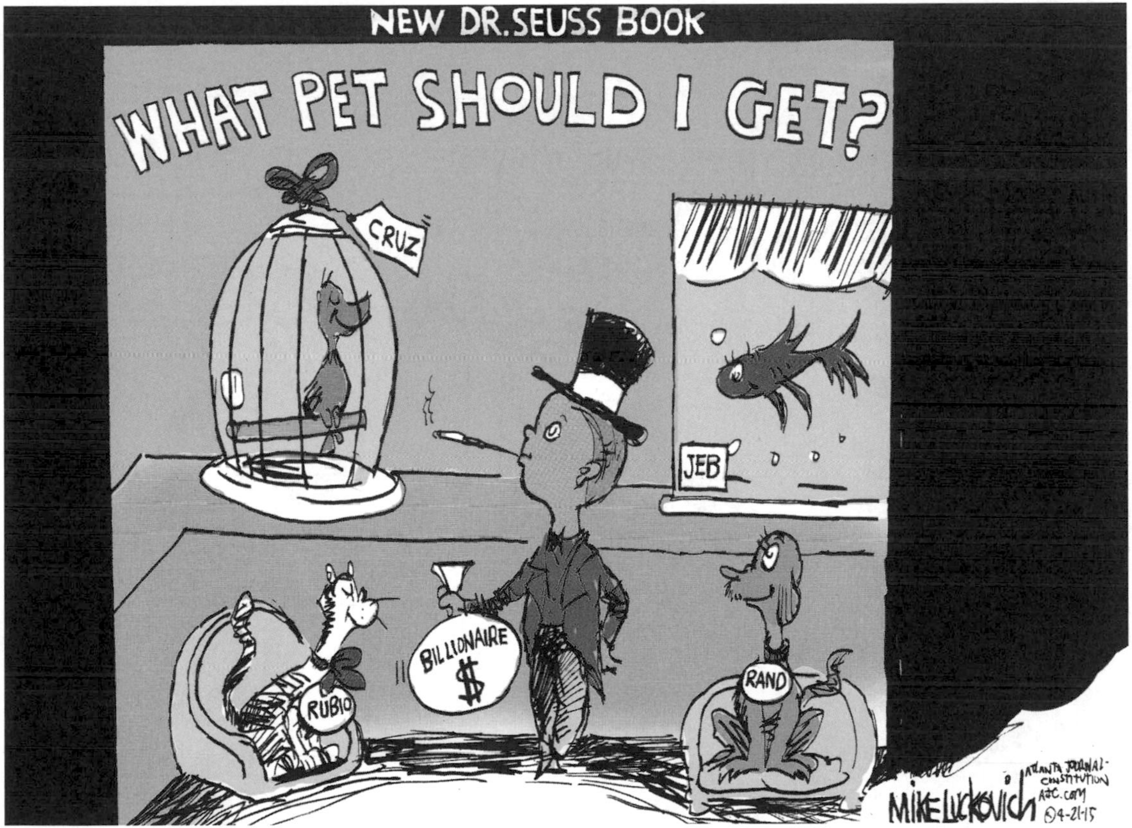
NEW DR. SEUSS BOOK
WHAT PET SHOULD I GET?
CRUZ
JEB
BILLIONAIRE $
RUBIO
RAND
MIKE LUCKOVICH
ATLANTA JOURNAL-CONSTITUTION
AJC.com
©4-21-15

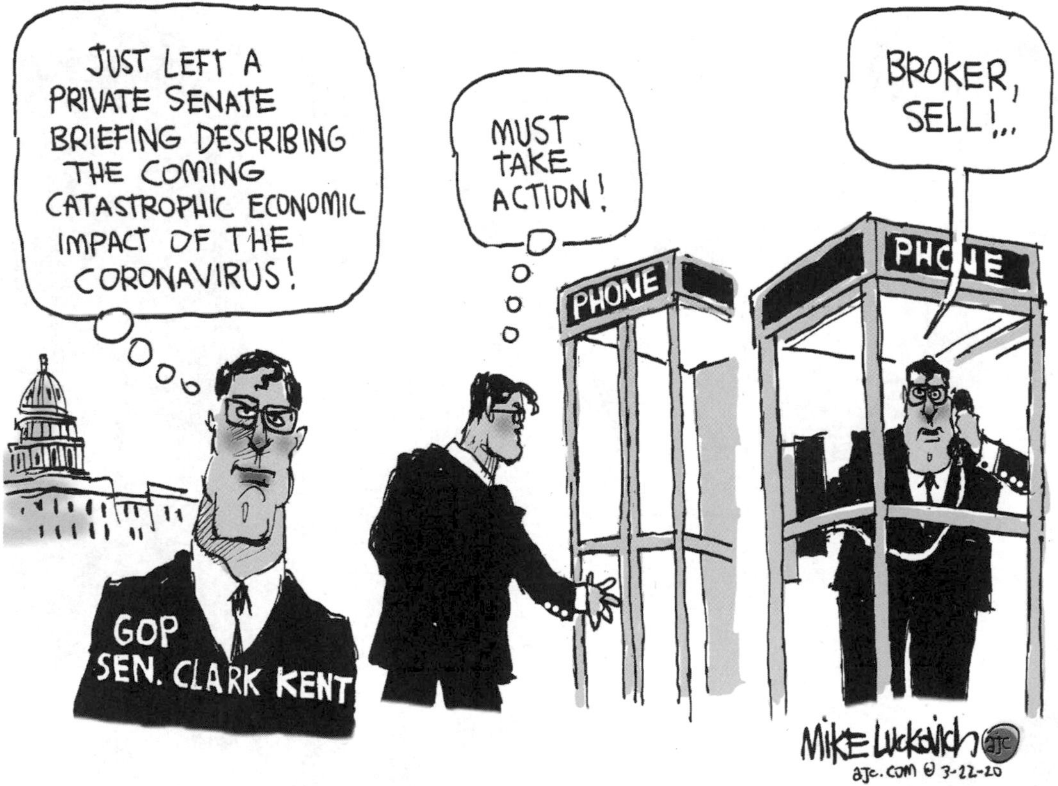
JUST LEFT A PRIVATE SENATE BRIEFING DESCRIBING THE COMING CATASTROPHIC ECONOMIC IMPACT OF THE CORONAVIRUS!
GOP SEN. CLARK KENT
MUST TAKE ACTION!
PHONE
BROKER, SELL!...
PHONE
MIKE LUCKOVICH
ajc.com © 3-22-20

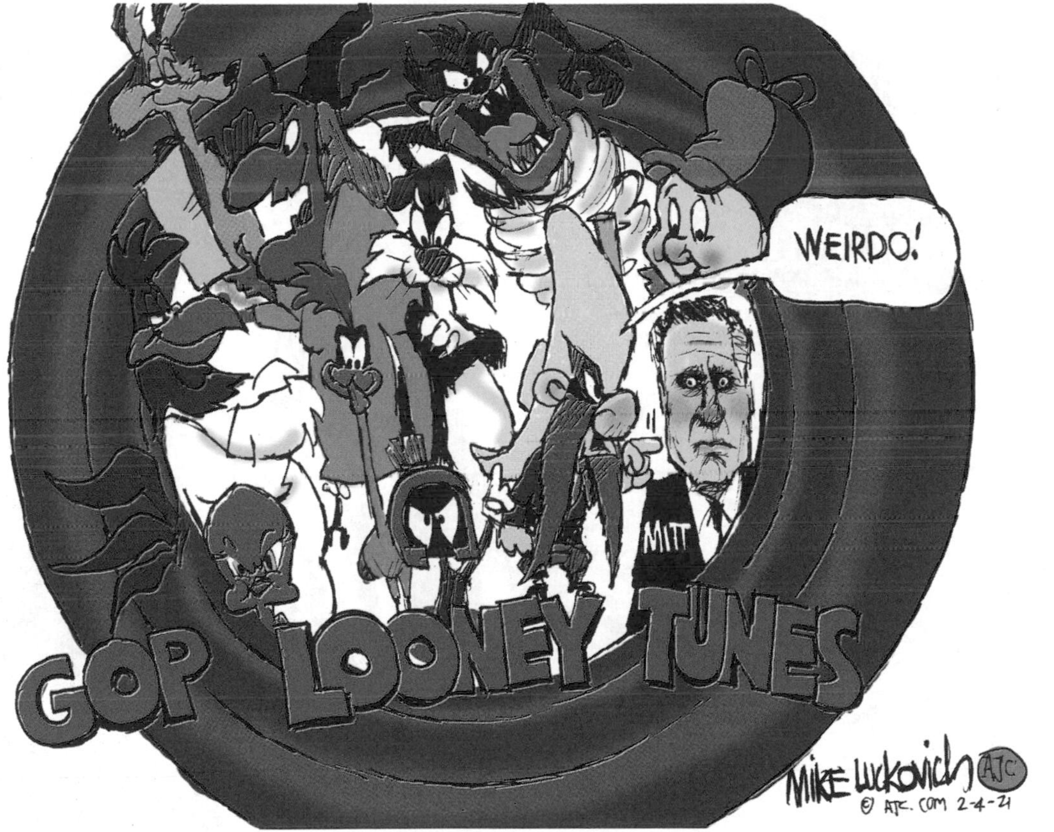
WEIRDO!
MITT
GOP LOONEY TUNES
MIKE LUCKOVICH AJC
© AJC.COM 2-4-21

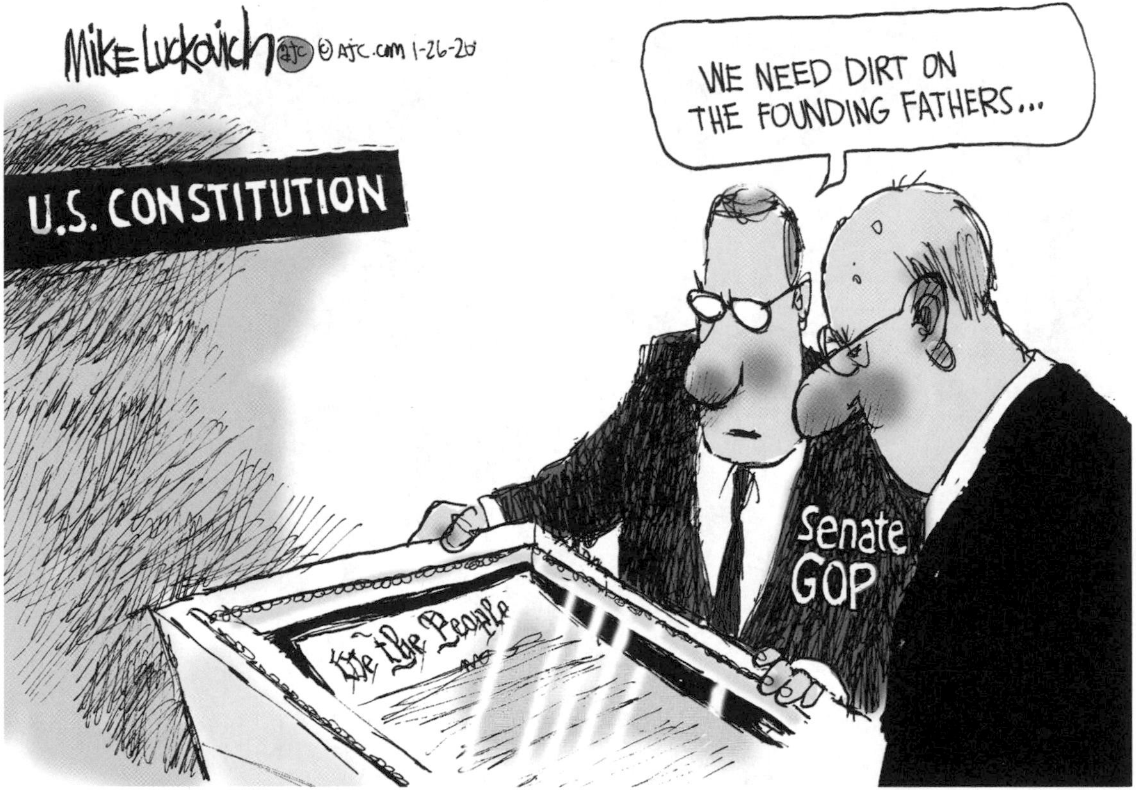
MIKE LUCKOVICH ajc © AJC.com 1-26-20
WE NEED DIRT ON THE FOUNDING FATHERS...
U.S. CONSTITUTION
We the People
Senate GOP

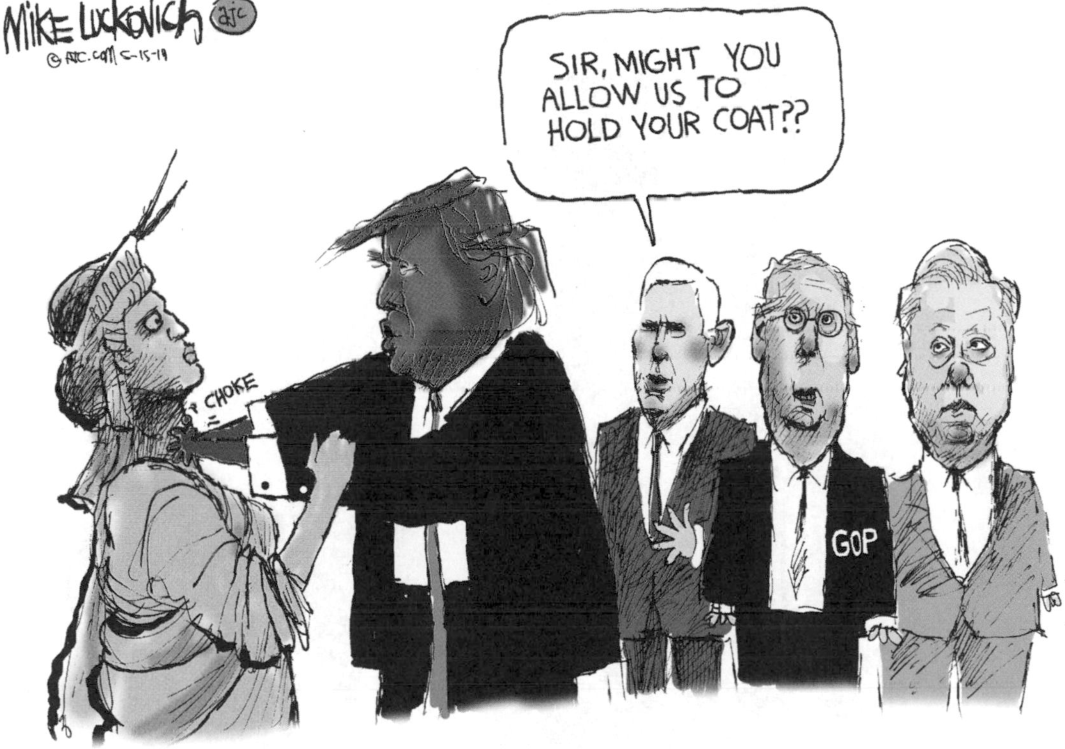
MIKE LUCKOVICH ajc
© AJC.com 5-15-19
SIR, MIGHT YOU
ALLOW US TO
HOLD YOUR COAT??
CHOKE
GOP

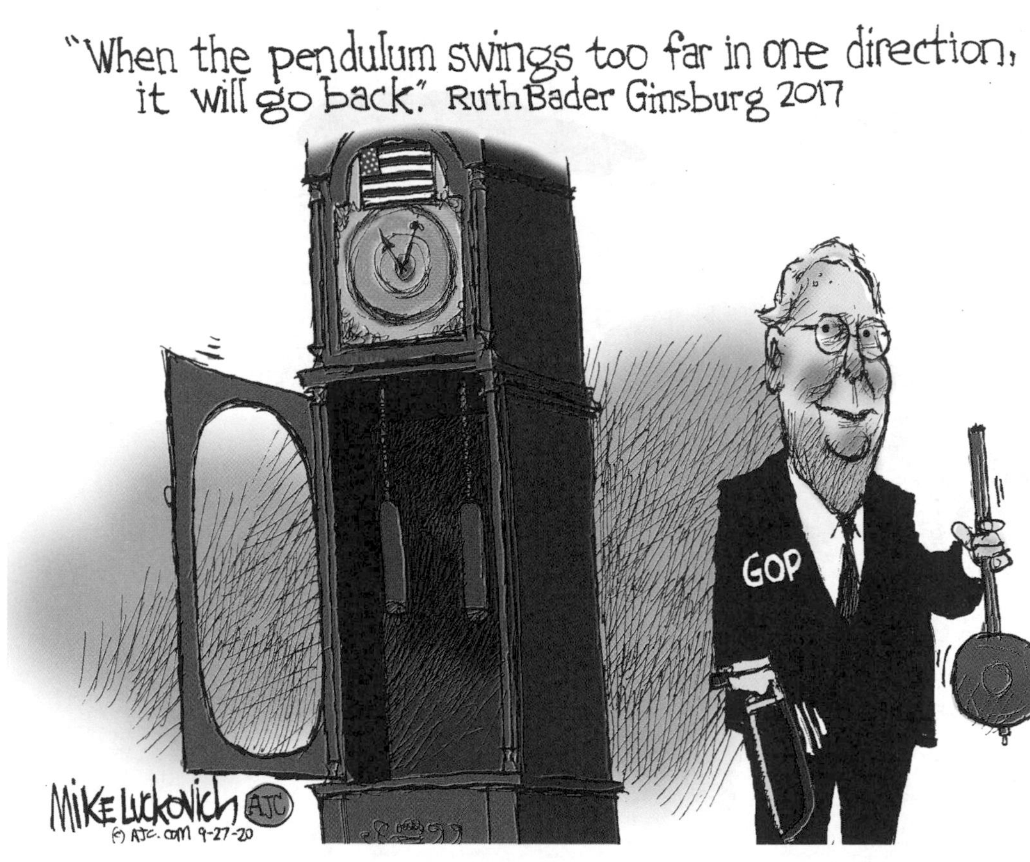
"When the pendulum swings too far in one direction, it will go back." Ruth Bader Ginsburg 2017
GOP
MIKE LUCKOVICH AJC
© AJC.com 9-27-20

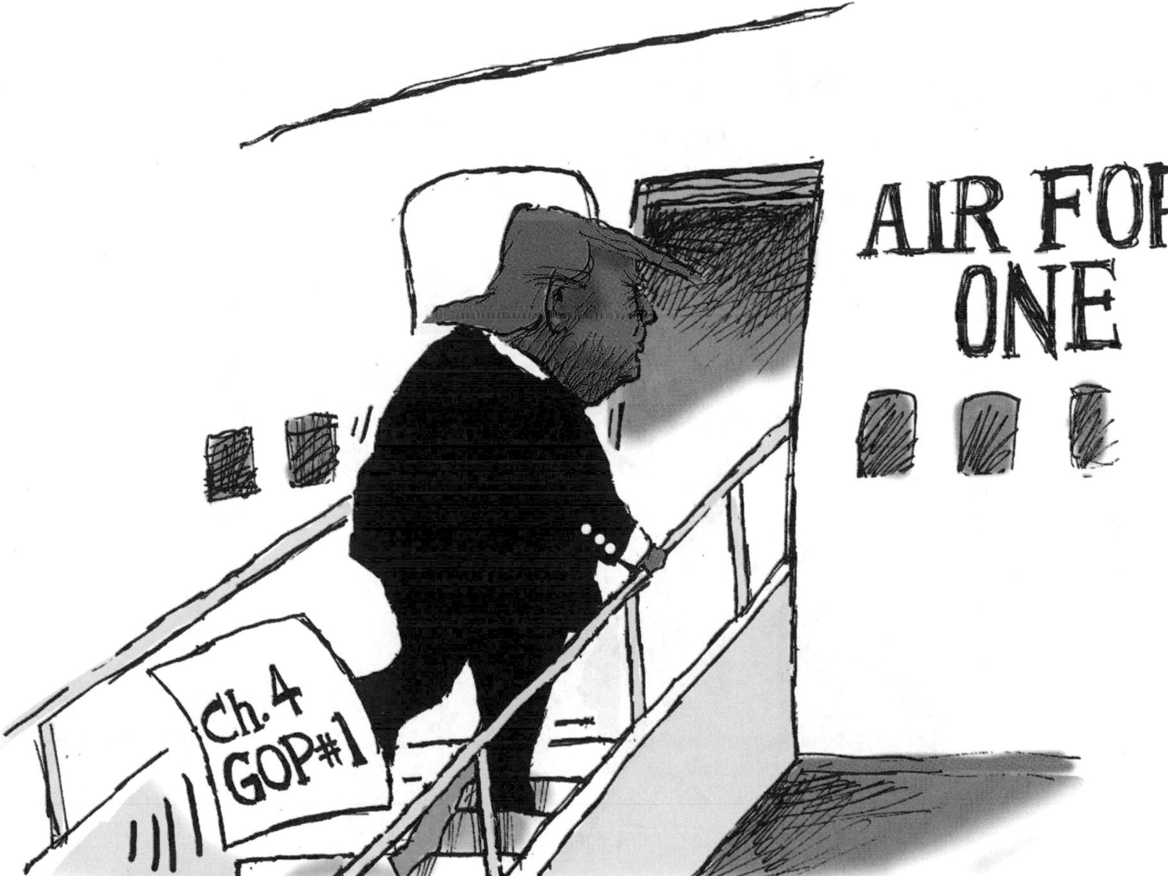
AIR FOR ONE
Ch. 4 GOP#1

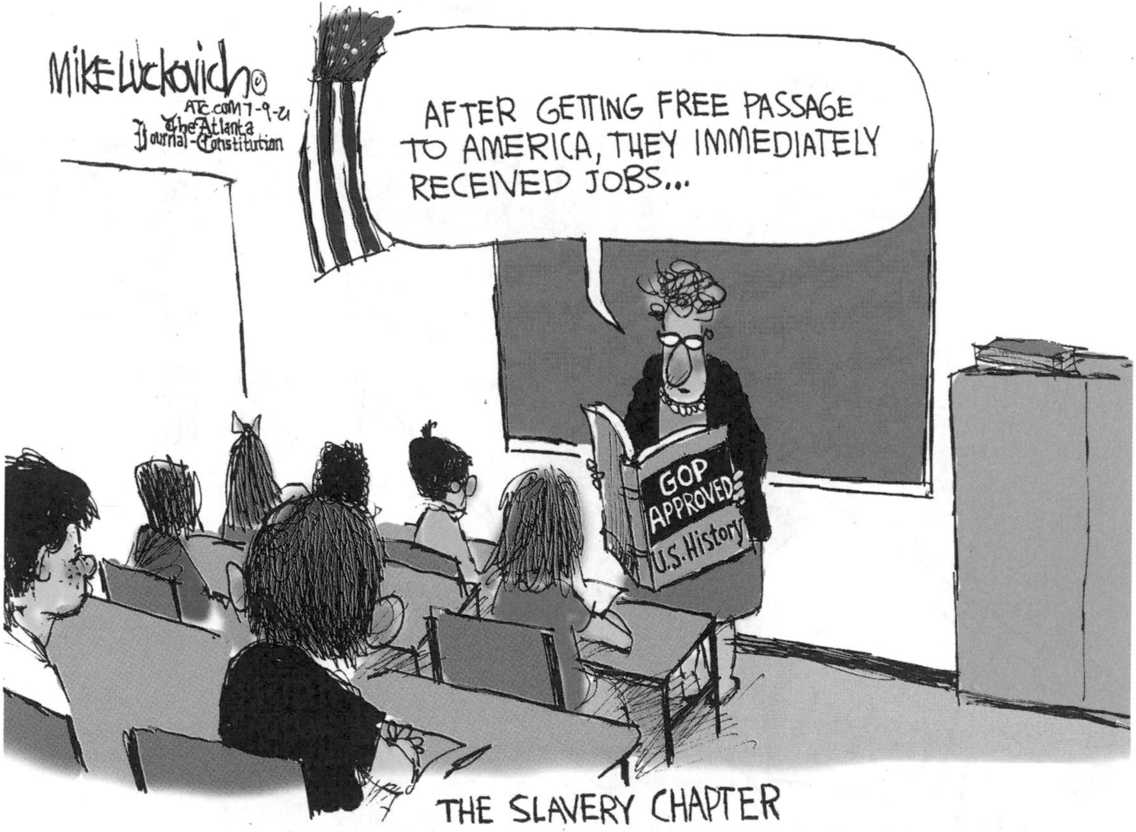
MIKE LUCKOVICH ©
AJC.COM 7-9-21
The Atlanta Journal-Constitution
AFTER GETTING FREE PASSAGE TO AMERICA, THEY IMMEDIATELY RECEIVED JOBS...
GOP APPROVED
U.S. History
THE SLAVERY CHAPTER

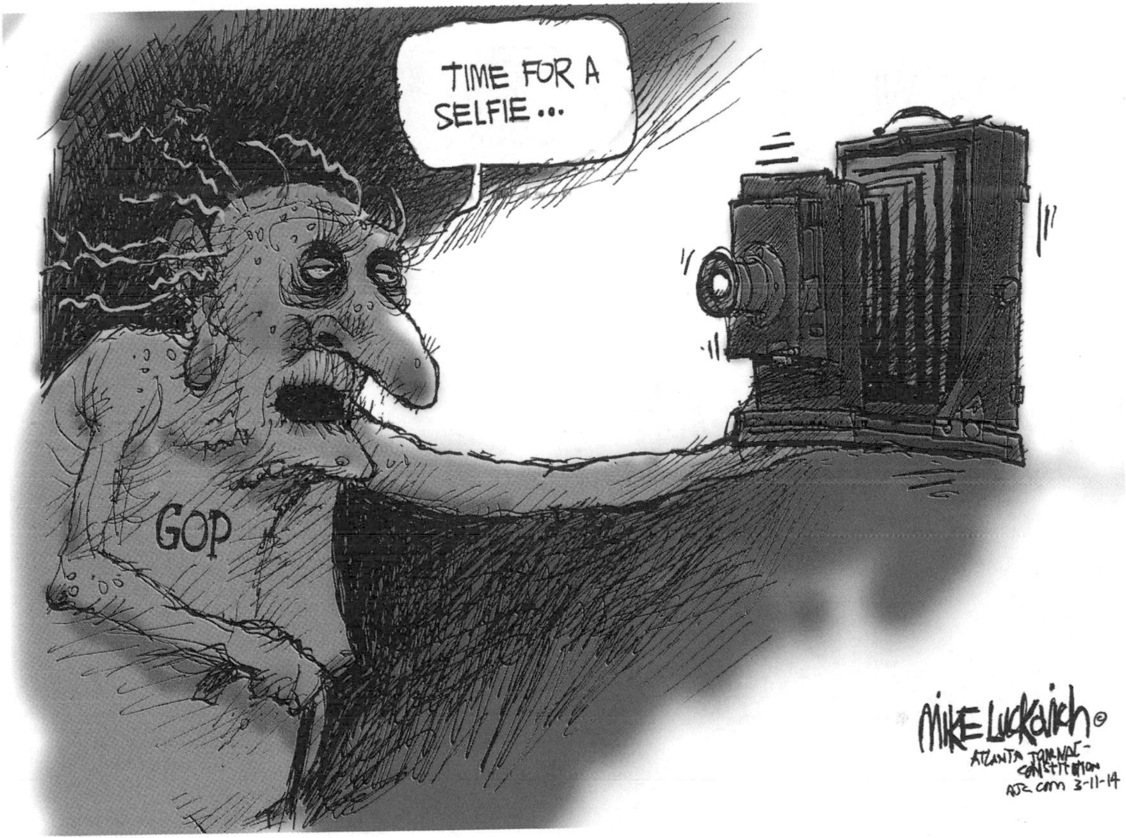
TIME FOR A SELFIE...
GOP
MIKE LUCKOVICH©
ATLANTA JOURNAL-CONSTITUTION
AJC.COM 3-11-14

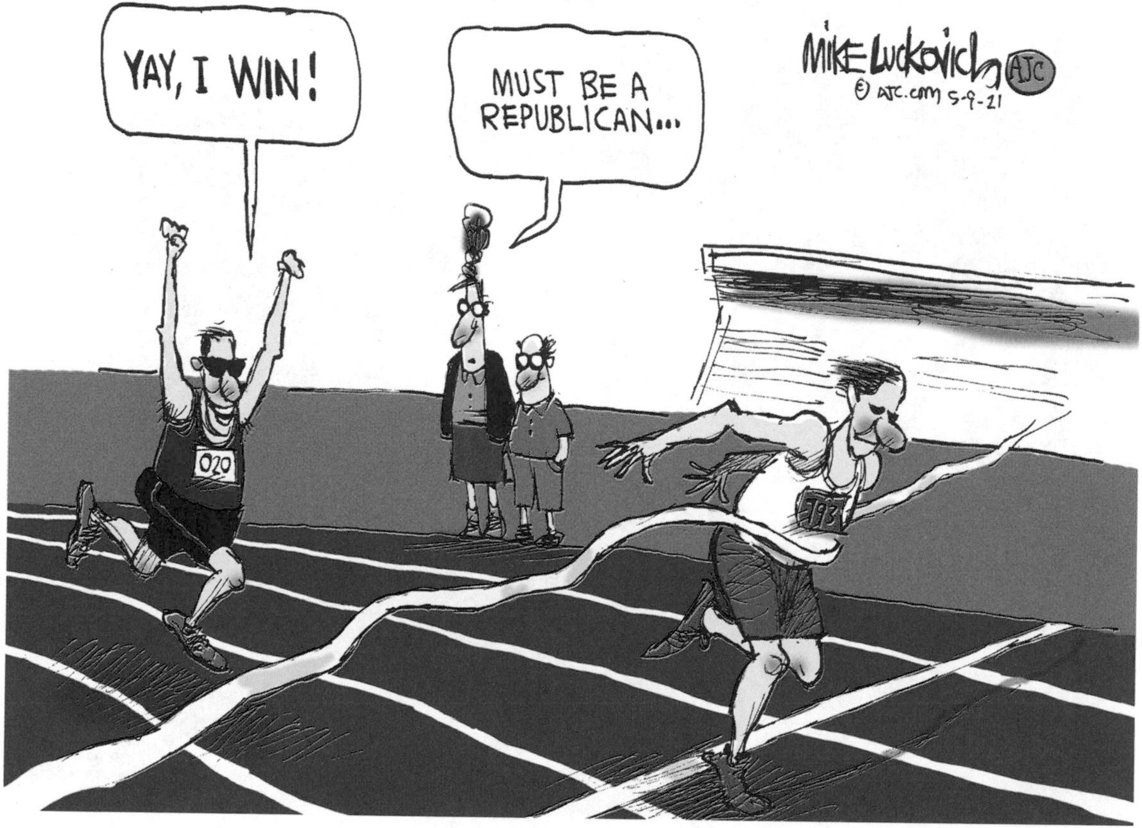
YAY, I WIN!
MUST BE A REPUBLICAN...
MIKE LUCKOVICH
AJC
© ajc.com 5-9-21
020
793

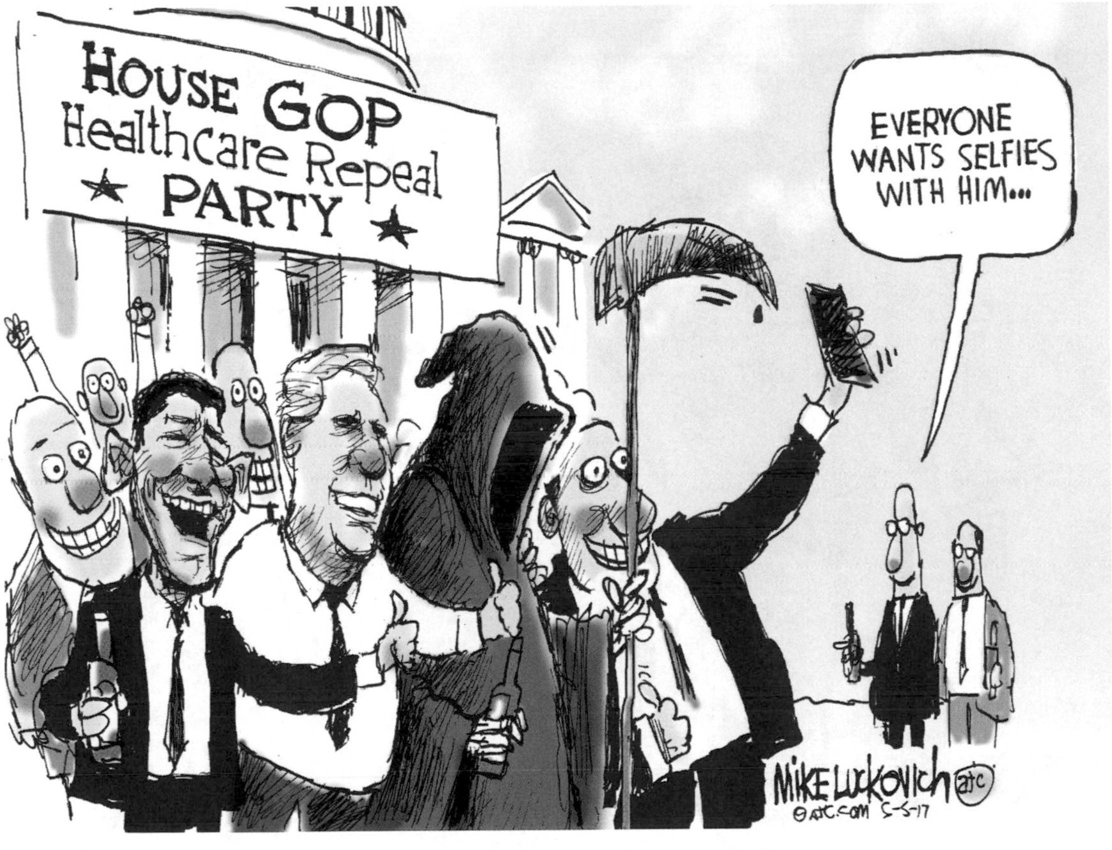
HOUSE GOP
Healthcare Repeal
PARTY
EVERYONE WANTS SELFIES WITH HIM...
MIKE LUCKOVICH
©AJC.COM 5-5-17

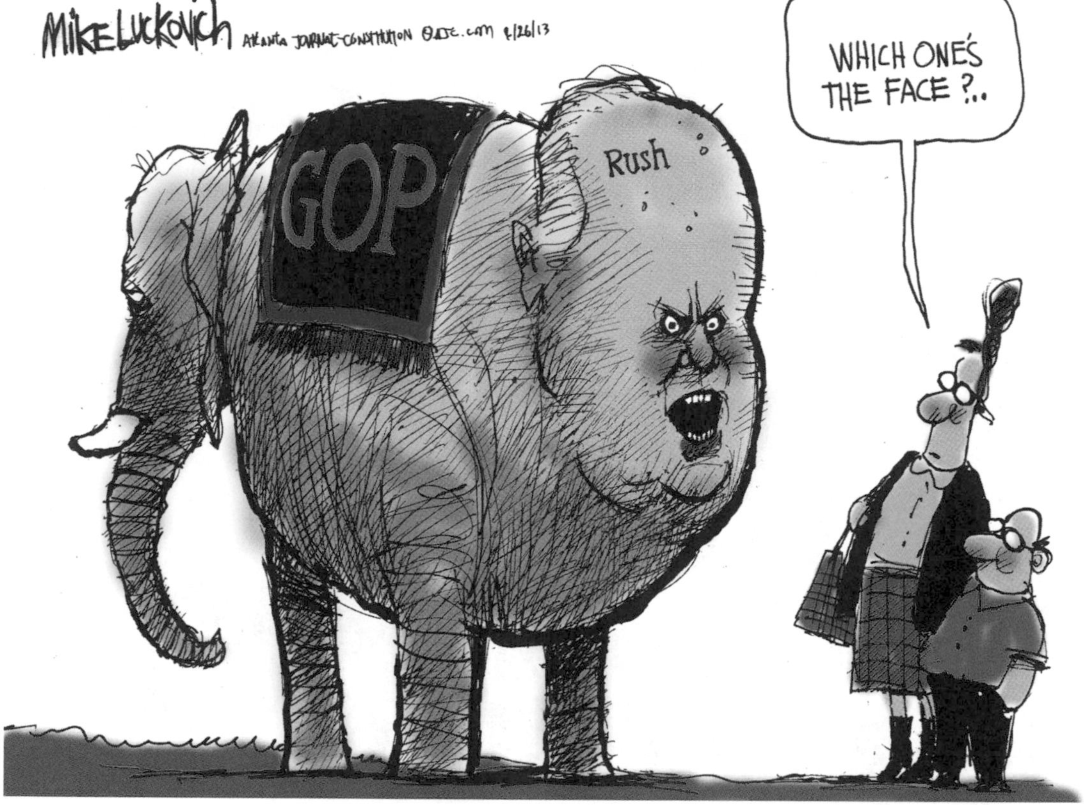
MIKE LUCKOVICH ATLANTA JOURNAL-CONSTITUTION @AJC.com 8/26/13
WHICH ONE'S THE FACE ?..
GOP
Rush

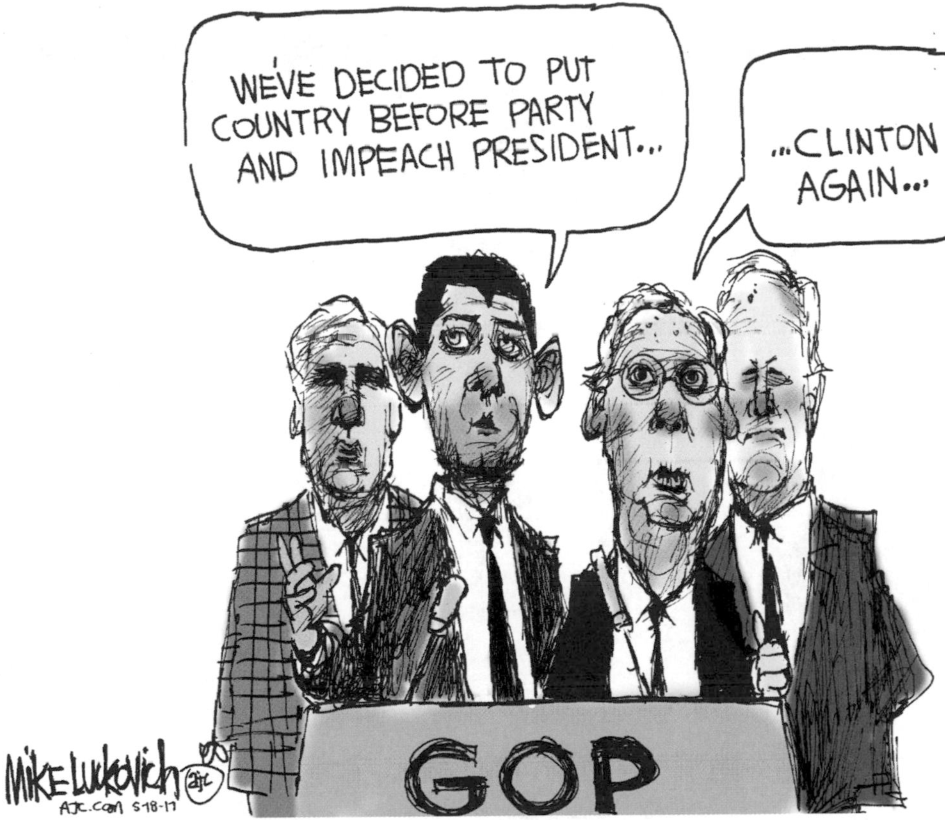
WE'VE DECIDED TO PUT COUNTRY BEFORE PARTY AND IMPEACH PRESIDENT...
...CLINTON AGAIN...
GOP
MIKE LUCKOVICH
AJC.com 5-18-17

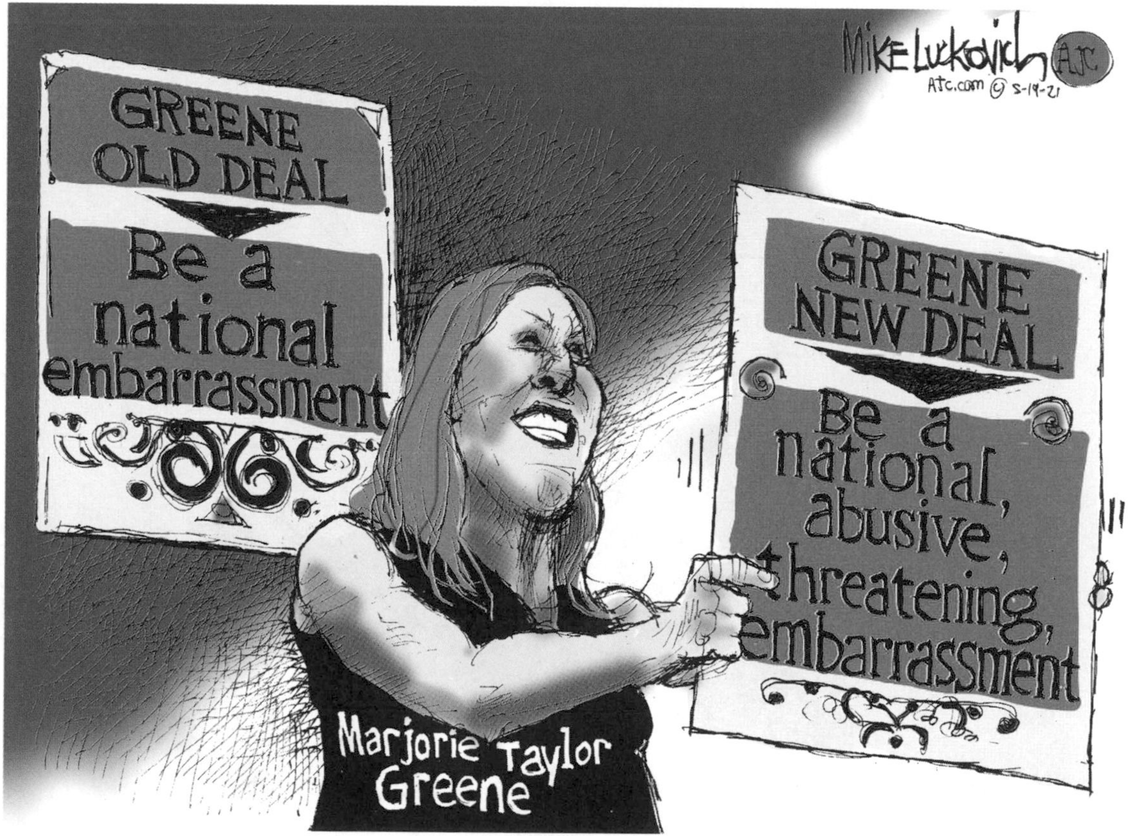
MIKE LUCKOVICH AJC
AJC.com © 5-19-21
GREENE OLD DEAL
Be a national embarrassment
GREENE NEW DEAL
Be a national, abusive, threatening, embarrassment
Marjorie Taylor Greene

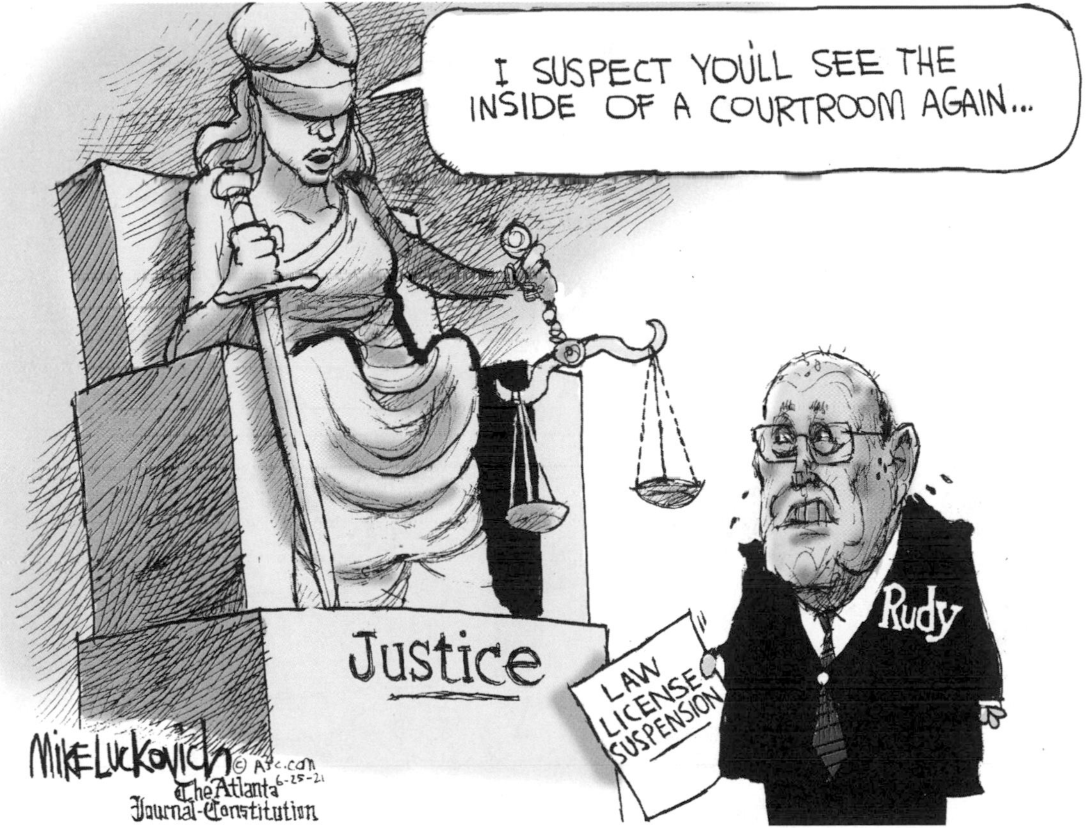
I SUSPECT YOU'LL SEE THE INSIDE OF A COURTROOM AGAIN...
Justice
LAW LICENSE SUSPENSION
Rudy
MIKE LUCKOVICH © AJC.com 6-25-21 The Atlanta Journal-Constitution

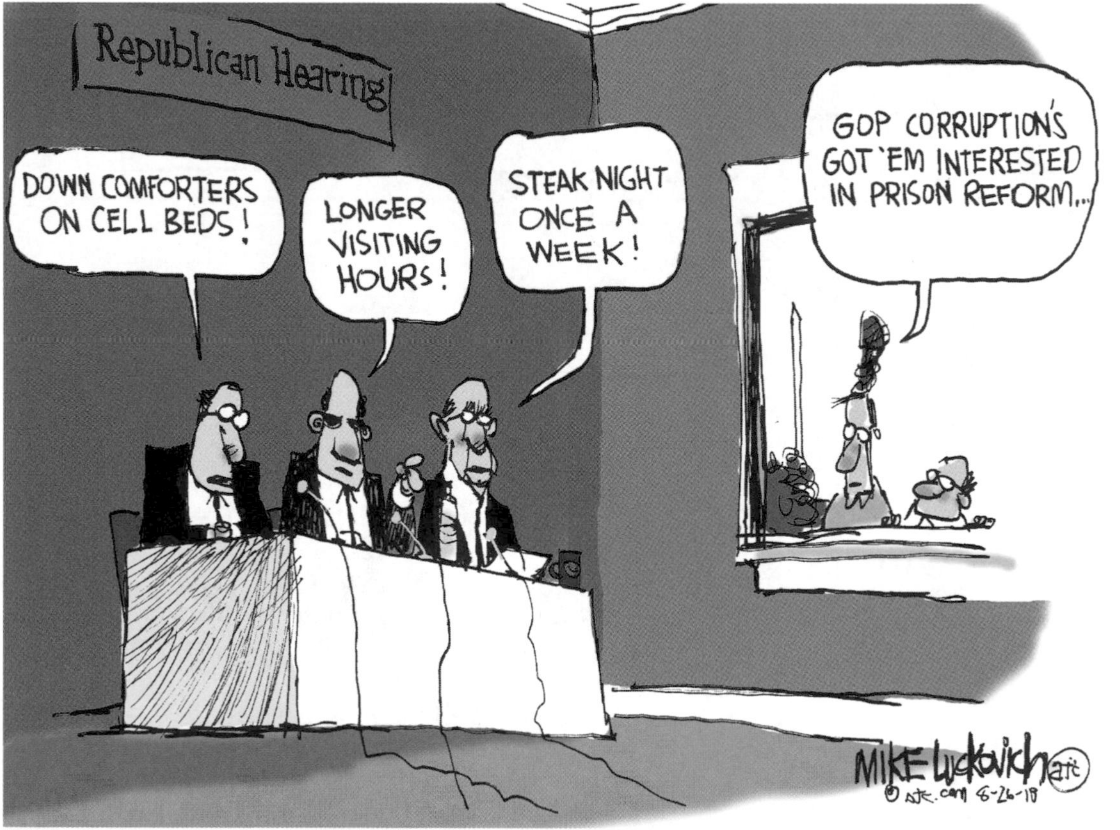
Republican Hearing
DOWN COMFORTERS ON CELL BEDS!
LONGER VISITING HOURS!
STEAK NIGHT ONCE A WEEK!
GOP CORRUPTION'S GOT 'EM INTERESTED IN PRISON REFORM...
MIKE LUCKOVICH
© ajc.com 6-26-18

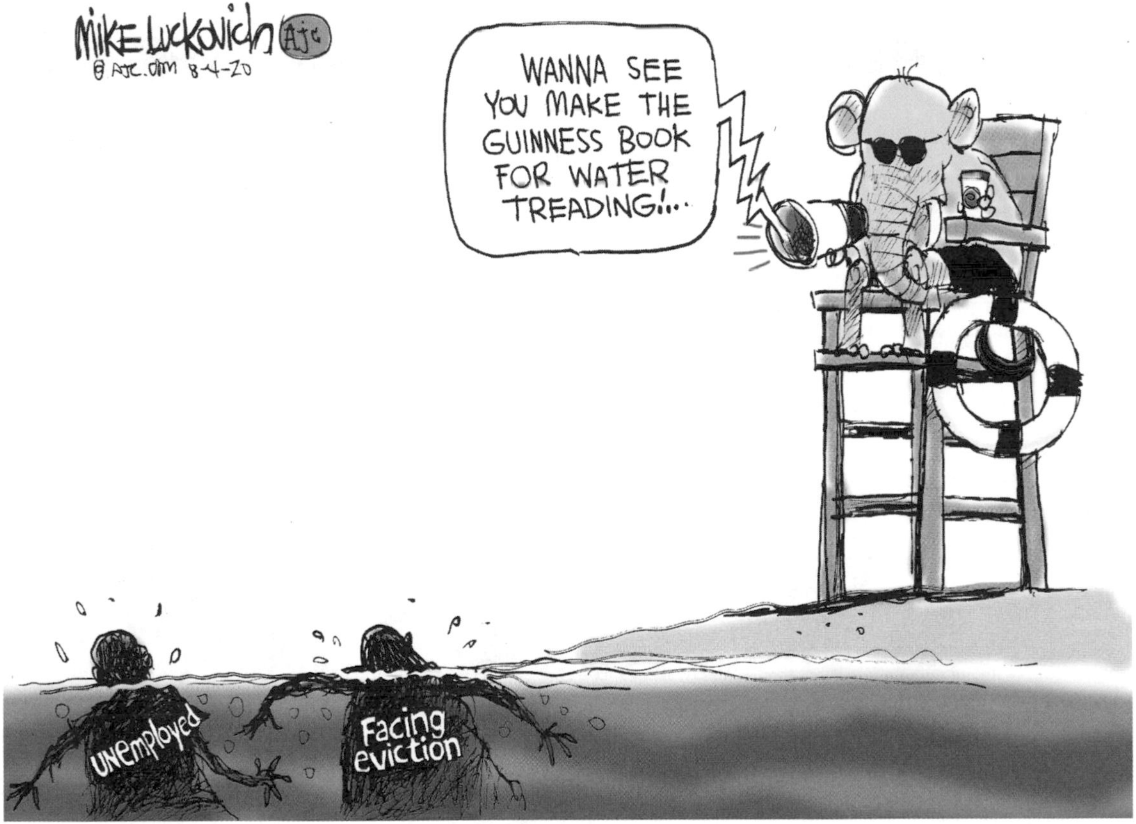
MIKE LUCKOVICH AJC
© AJC.com 8-4-20
WANNA SEE YOU MAKE THE GUINNESS BOOK FOR WATER TREADING!...
unemployed
Facing eviction

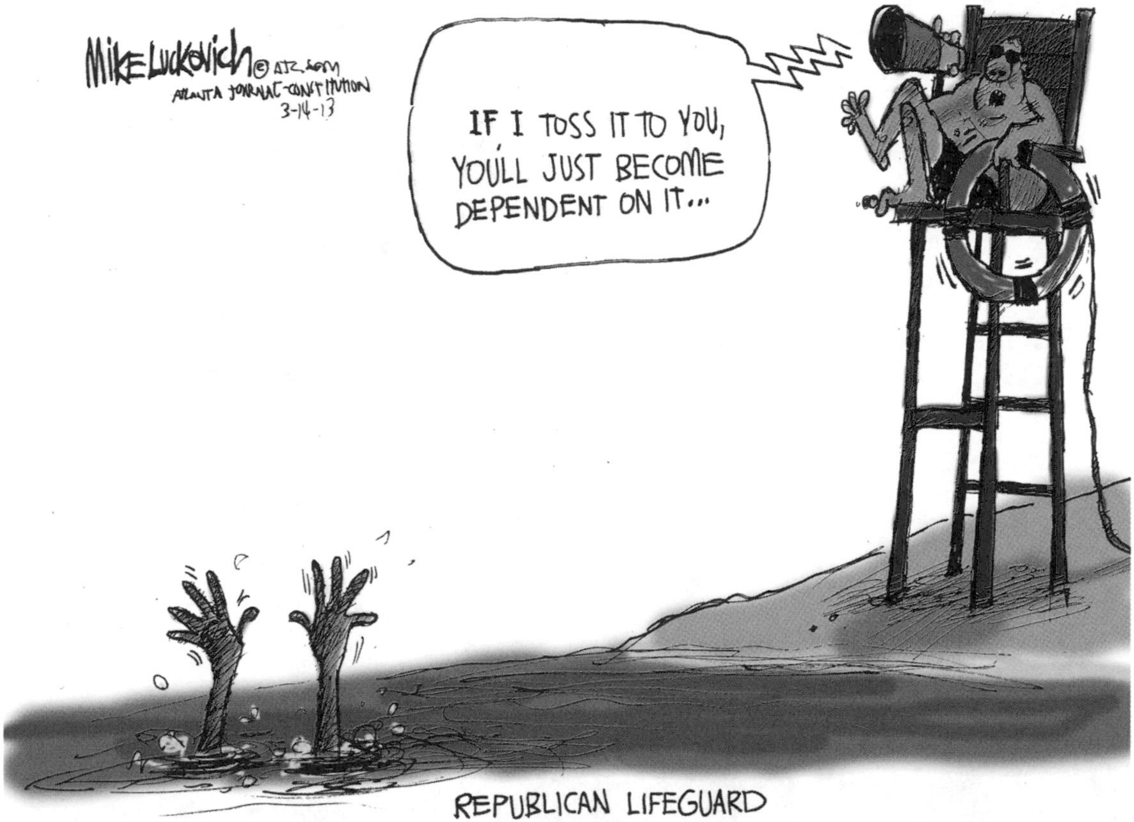
MIKE LUCKOVICH © AJC.COM
ATLANTA JOURNAL-CONSTITUTION
3-14-13
IF I TOSS IT TO YOU, YOU'LL JUST BECOME DEPENDENT ON IT...
REPUBLICAN LIFEGUARD

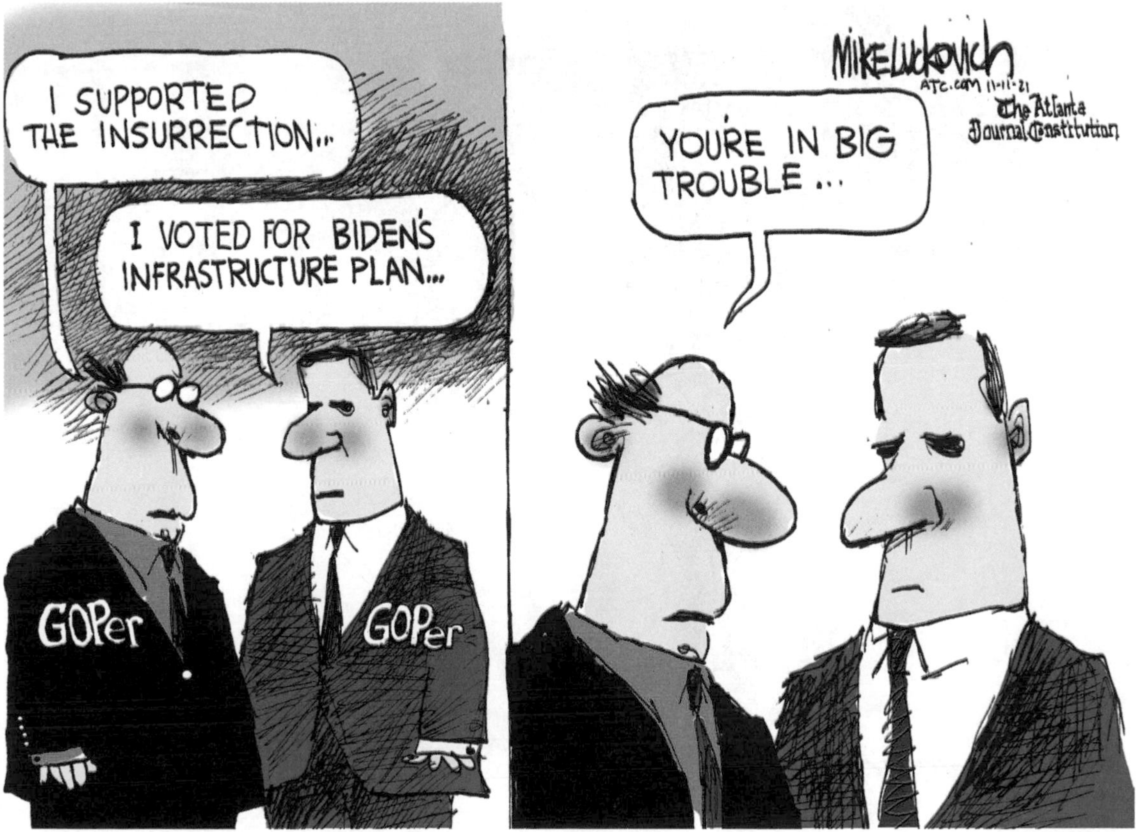
I SUPPORTED THE INSURRECTION...
I VOTED FOR BIDEN'S INFRASTRUCTURE PLAN...
GOPer
GOPer
MIKELUCKOVICH
AJC.com 11-11-21
The Atlanta Journal-Constitution
YOU'RE IN BIG TROUBLE ...

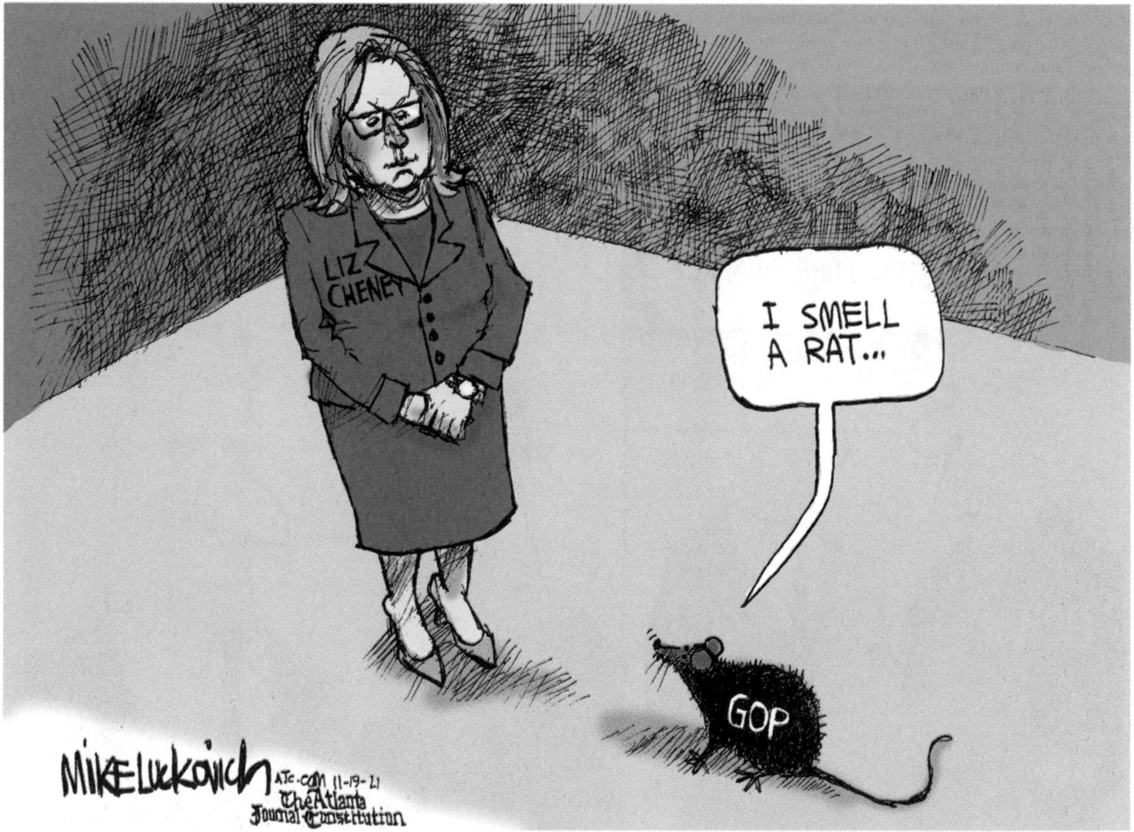
LIZ CHENEY
I SMELL A RAT...
GOP
MIKE LUCKOVICH AJC.COM 11-19-21
The Atlanta Journal-Constitution

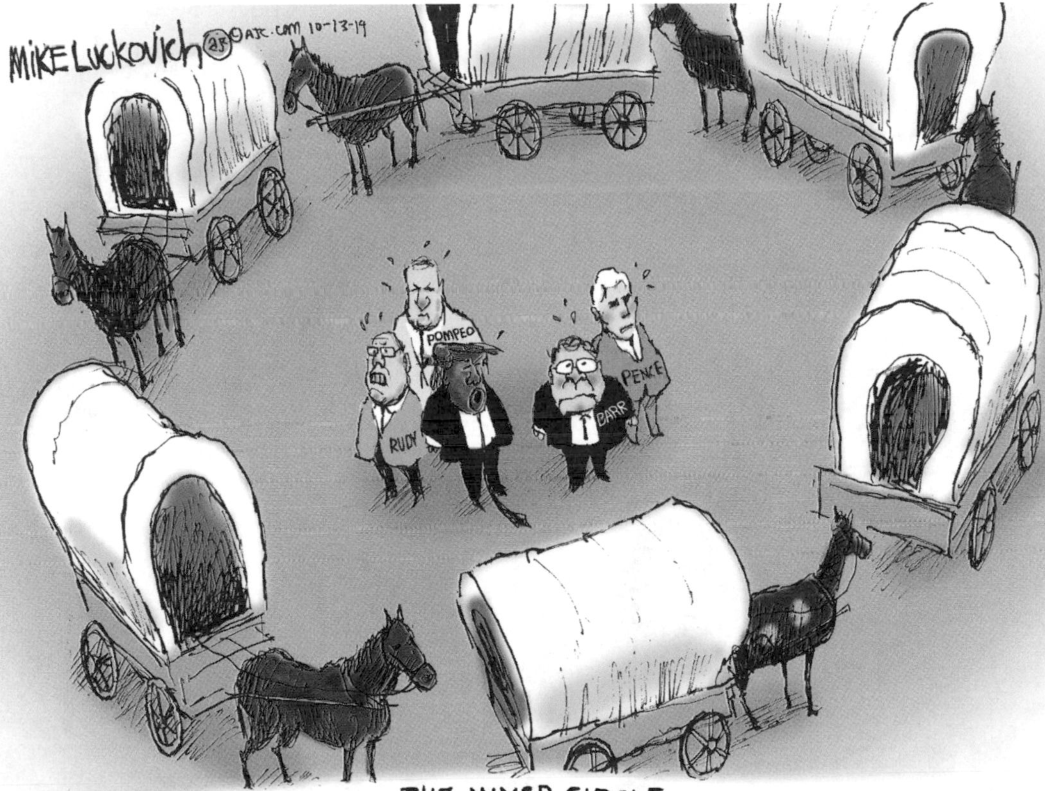
MIKE LUCKOVICH
©AJC.com 10-13-19
POMPEO
RUDY
BARR
PENCE

THE INNER CIRCLE

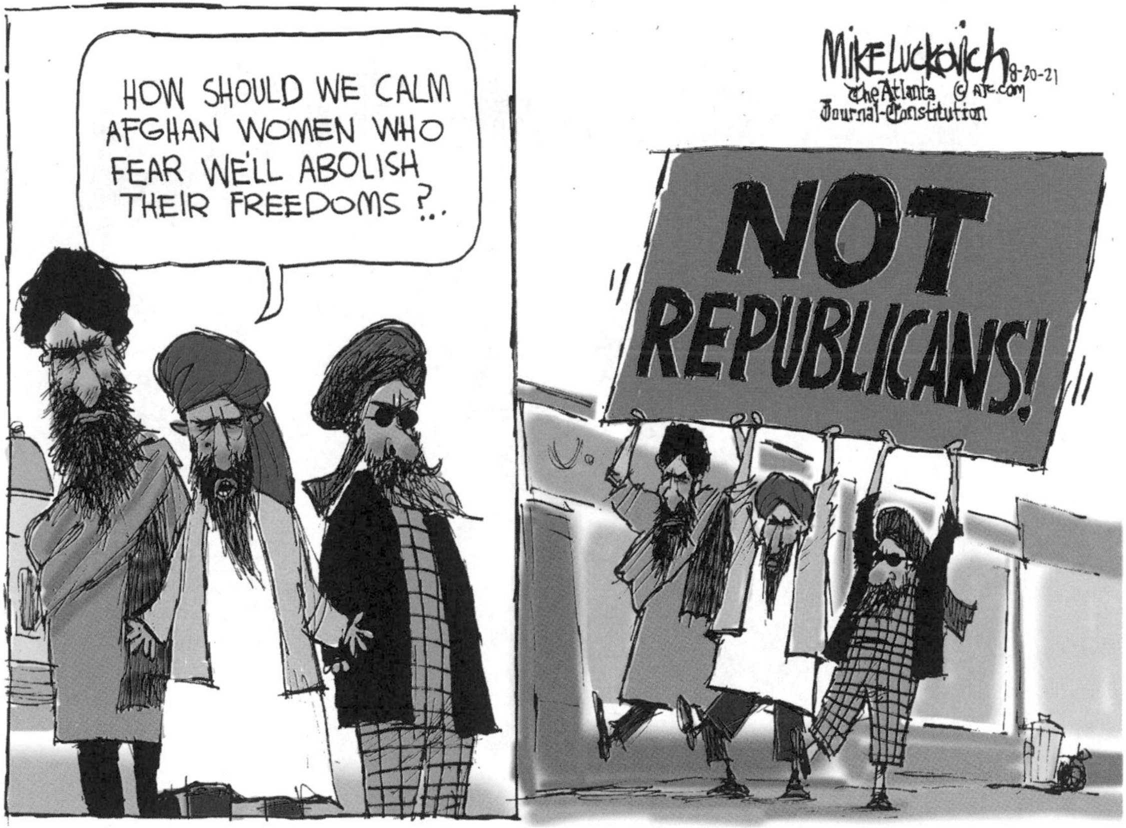
HOW SHOULD WE CALM AFGHAN WOMEN WHO FEAR WE'LL ABOLISH THEIR FREEDOMS ?..
MIKE LUCKOVICH 8-20-21
The Atlanta Journal-Constitution © AJC.com
NOT REPUBLICANS!

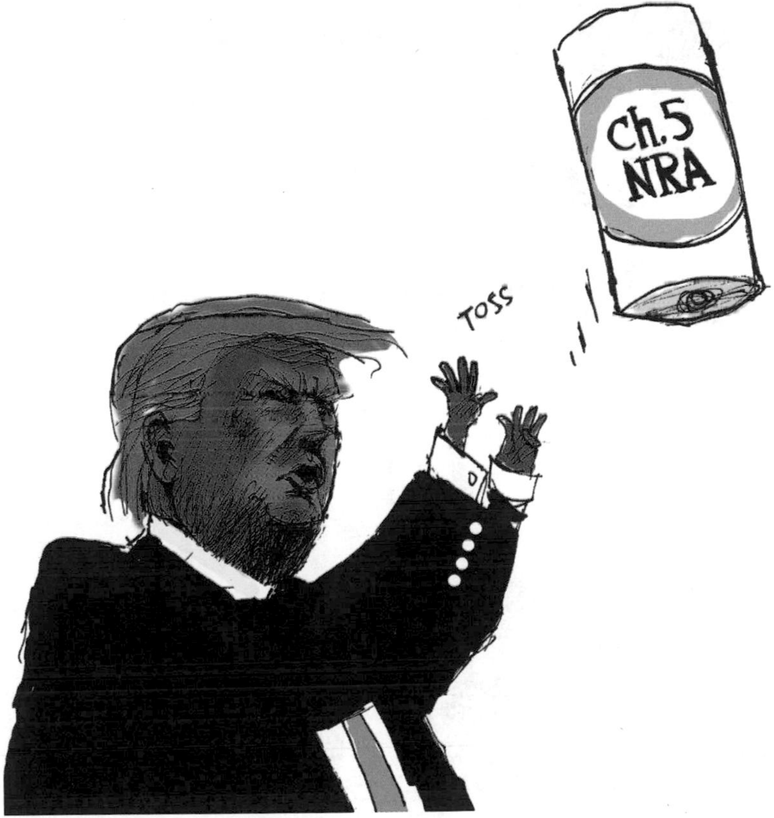
Ch.5
NRA
TOSS

I'm sick of the National Rifle Association (NRA). Whenever there's a mass shooting, the NRA's response is there needs to be more guns. If that was the solution, with Americans currently owning nearly four hundred million guns, we should be the safest country on Earth. I'm also sick of Republican members of Congress who receive NRA donations and whose stock reply after a mass shooting is "thoughts and prayers" to the victims and their families. Republicans don't regulate guns, just uteruses.

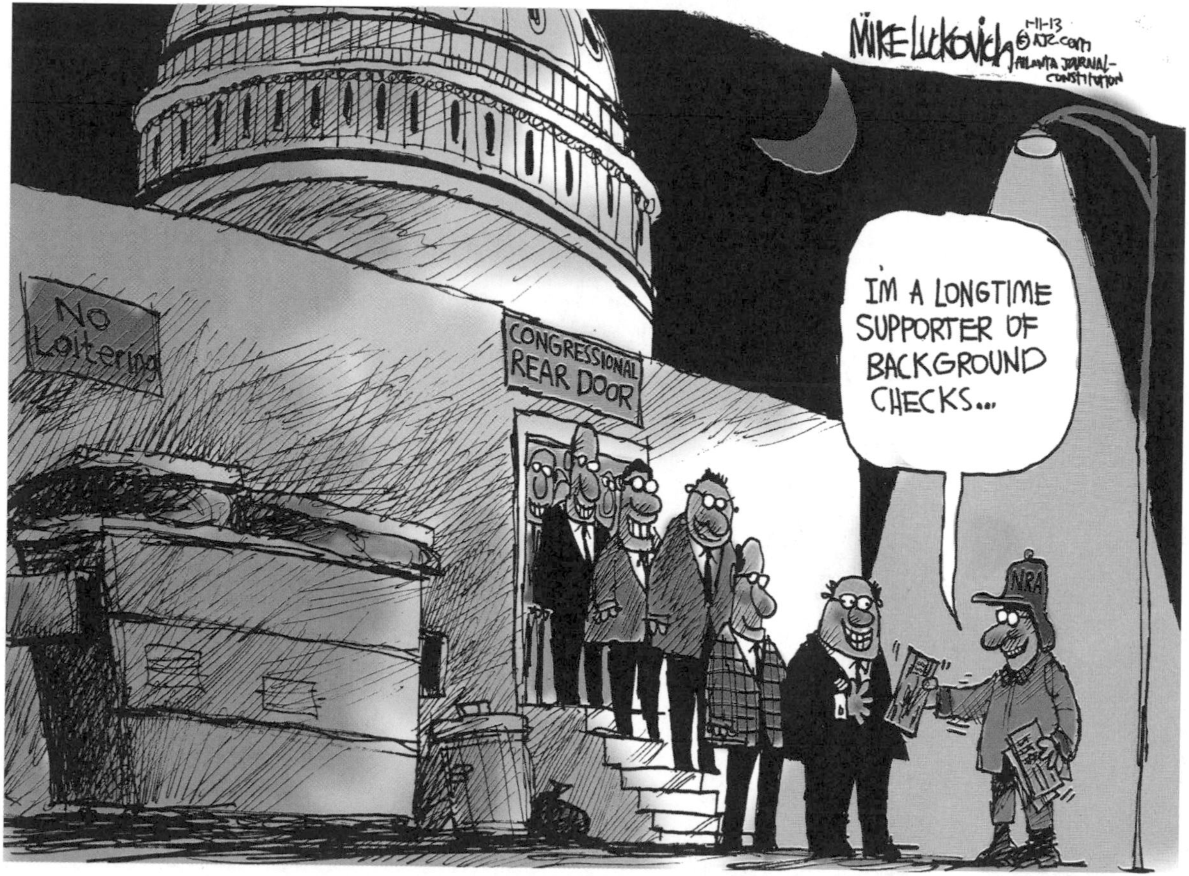
MIKE LUCKOVICH
1-11-13
© AJC.com
ATLANTA JOURNAL-CONSTITUTION
NO Loitering
CONGRESSIONAL REAR DOOR
I'M A LONGTIME SUPPORTER OF BACKGROUND CHECKS...
NRA

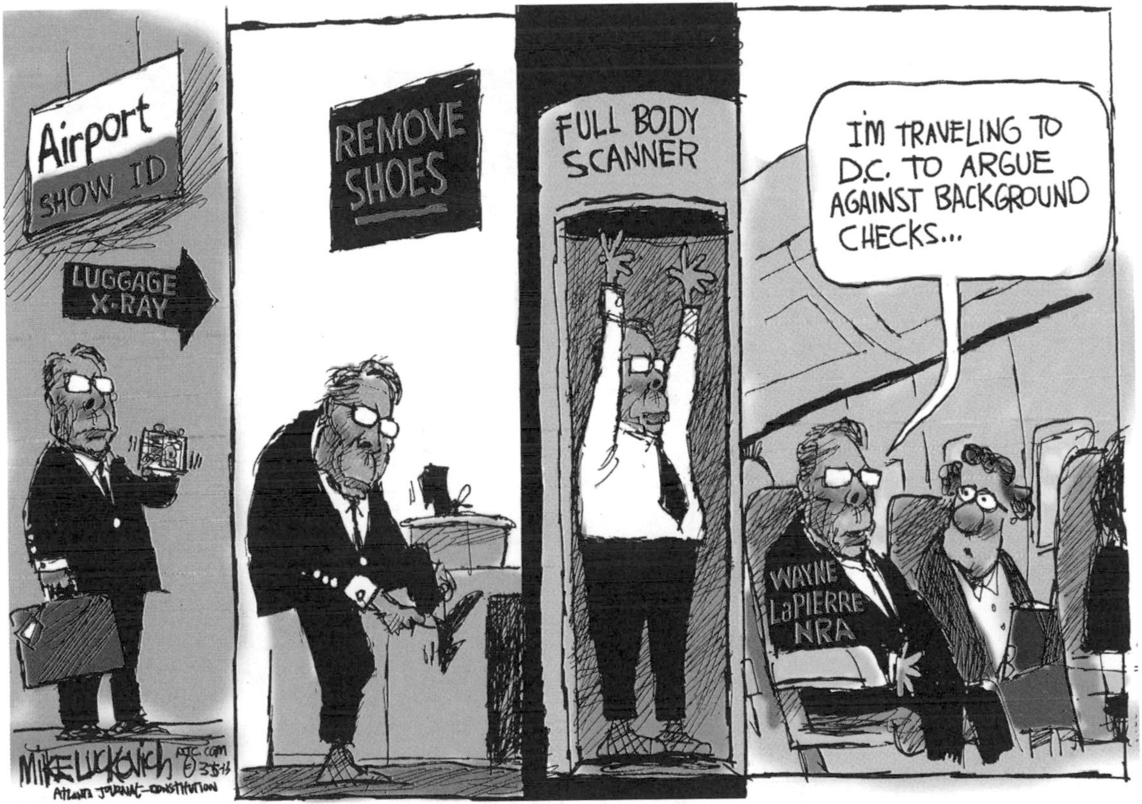
Airport
SHOW ID
LUGGAGE X-RAY
REMOVE SHOES
FULL BODY SCANNER
I'M TRAVELING TO D.C. TO ARGUE AGAINST BACKGROUND CHECKS...
WAYNE LaPIERRE NRA
MIKE LUCKOVICH
AJC.COM
Atlanta Journal-Constitution

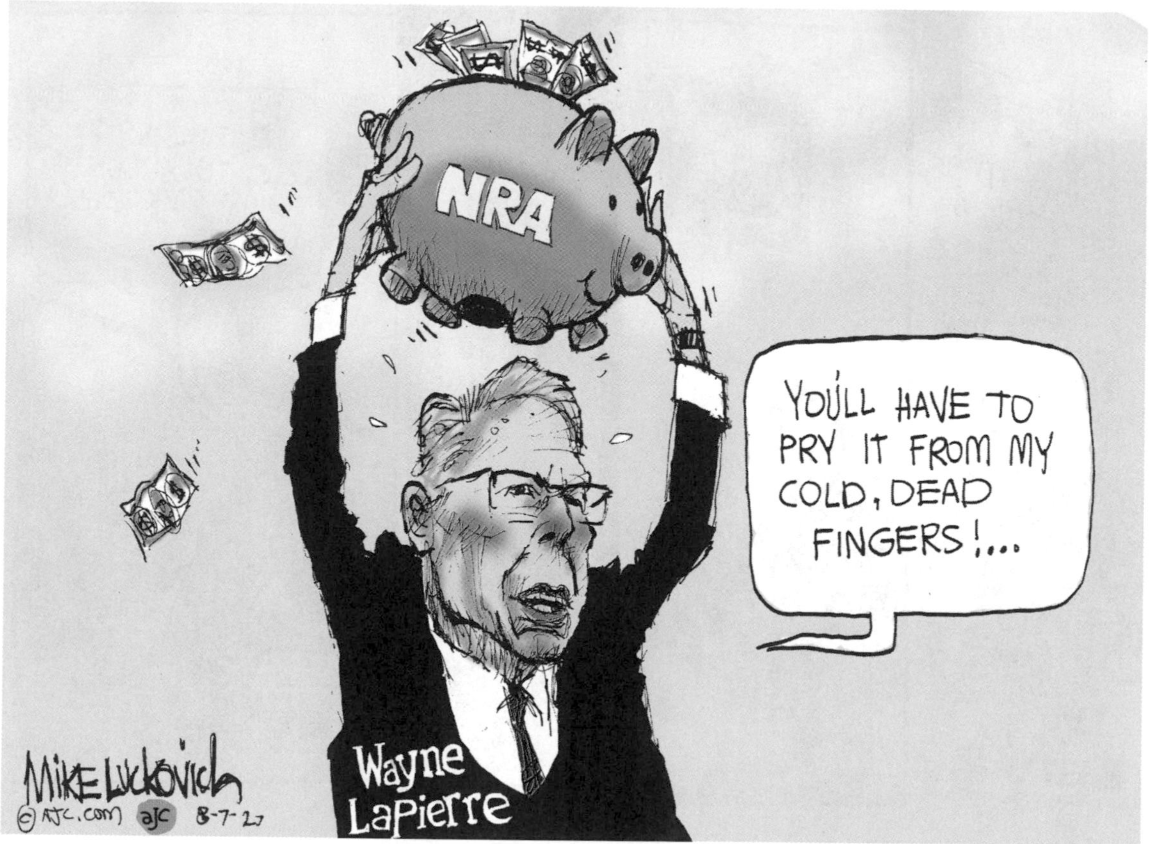
NRA
YOU'LL HAVE TO PRY IT FROM MY COLD, DEAD FINGERS!...
Wayne LaPierre
MIKE LUCKOVICH
© AJC.com ajc 8-7-21

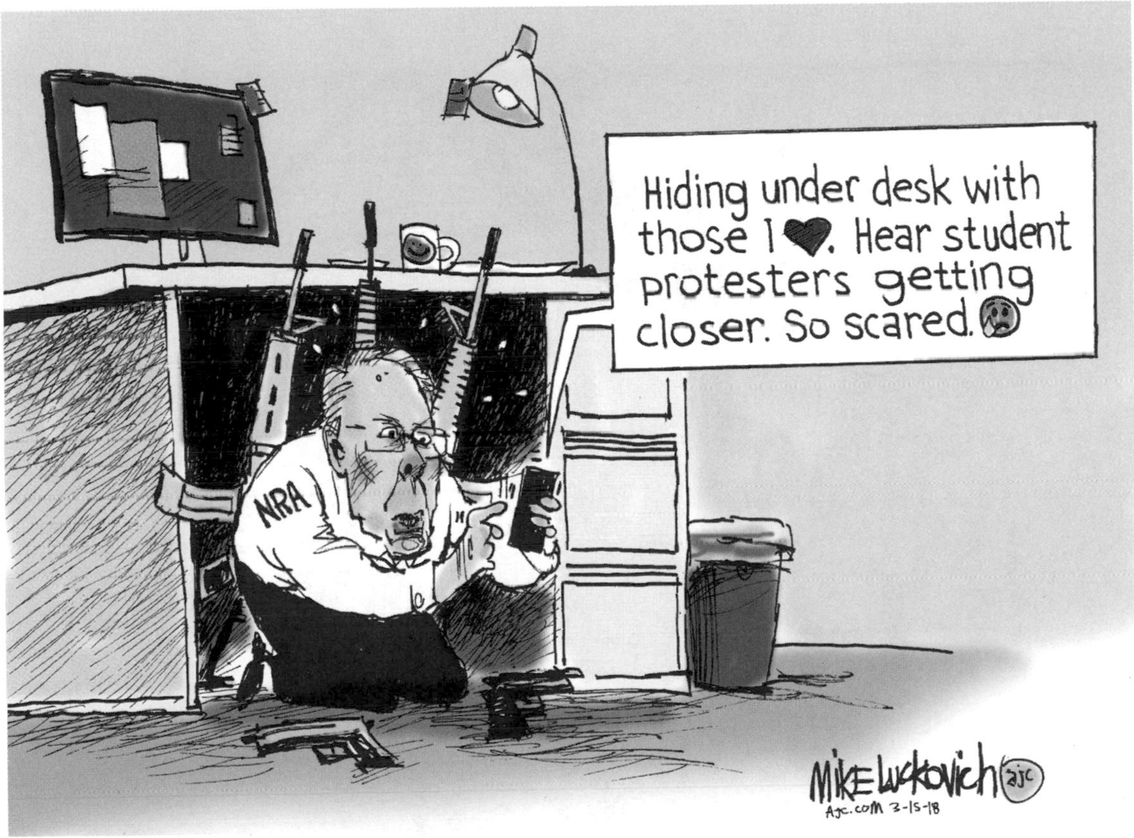
Hiding under desk with those I ♥. Hear student protesters getting closer. So scared.
NRA
MIKE LUCKOVICH
ajc
AJC.COM 3-15-18

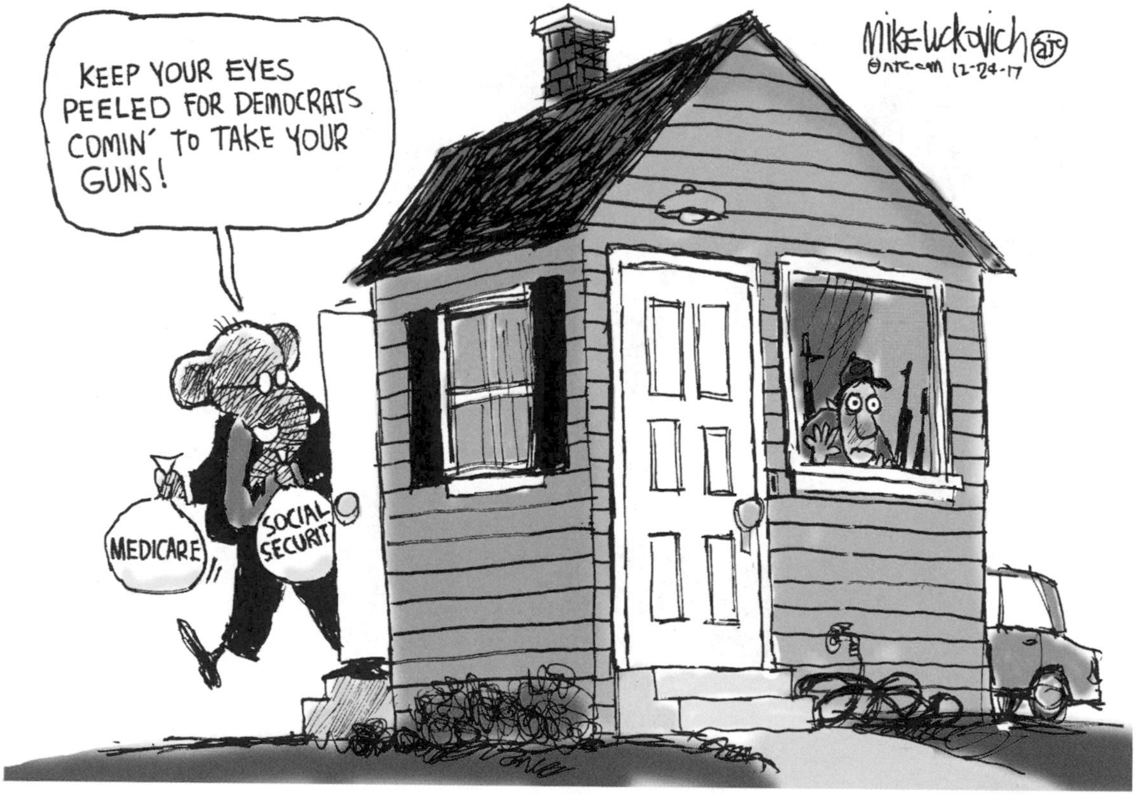
KEEP YOUR EYES PEELED FOR DEMOCRATS COMIN´ TO TAKE YOUR GUNS!
MEDICARE
SOCIAL SECURITY
MIKE LUCKOVICH
12-24-17

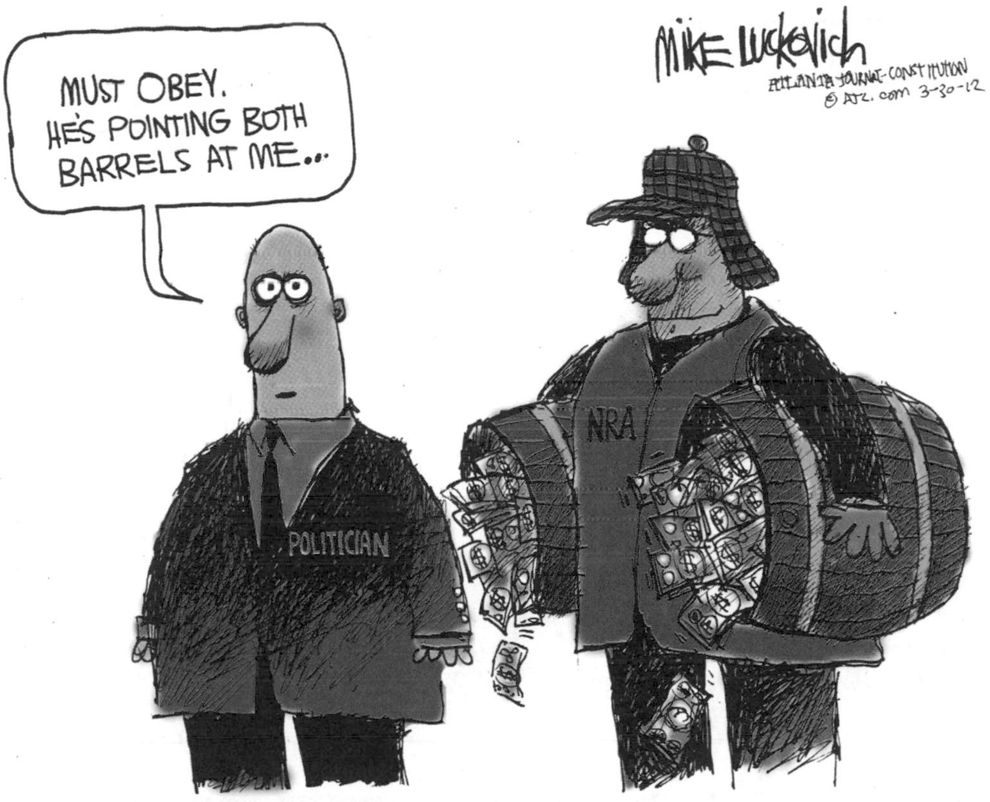
MUST OBEY.
HE'S POINTING BOTH
BARRELS AT ME...
MIKE LUCKOVICH
ATLANTA JOURNAL-CONSTITUTION
© AJC.com 3-30-12
NRA
POLITICIAN

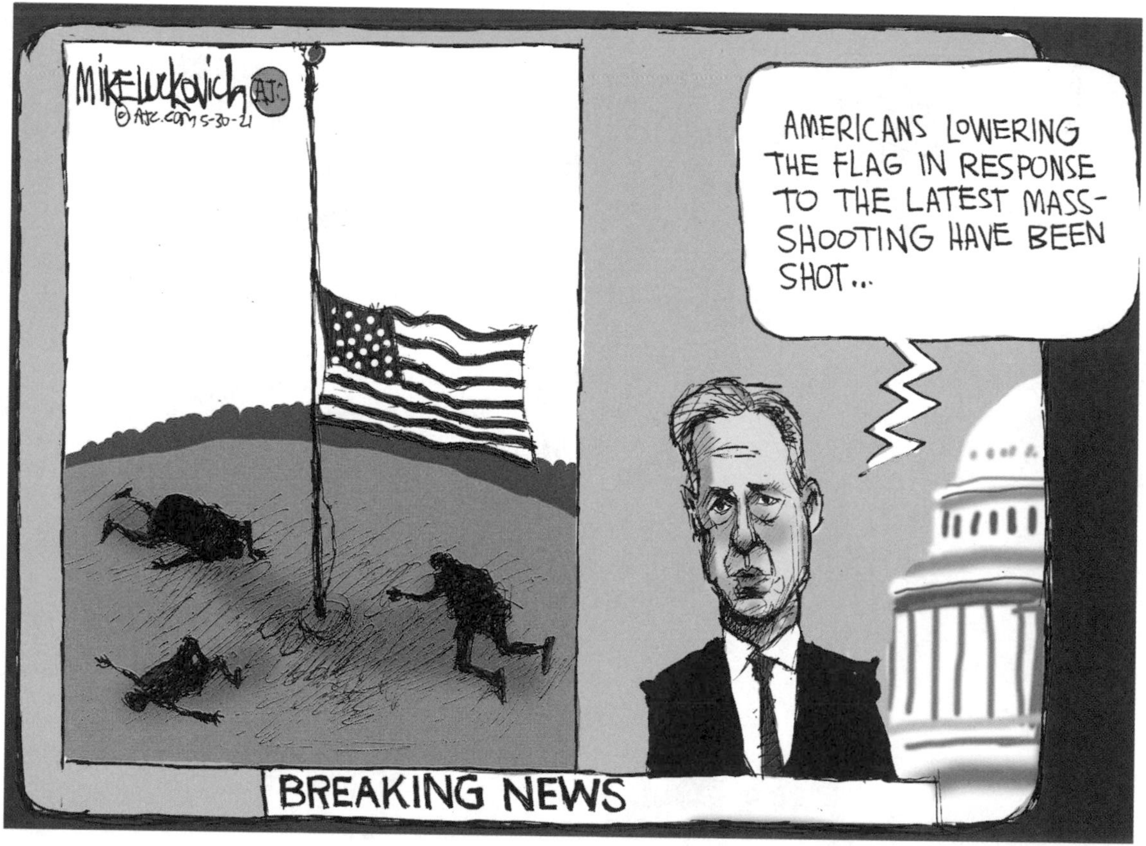
MIKELUCKOVICH AJC
© AJC.com 5-30-21
AMERICANS LOWERING THE FLAG IN RESPONSE TO THE LATEST MASS-SHOOTING HAVE BEEN SHOT...
BREAKING NEWS

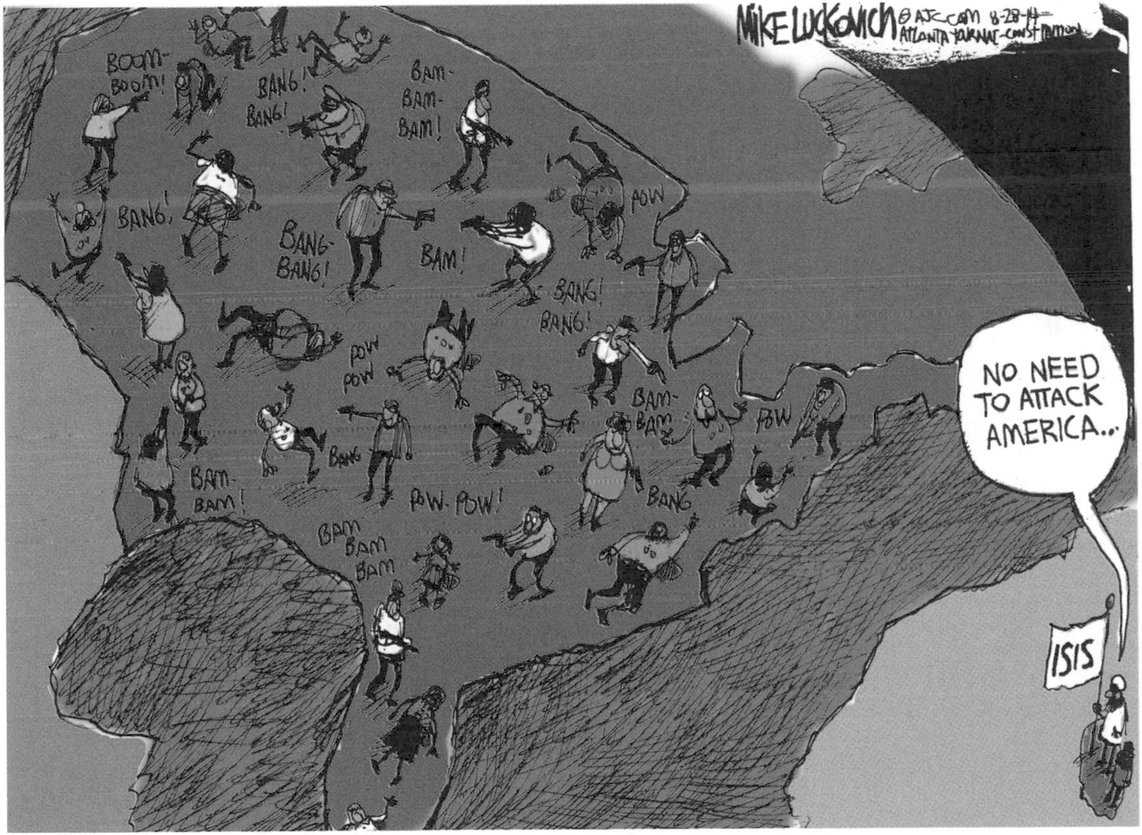
MIKE LUCKOVICH ©AJC.com 8-28-14
ATLANTA JOURNAL-CONSTITUTION
BOOM-BOOM!
BANG! BANG!
BAM-BAM-BAM!
BANG!
POW
BANG-BANG!
BAM!
BANG! BANG!
POW POW
BAM-BAM
POW
BANG
BAM-BAM!
POW-POW!
BANG
BAM BAM BAM
NO NEED TO ATTACK AMERICA...
ISIS

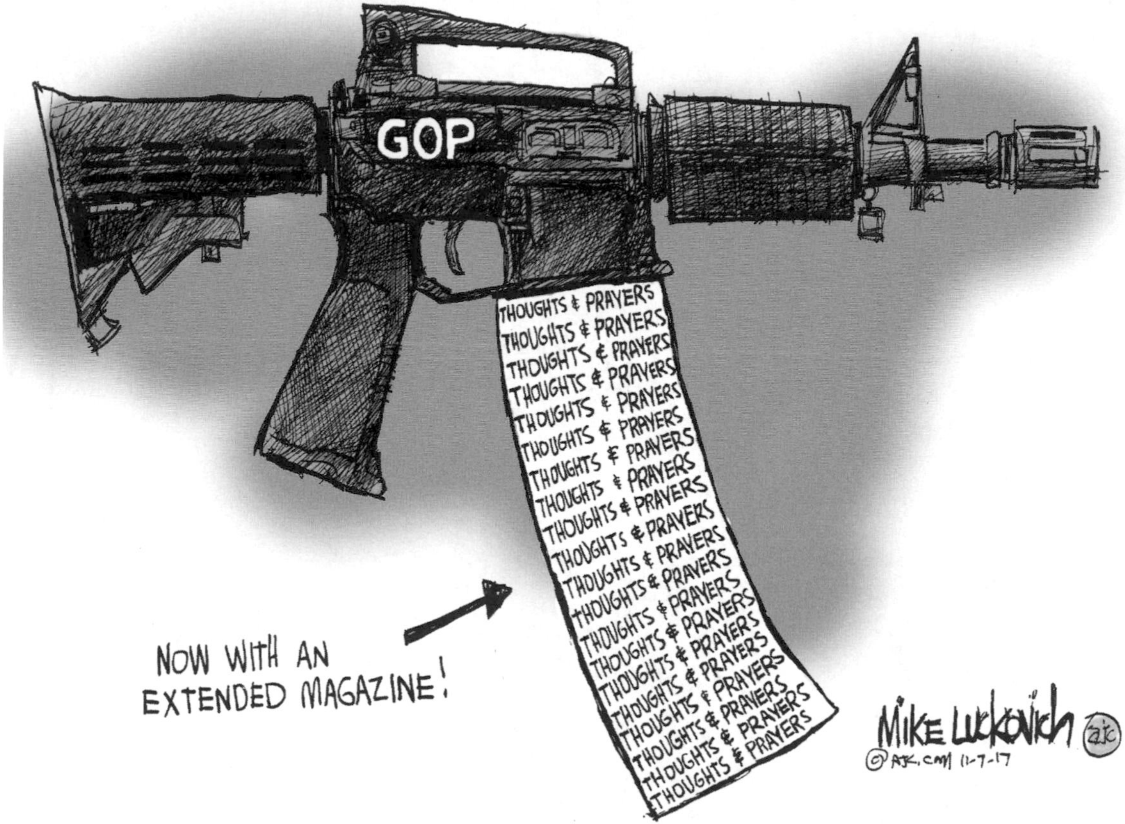
GOP
THOUGHTS & PRAYERS
THOUGHTS & PRAYERS
THOUGHTS & PRAYERS
THOUGHTS & PRAYERS
THOUGHTS & PRAYERS
THOUGHTS & PRAYERS
THOUGHTS & PRAYERS
THOUGHTS & PRAYERS
THOUGHTS & PRAYERS
THOUGHTS & PRAYERS
THOUGHTS & PRAYERS
THOUGHTS & PRAYERS
THOUGHTS & PRAYERS
THOUGHTS & PRAYERS
THOUGHTS & PRAYERS
THOUGHTS & PRAYERS
THOUGHTS & PRAYERS
THOUGHTS & PRAYERS
THOUGHTS & PRAYERS
THOUGHTS & PRAYERS
THOUGHTS & PRAYERS
THOUGHTS & PRAYERS
NOW WITH AN EXTENDED MAGAZINE!
MIKE LUCKOVICH
AJC
© AJC.com 11-7-17

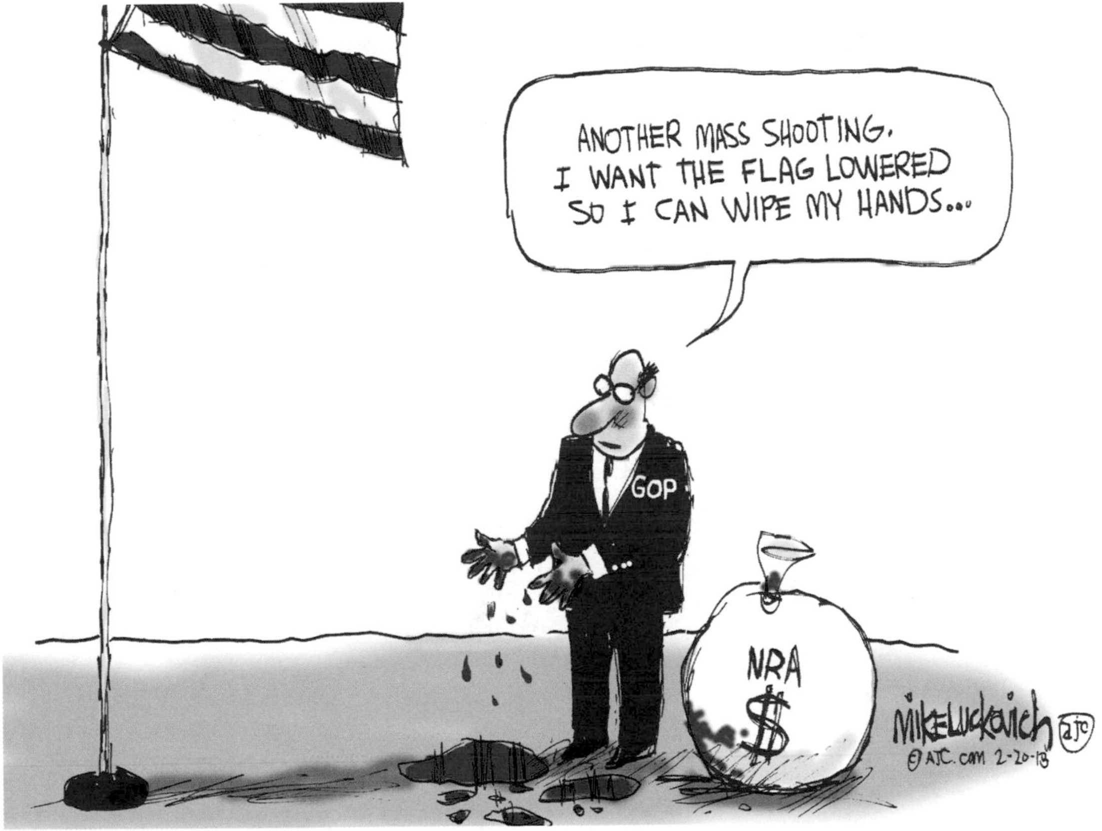
ANOTHER MASS SHOOTING.
I WANT THE FLAG LOWERED
SO I CAN WIPE MY HANDS...
GOP
NRA
$
MIKELUCKOVICH
©AJC.com 2-20-18

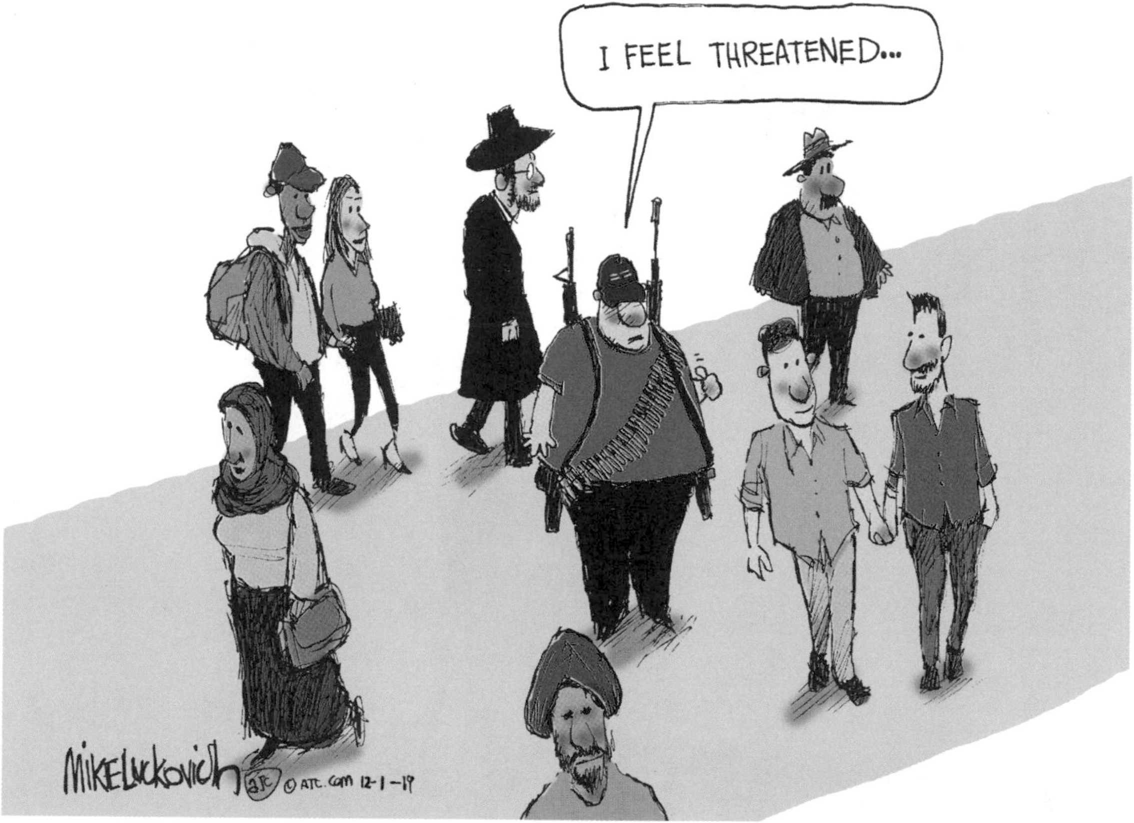
I FEEL THREATENED...
MIKELUCKOVICH
AJC © AJC.com 12-1-19

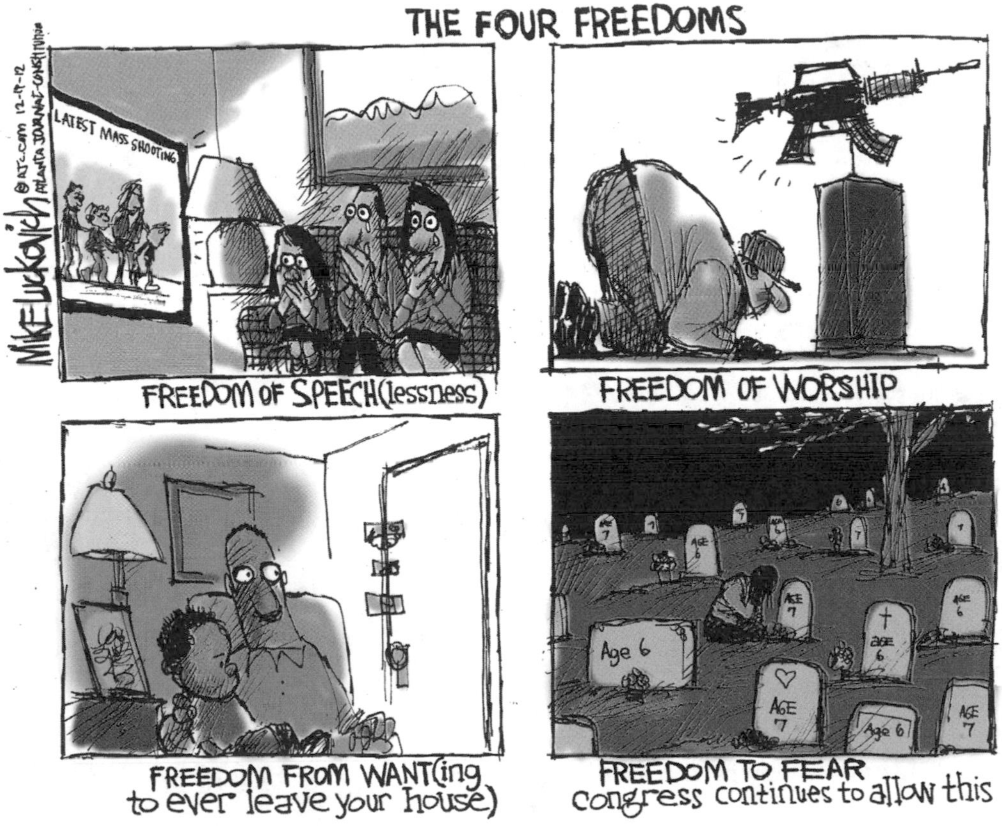
THE FOUR FREEDOMS
MIKE LUCKOVICH
LATEST MASS SHOOTING
FREEDOM OF SPEECH(lessness)
FREEDOM OF WORSHIP
FREEDOM FROM WANT(ing to ever leave your house)
Age 6
AGE 7
AGE 6
FREEDOM TO FEAR
congress continues to allow this

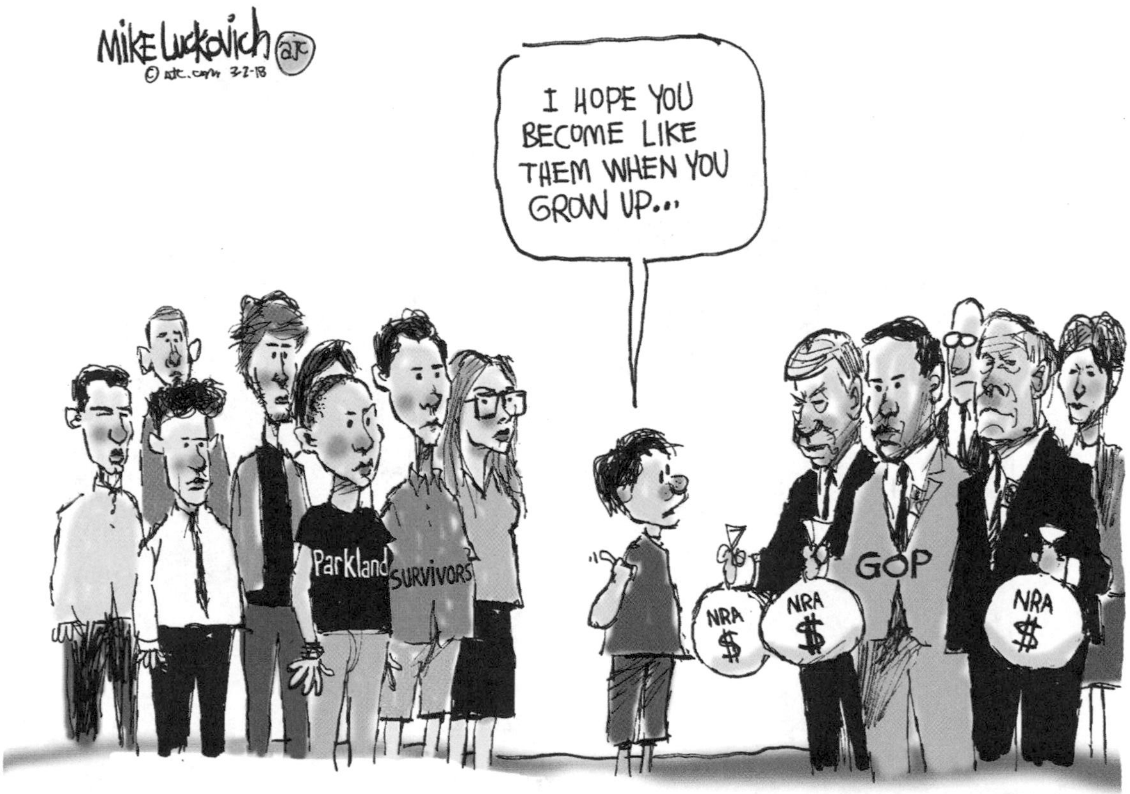
MIKE LUCKOVICH
© ajc.com 3-2-18
I HOPE YOU BECOME LIKE THEM WHEN YOU GROW UP...
Parkland
SURVIVORS
NRA $
NRA $
GOP
NRA $

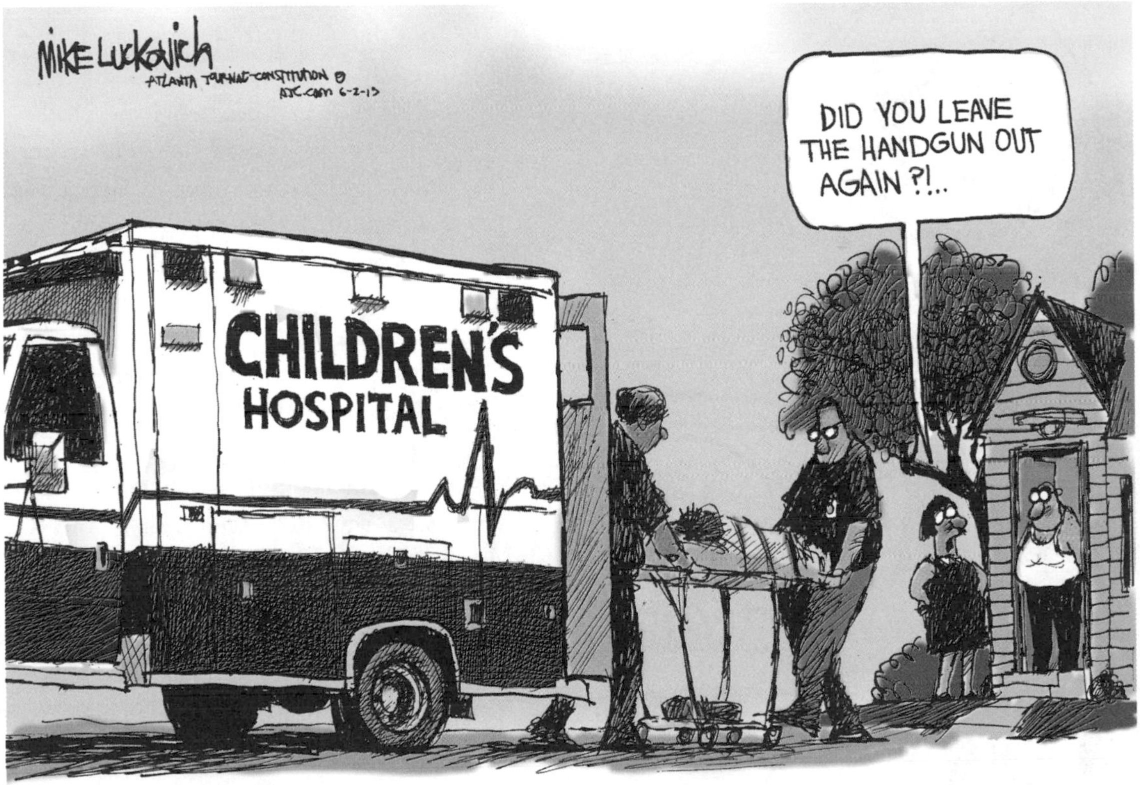
MIKE LUCKOVICH
DID YOU LEAVE THE HANDGUN OUT AGAIN ?!..
CHILDREN'S HOSPITAL

FLUSH

Ch. 6 Voting Rights

As a young cartoonist, my cartoons were, for the most part, humorous, lighter takes on what was occurring in America. Even though it had problems and challenges, I viewed the United States as basically on the right path — almost like a plane on autopilot. I thought we would continue forming a more perfect union. I began seeing America change in the late '90s with the rise of Fox News, Rush Limbaugh and Newt Gingrich as House Speaker. This is when civility and truth began to die. Gingrich, Rush and Fox News were demonizing and lying about Democrats in a way I'd never seen before. George W. Bush, Trump, Mitch McConnell and social media have accelerated this trend to the point that I fear for America's future. While I still occasionally use humor in my cartoons, they've become more urgent, more about waking up my fellow citizens to what's happening.

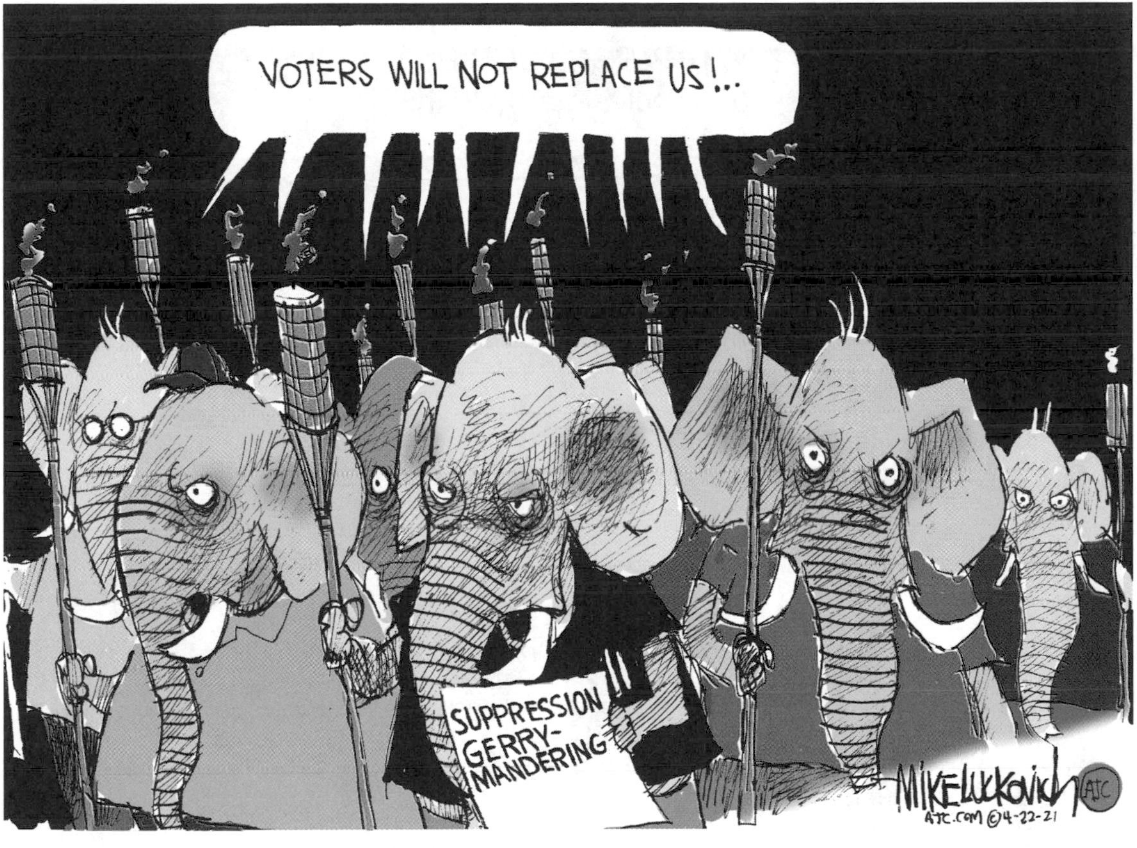
VOTERS WILL NOT REPLACE US!..
SUPPRESSION
GERRY-
MANDERING
MIKELUCKOVICH
AJC
AJC.com ©4-22-21

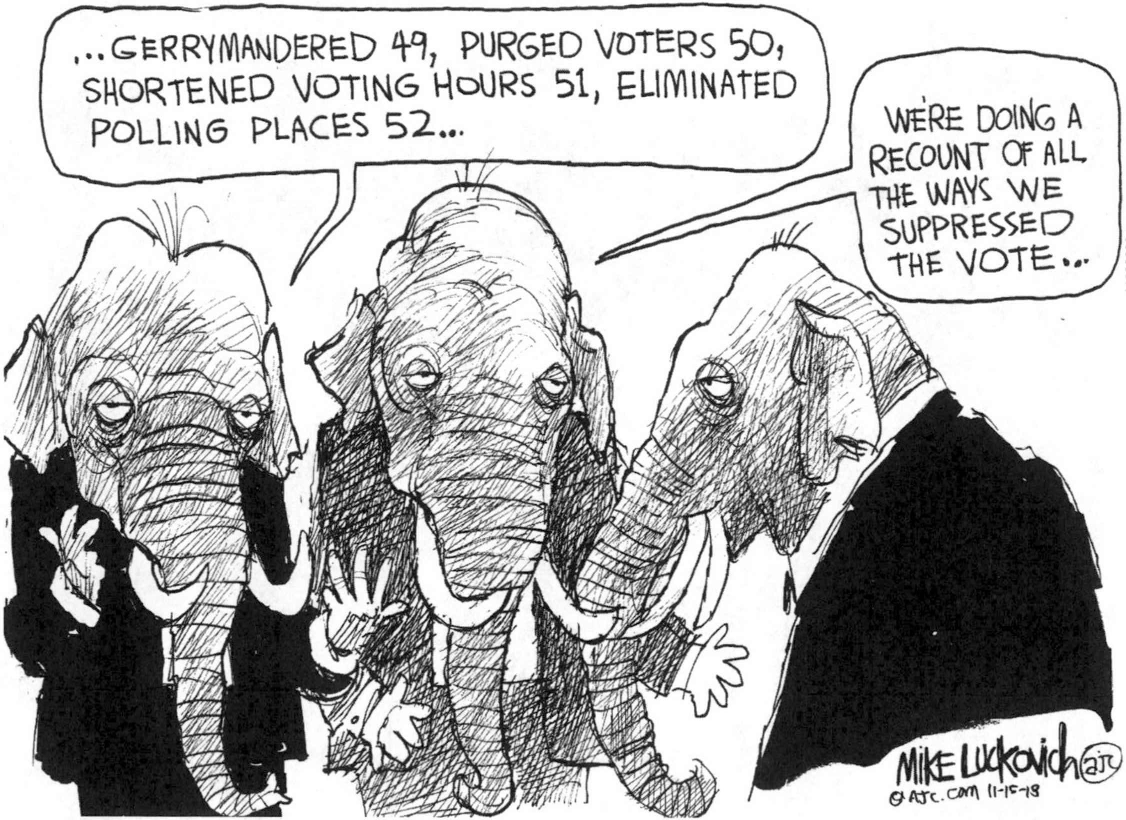
...GERRYMANDERED 49, PURGED VOTERS 50, SHORTENED VOTING HOURS 51, ELIMINATED POLLING PLACES 52...
WE'RE DOING A RECOUNT OF ALL THE WAYS WE SUPPRESSED THE VOTE...
MIKE LUCKOVICH AJC
©AJC.COM 11-15-18

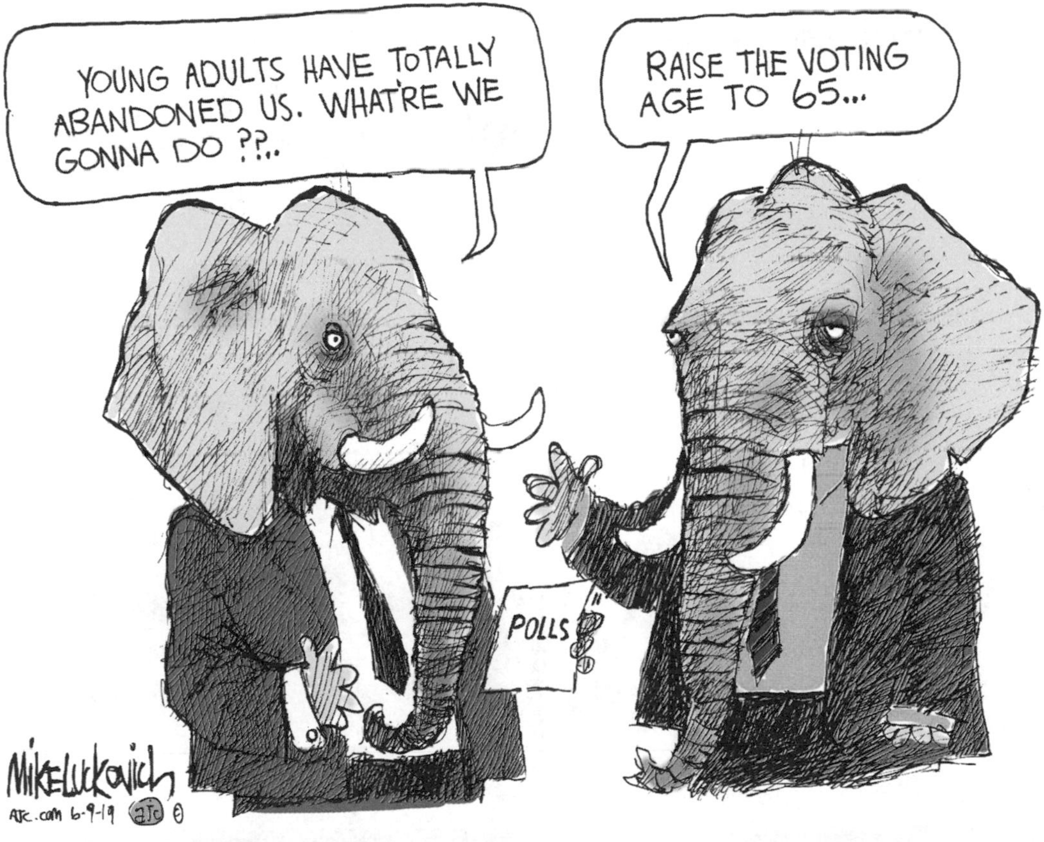
YOUNG ADULTS HAVE TOTALLY ABANDONED US. WHAT'RE WE GONNA DO ??..
RAISE THE VOTING AGE TO 65...
POLLS
MIKELUCKOVICH
AJC.com 6-9-19

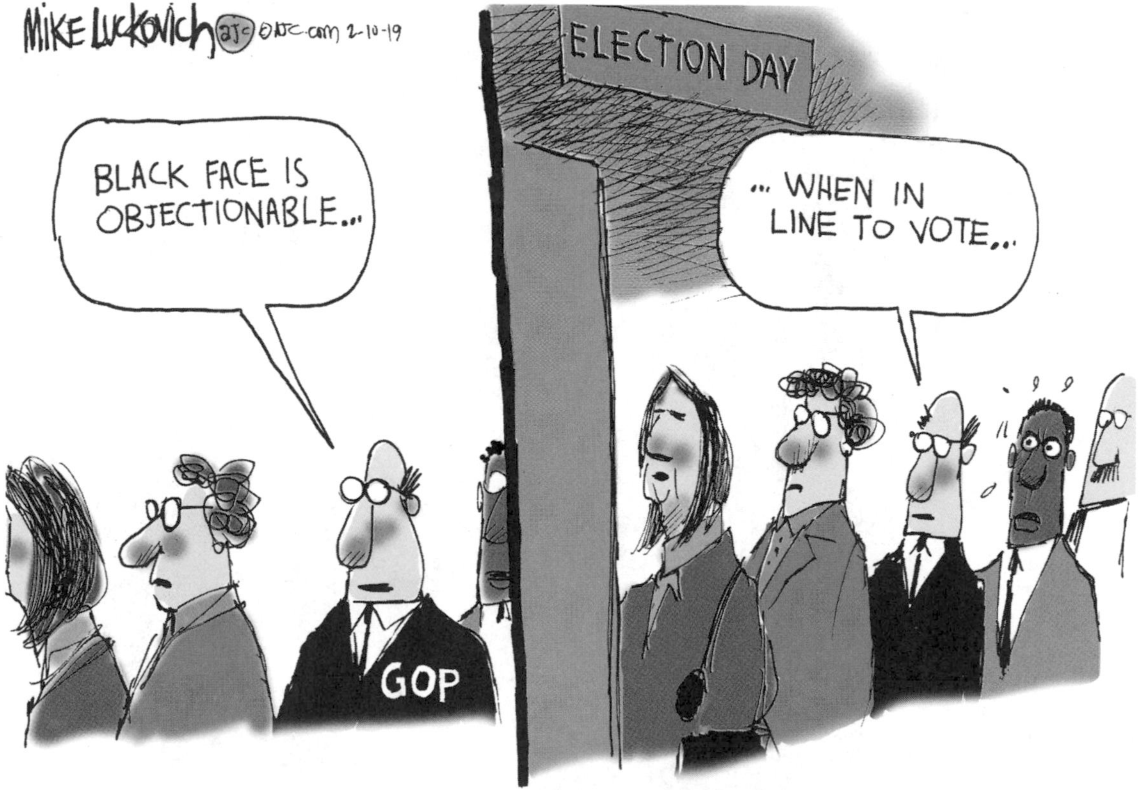
MIKE LUCKOVICH ajc ©AJC.com 2-10-19
BLACK FACE IS OBJECTIONABLE...
GOP
ELECTION DAY
... WHEN IN LINE TO VOTE...

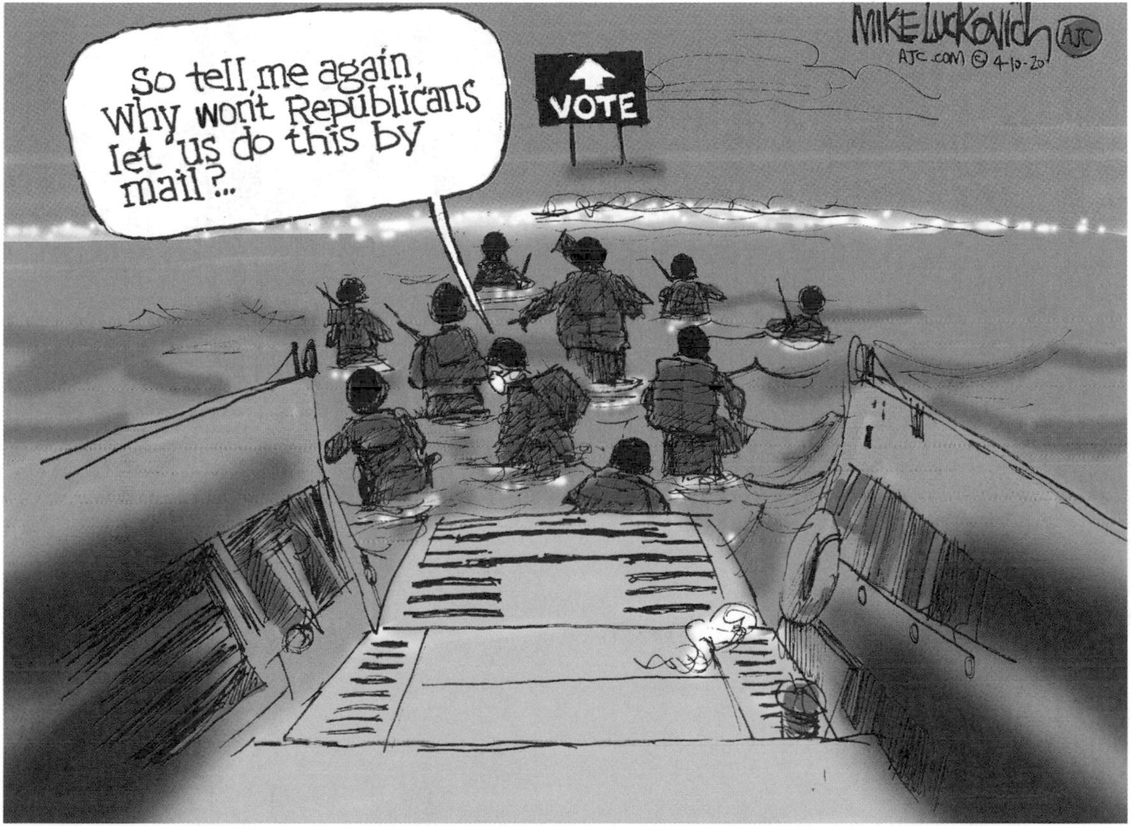
So tell me again, Why won't Republicans let us do this by mail?..
VOTE
MIKE LUCKOVICH
AJC.COM © 4-10-20

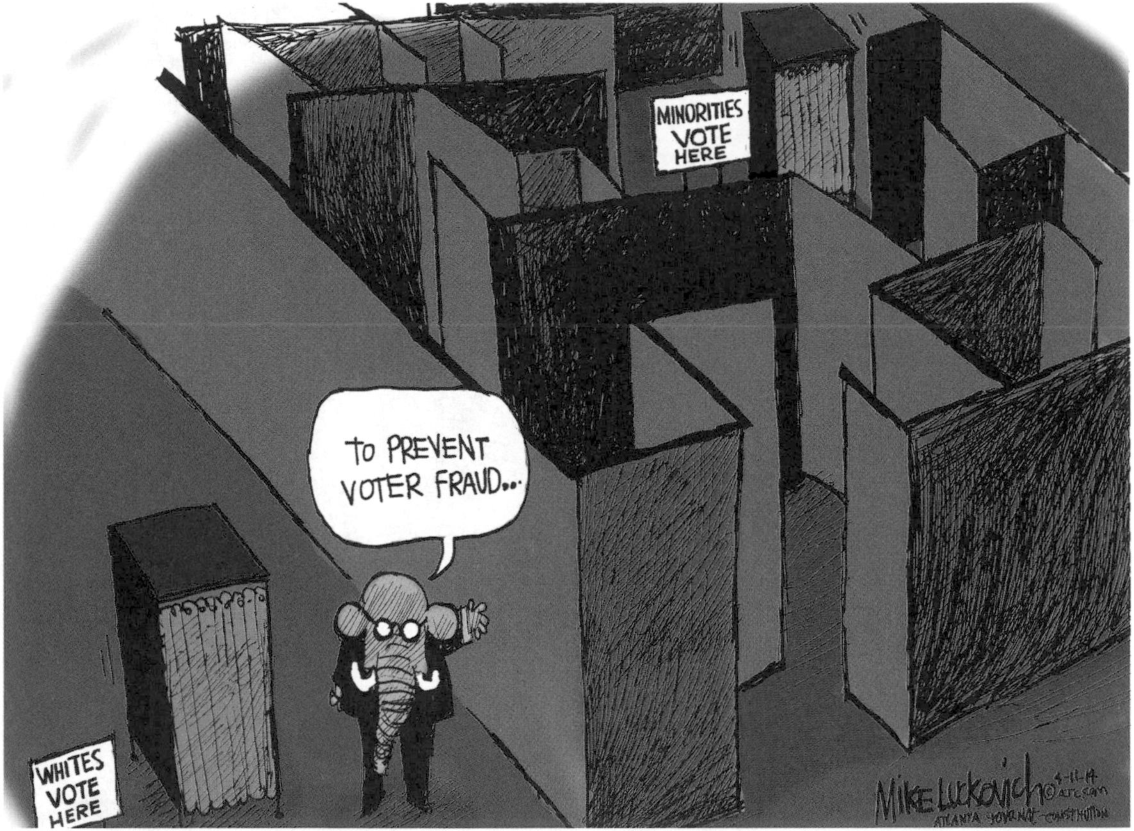
MINORITIES VOTE HERE
TO PREVENT VOTER FRAUD...
WHITES VOTE HERE
MIKE LUCKOVICH
ATLANTA JOURNAL-CONSTITUTION

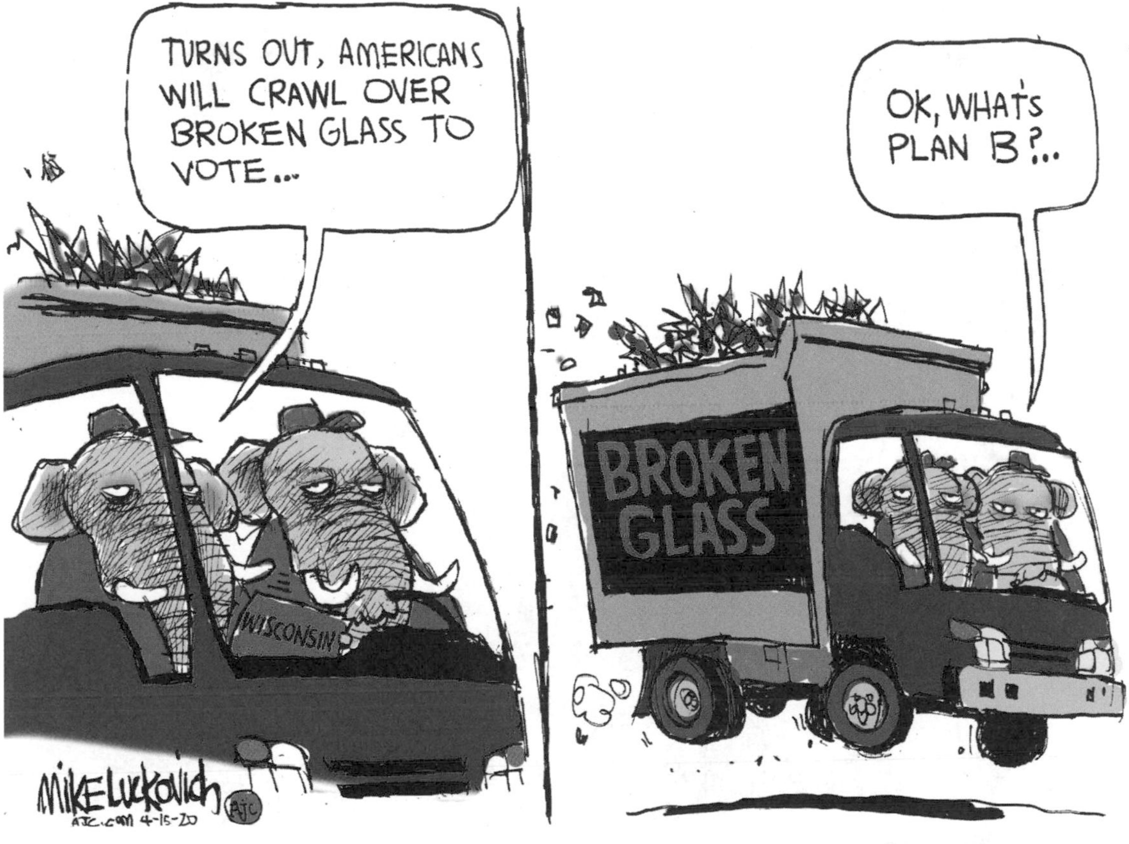
TURNS OUT, AMERICANS WILL CRAWL OVER BROKEN GLASS TO VOTE...
WISCONSIN
MIKE LUCKOVICH
AJC.com 4-15-20
AJC
BROKEN GLASS
OK, WHAT'S PLAN B?...

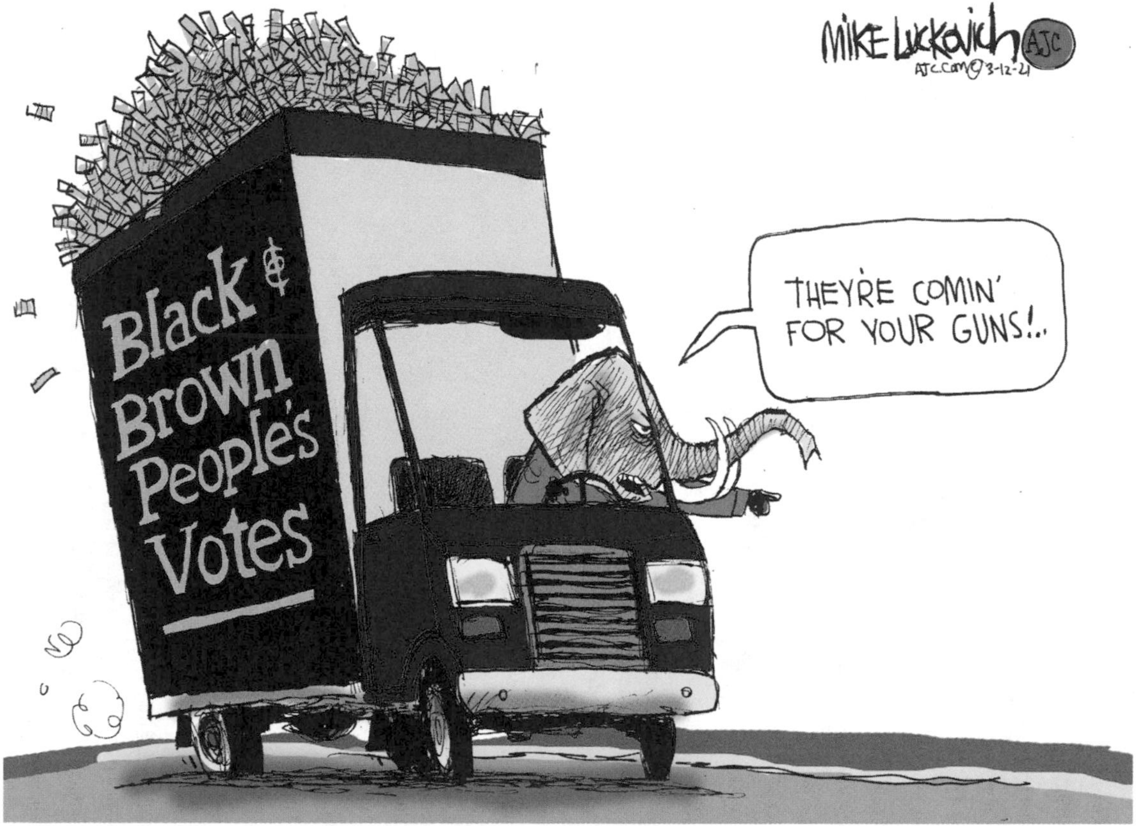
MIKE LUCKOVICH AJC
AJC.com © 3-12-21
Black & Brown People's Votes
THEY'RE COMIN' FOR YOUR GUNS!..

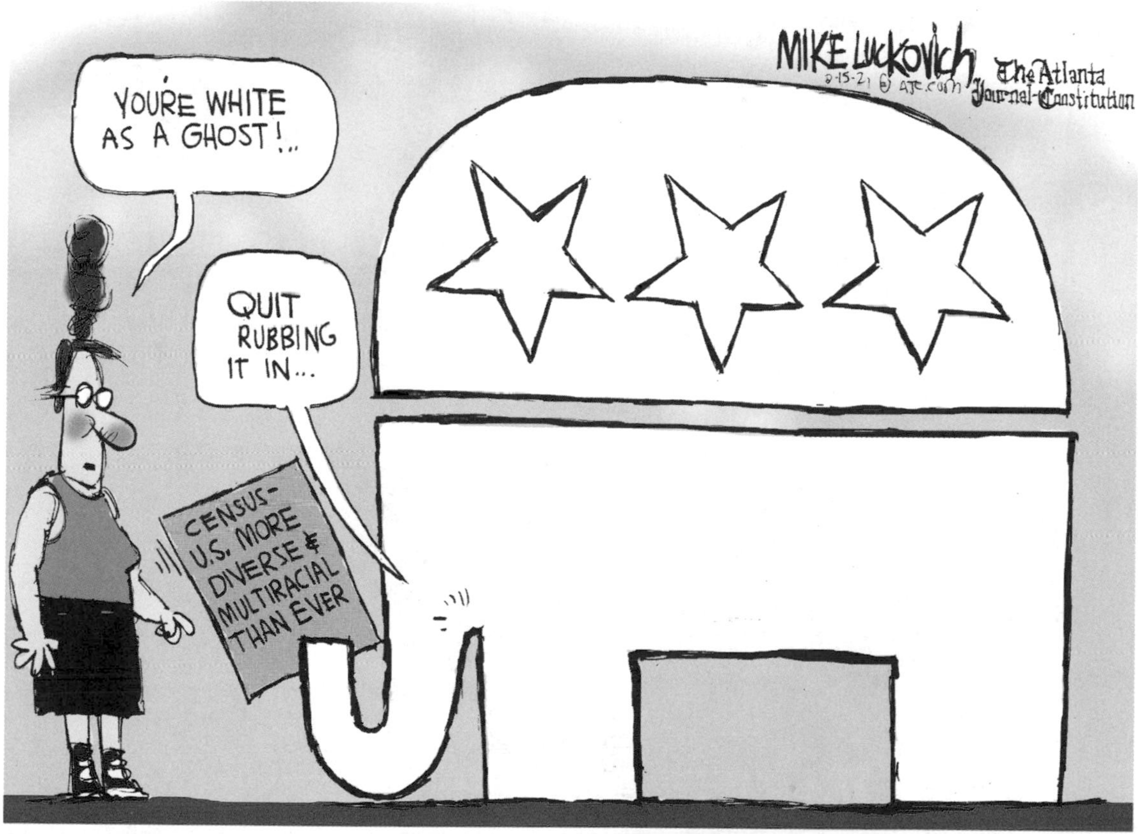
MIKE LUCKOVICH
2-15-21 © AJC.com
The Atlanta Journal-Constitution
YOU'RE WHITE AS A GHOST!...
QUIT RUBBING IT IN...
CENSUS- U.S. MORE DIVERSE & MULTIRACIAL THAN EVER

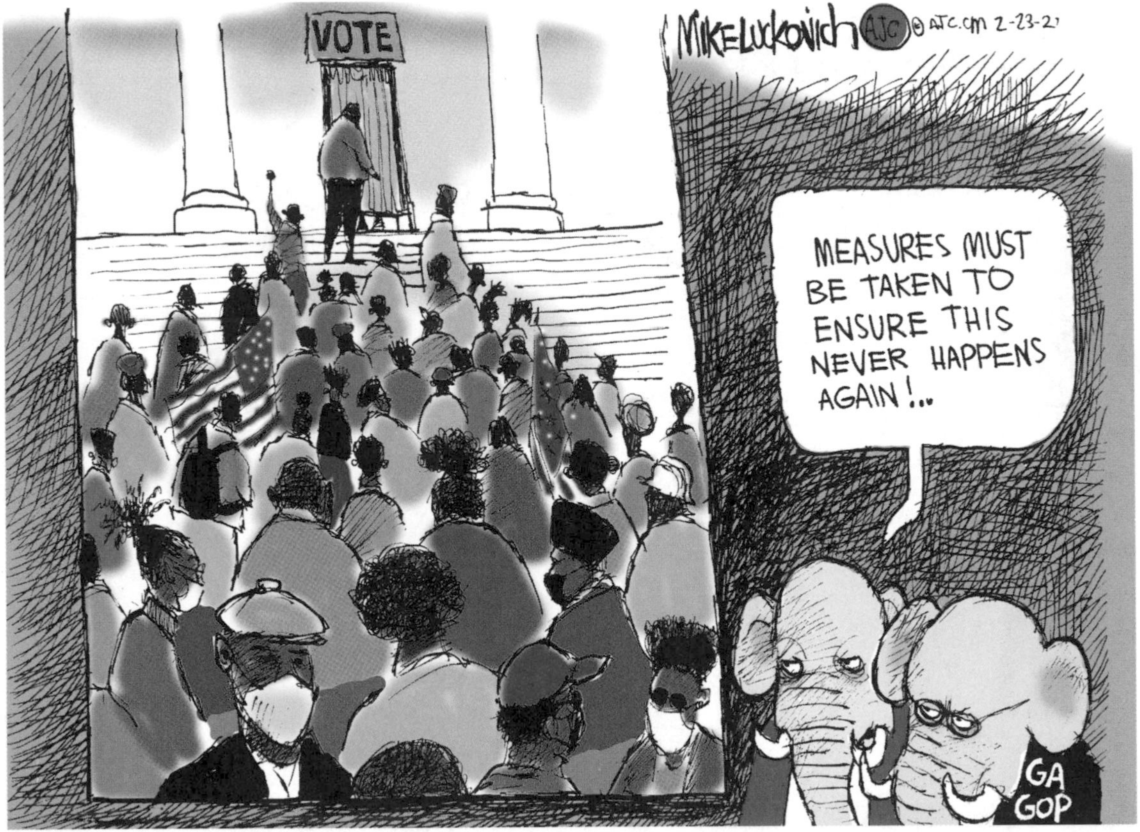
VOTE
MIKE LUCKOVICH AJC © AJC.com 2-23-21
MEASURES MUST BE TAKEN TO ENSURE THIS NEVER HAPPENS AGAIN!..
GA GOP

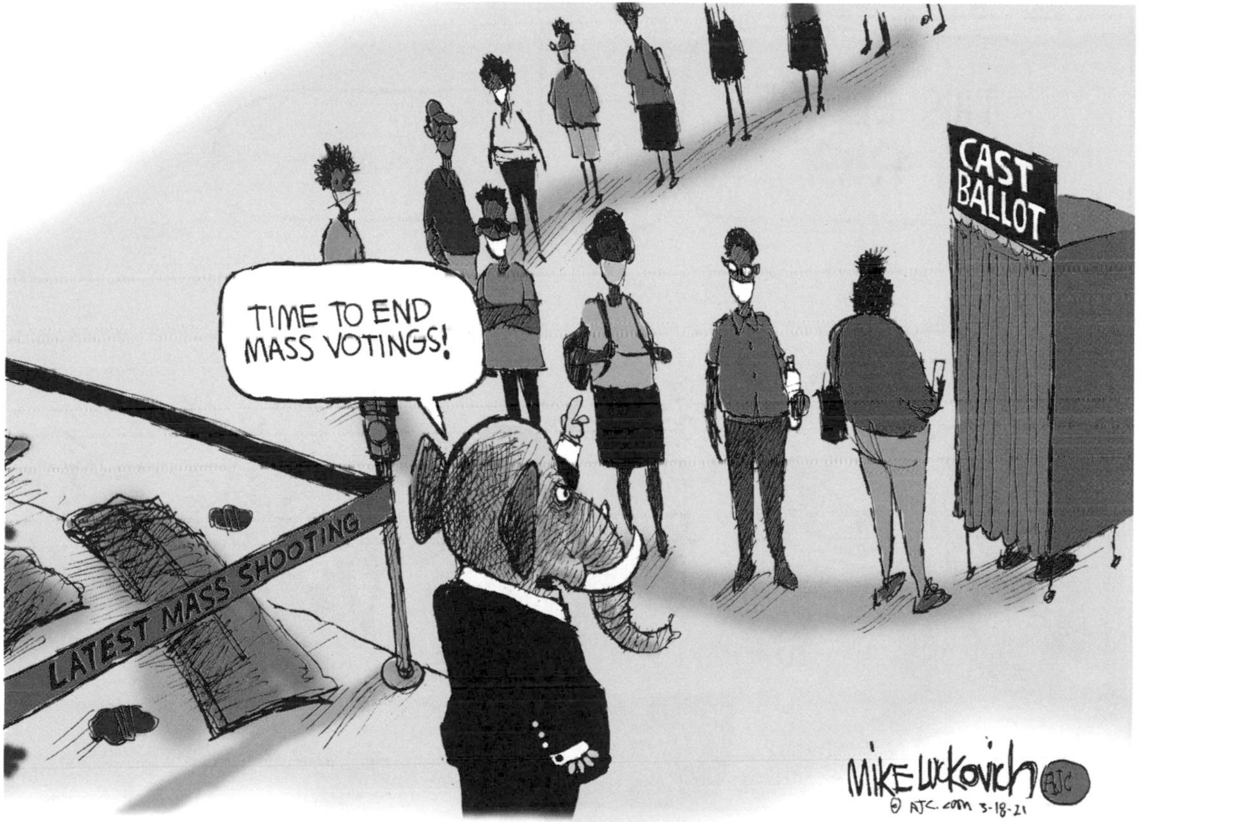
CAST BALLOT
TIME TO END MASS VOTINGS!
LATEST MASS SHOOTING
MIKE LUCKOVICH
© AJC.com 3-18-21

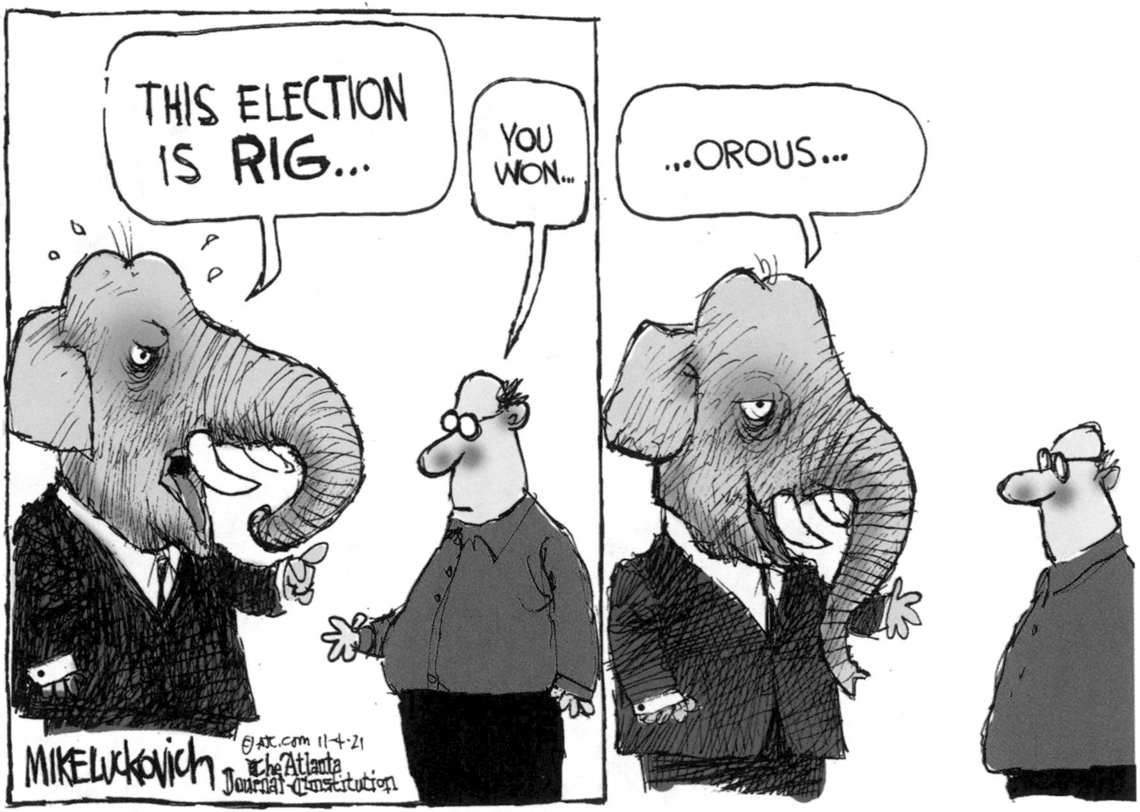
THIS ELECTION IS RIG...
YOU WON...
...OROUS...
MIKELUCKOVICH
©AJC.com 11-4-21
The Atlanta Journal-Constitution

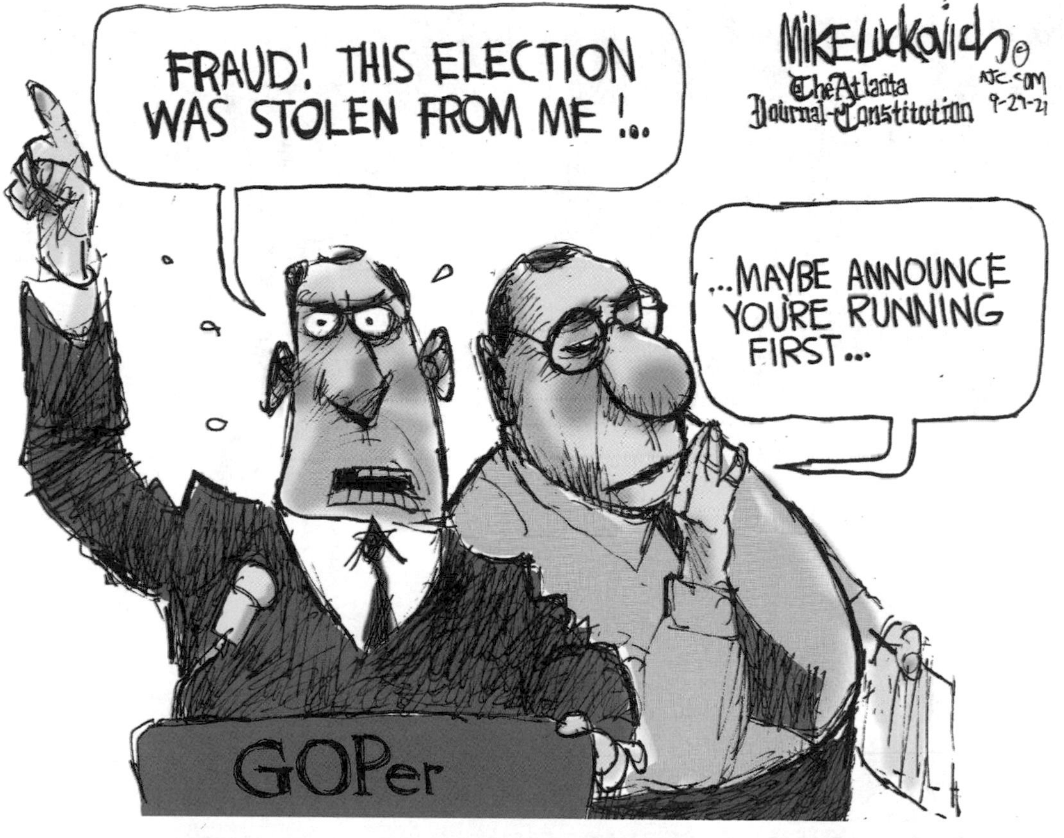
FRAUD! THIS ELECTION WAS STOLEN FROM ME !...
...MAYBE ANNOUNCE YOU'RE RUNNING FIRST...
GOPer
MIKE LUCKOVICH ©
The Atlanta Journal-Constitution
AJC.COM
9-29-21

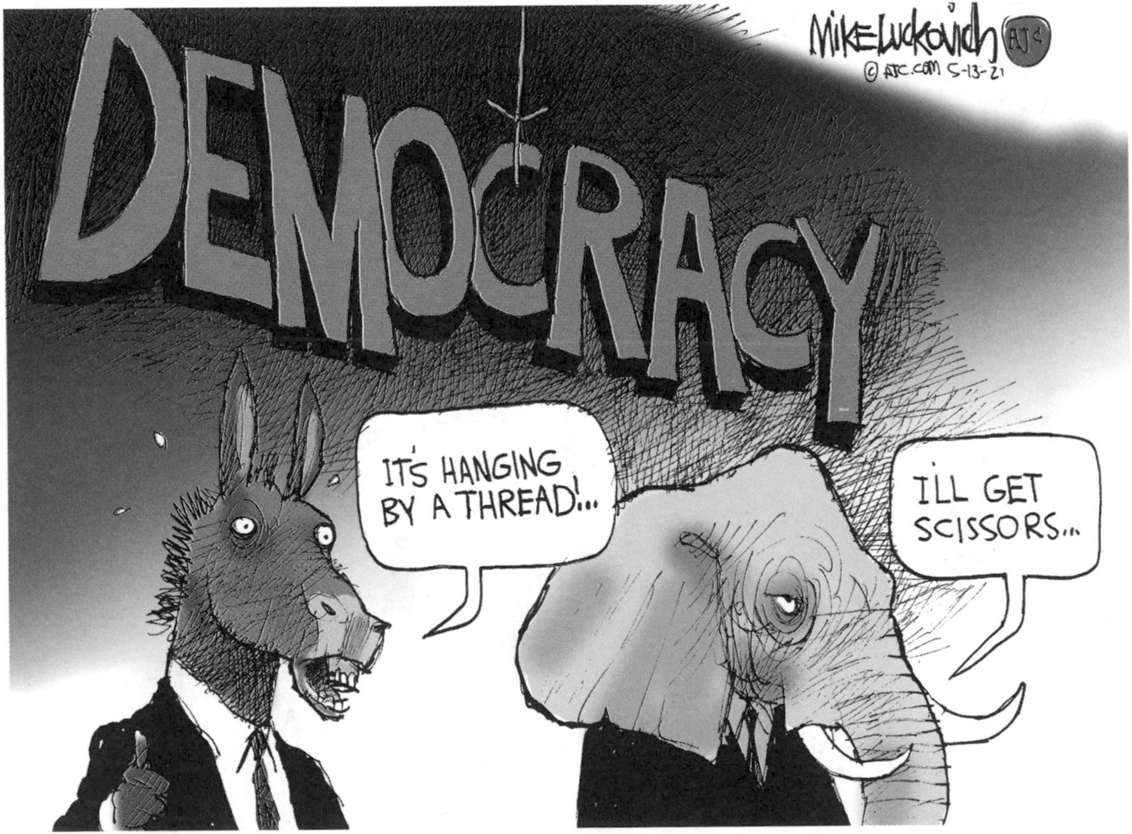
DEMOCRACY
MIKE LUCKOVICH AJC
© AJC.com 5-13-21
IT'S HANGING BY A THREAD!...
I'LL GET SCISSORS...

CHEW CHEW

Ch. 7
Immigration

Want to know one of the best things the U.S. economy has going for it? Immigrants. Immigrants keep the economy growing and help maintain a healthy working-age to senior ratio, keeping Social Security going for America's aging population. The birth rate in the U.S. has slowed. We need a steady influx of immigrants to make up for this. Limiting immigration hurts America, but you wouldn't know this if you listened to Republicans and Fox News. They make immigrants out to be scary threats, headed in caravans towards our border, bringing crime and disease. America needs a path to citizenship for those who want to come to America and for those already here. It would be a win-win for everyone except the right-wing, who would lose one of their biggest fake talking points.

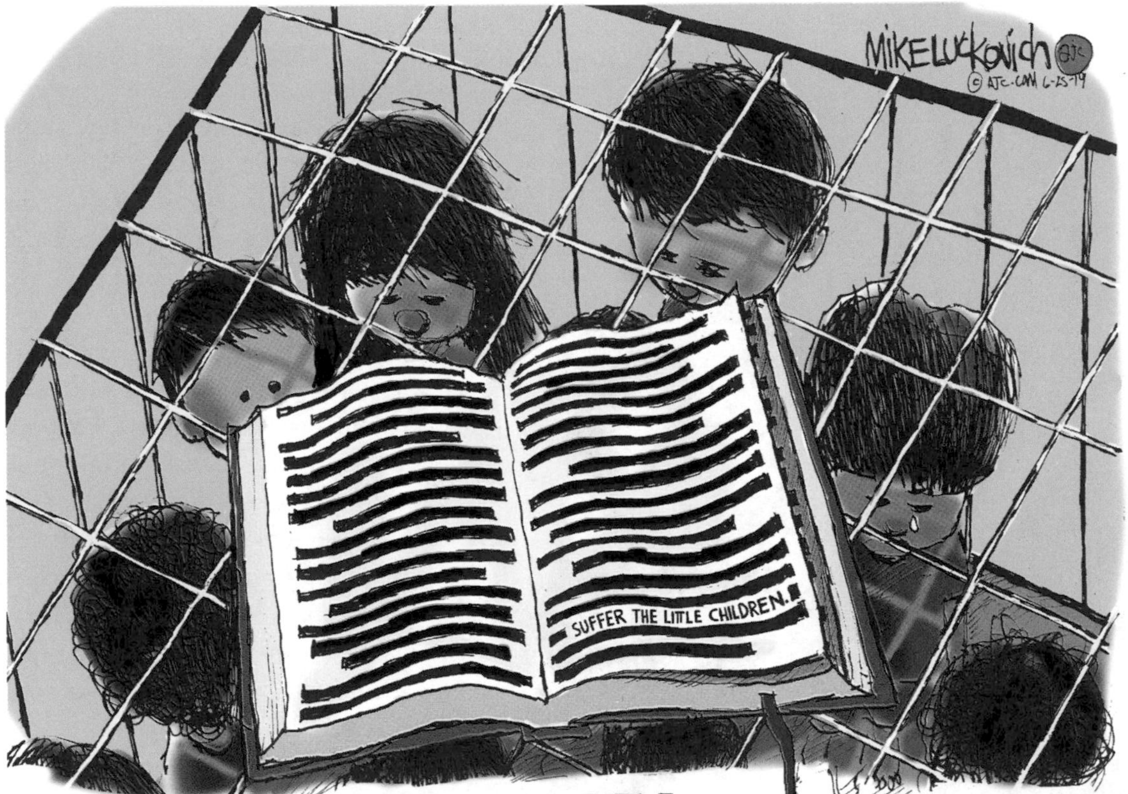
MIKELUCKOVICH
© AJC.COM 6-25-19
SUFFER THE LITTLE CHILDREN.

TRUMP-PENCE BIBLE

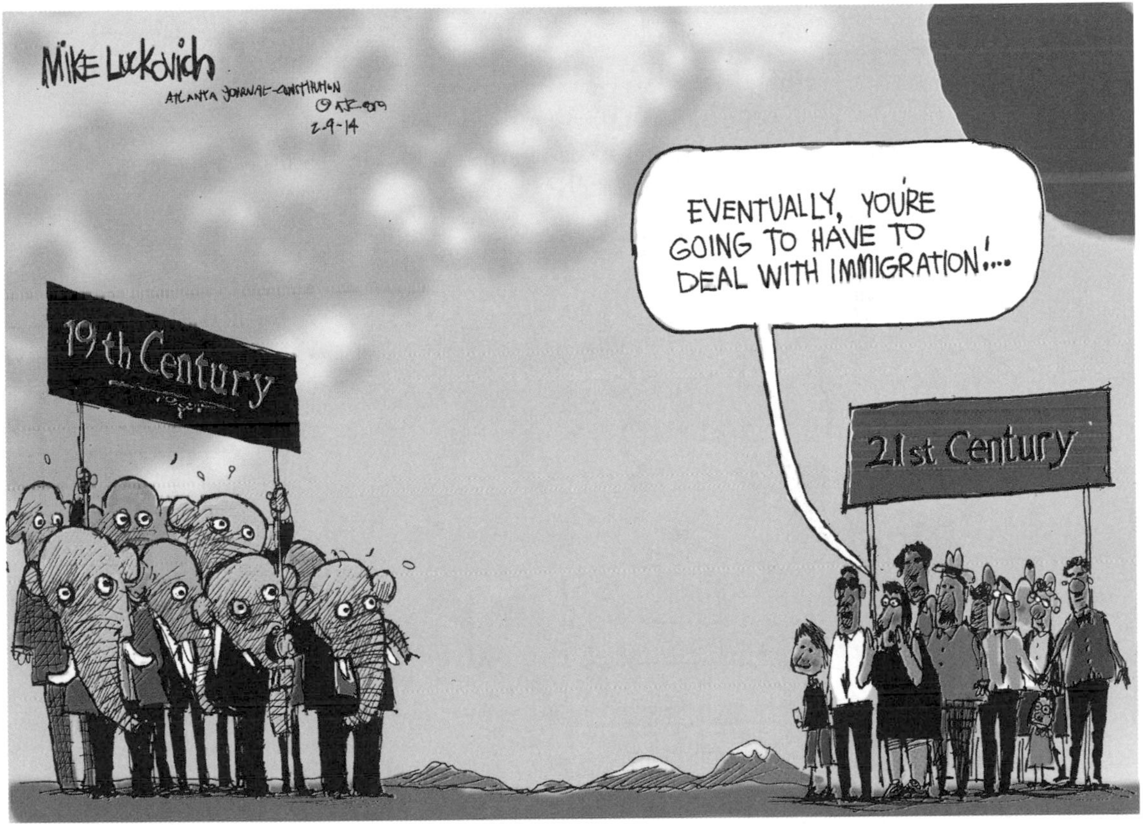
MIKE LUCKOVICH
ATLANTA JOURNAL-CONSTITUTION
2-9-14
19th Century
EVENTUALLY, YOU'RE GOING TO HAVE TO DEAL WITH IMMIGRATION!...
21st Century

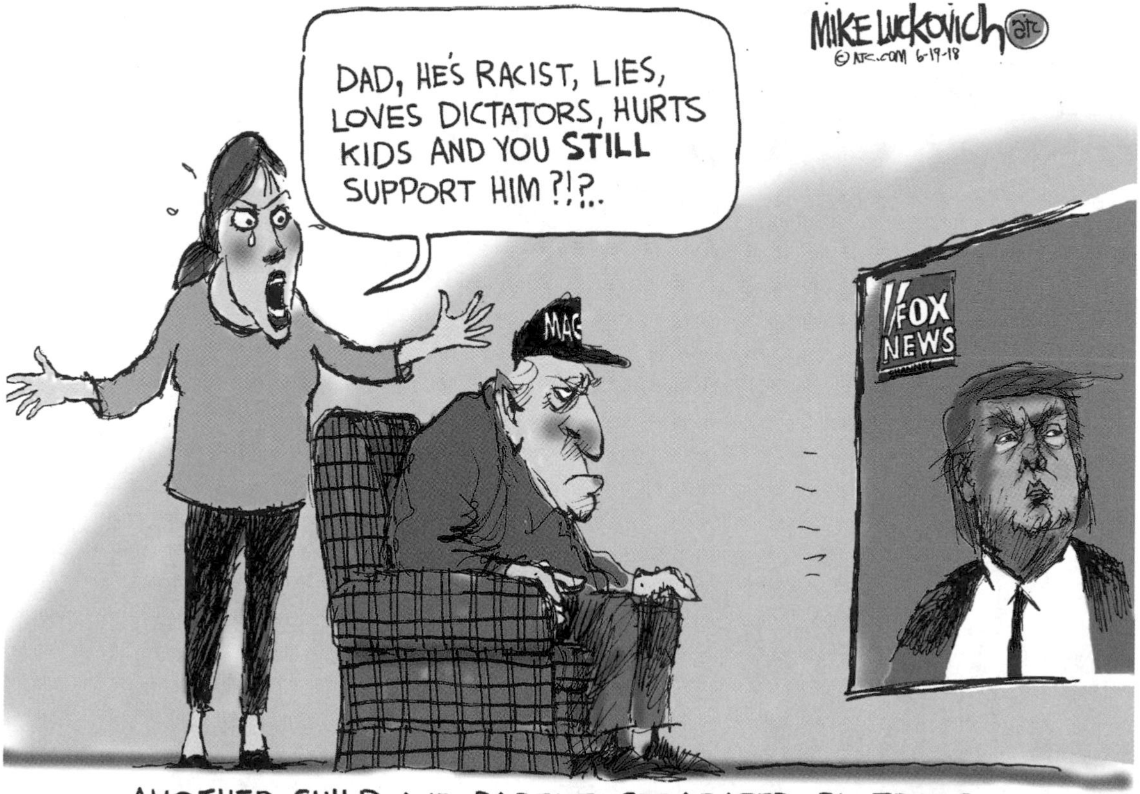
DAD, HE'S RACIST, LIES, LOVES DICTATORS, HURTS KIDS AND YOU **STILL** SUPPORT HIM ?!?..
MIKE LUCKOVICH
© AJC.COM 6-19-18
MAG
FOX NEWS

ANOTHER CHILD AND PARENT SEPARATED BY TRUMP

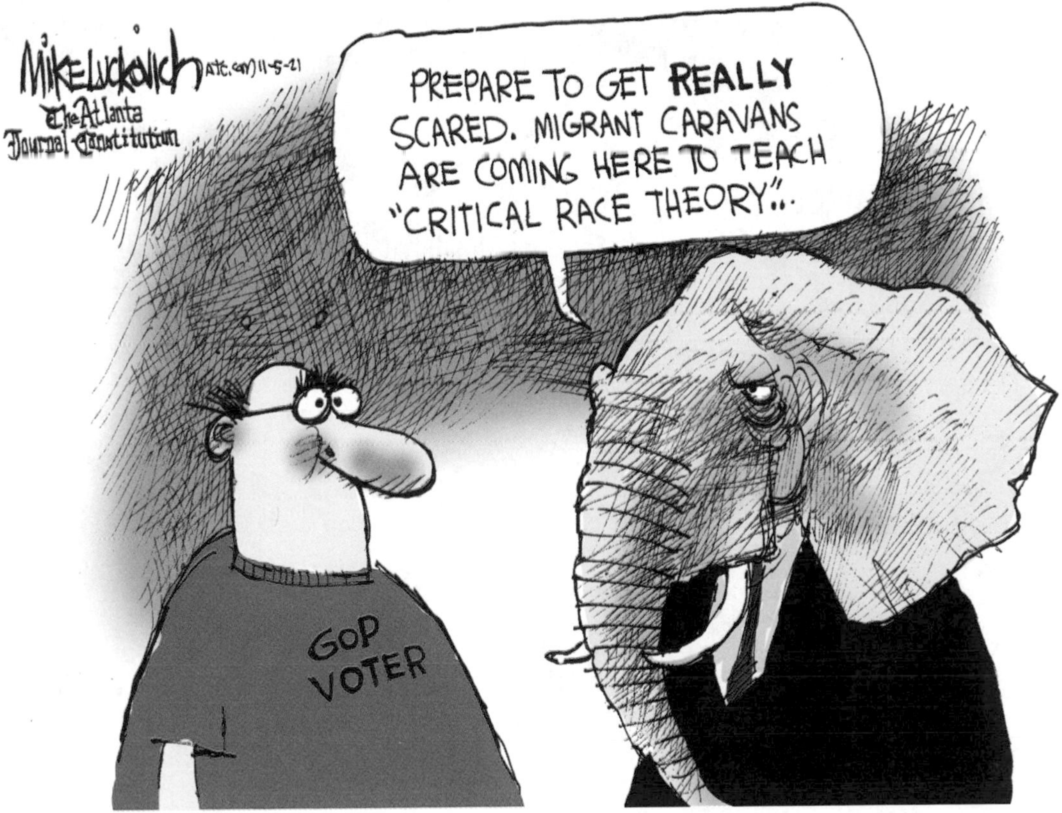
MIKELUCKOVICH AJC.com 11-5-21
The Atlanta Journal Constitution
PREPARE TO GET **REALLY** SCARED. MIGRANT CARAVANS ARE COMING HERE TO TEACH "CRITICAL RACE THEORY"...
GOP VOTER

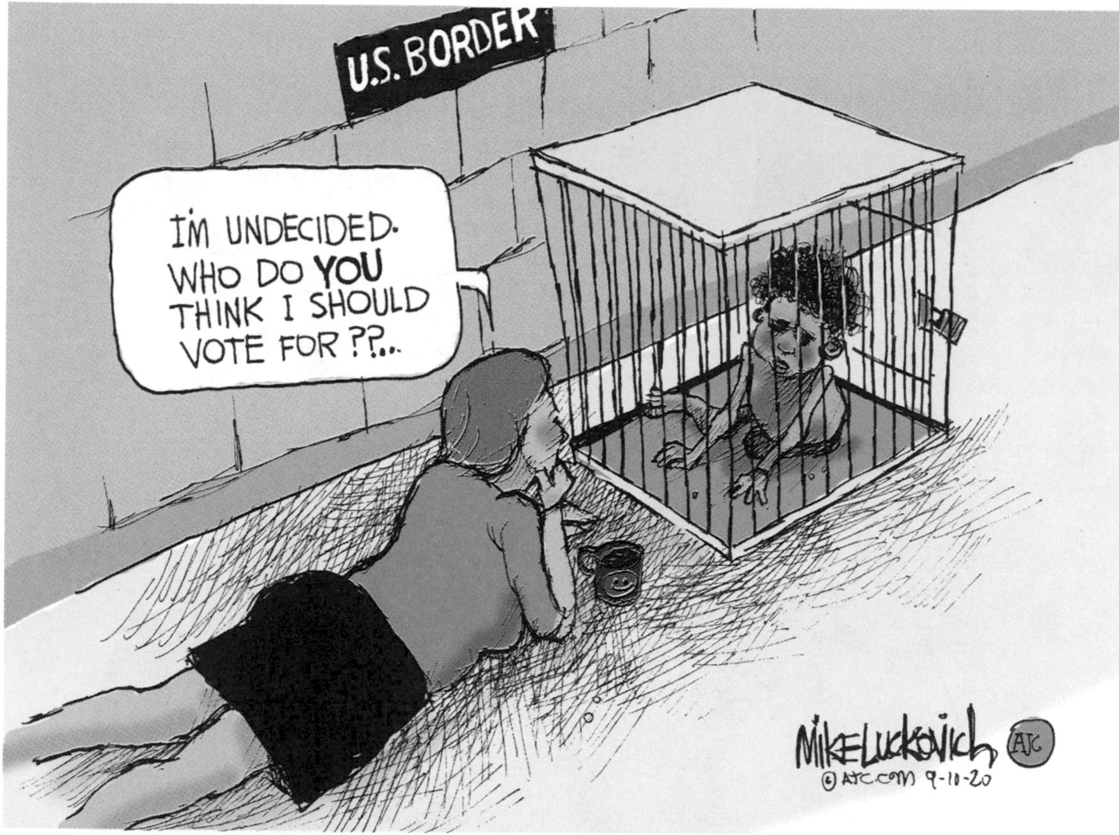
U.S. BORDER
I'M UNDECIDED. WHO DO YOU THINK I SHOULD VOTE FOR ??..
MIKELUCKOVICH
AJC
© AJC.COM 9-10-20

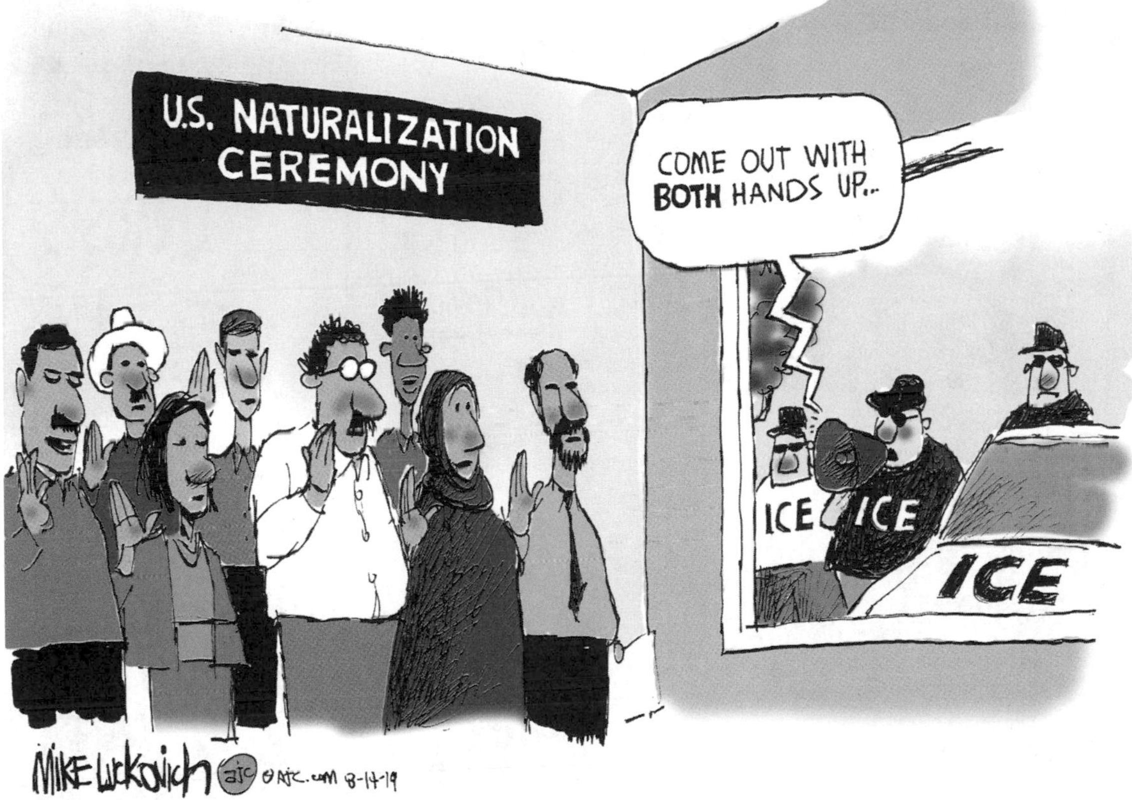
U.S. NATURALIZATION CEREMONY
COME OUT WITH BOTH HANDS UP...
ICE
ICE
ICE
MIKE LUCKOVICH
ajc
©AJC.com 8-14-19

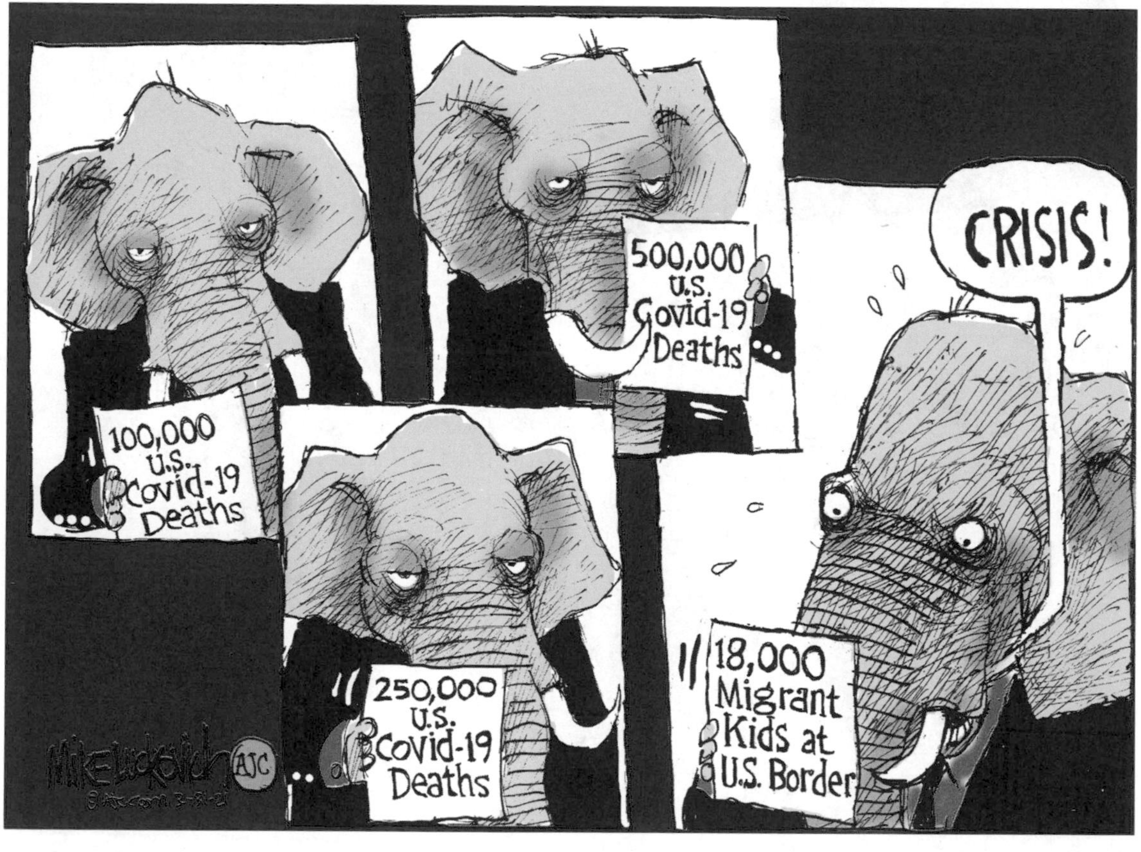
100,000
U.S.
Covid-19
Deaths
500,000
U.S.
Covid-19
Deaths
250,000
U.S.
Covid-19
Deaths
CRISIS!
18,000
Migrant
Kids at
U.S. Border
MIKE LUCKOVICH
AJC

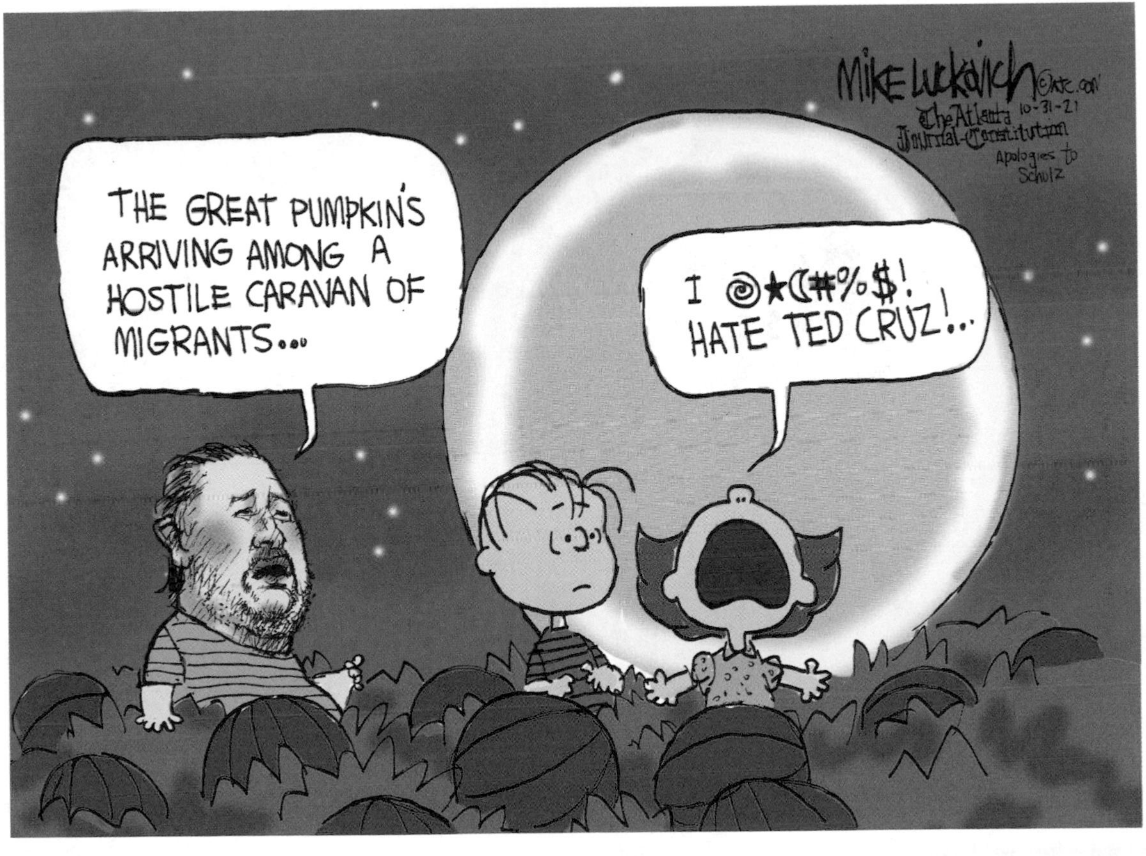
MIKE LUCKOVICH ©AJC.COM
The Atlanta Journal-Constitution 10-31-21
Apologies to Schulz
THE GREAT PUMPKIN'S ARRIVING AMONG A HOSTILE CARAVAN OF MIGRANTS...
I @★☾#%$! HATE TED CRUZ!...

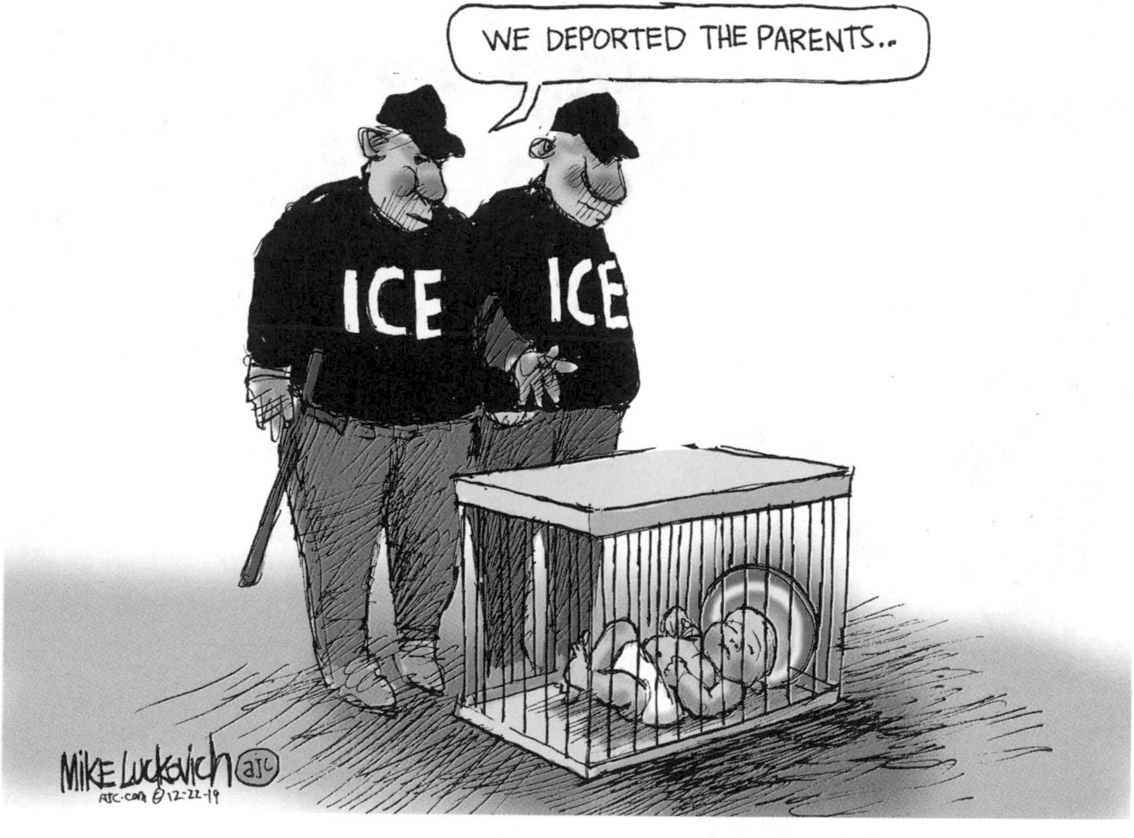
WE DEPORTED THE PARENTS..
ICE
ICE
MIKE LUCKOVICH
AJC
AJC.com ©12-22-19

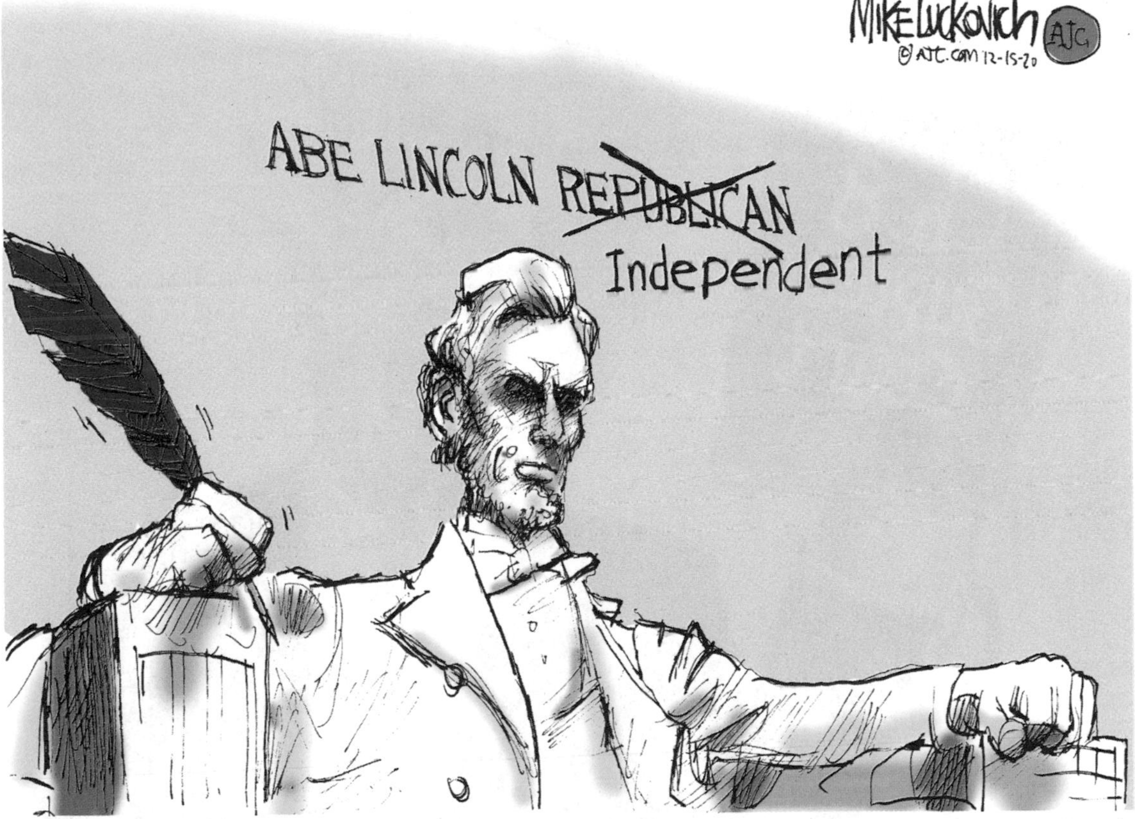
MIKE LUCKOVICH
AJC
© AJC.com 12-15-20
ABE LINCOLN REPUBLICAN
Independent

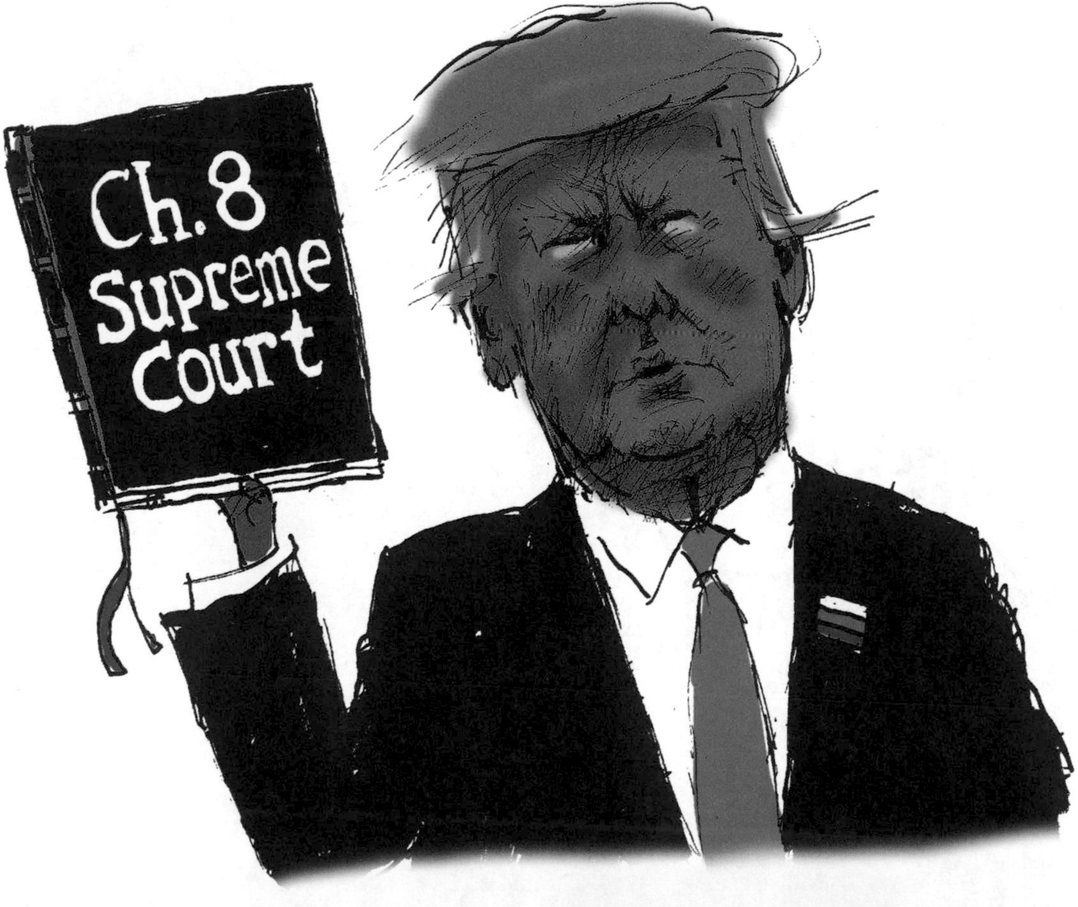
Ch. 8
Supreme
Court

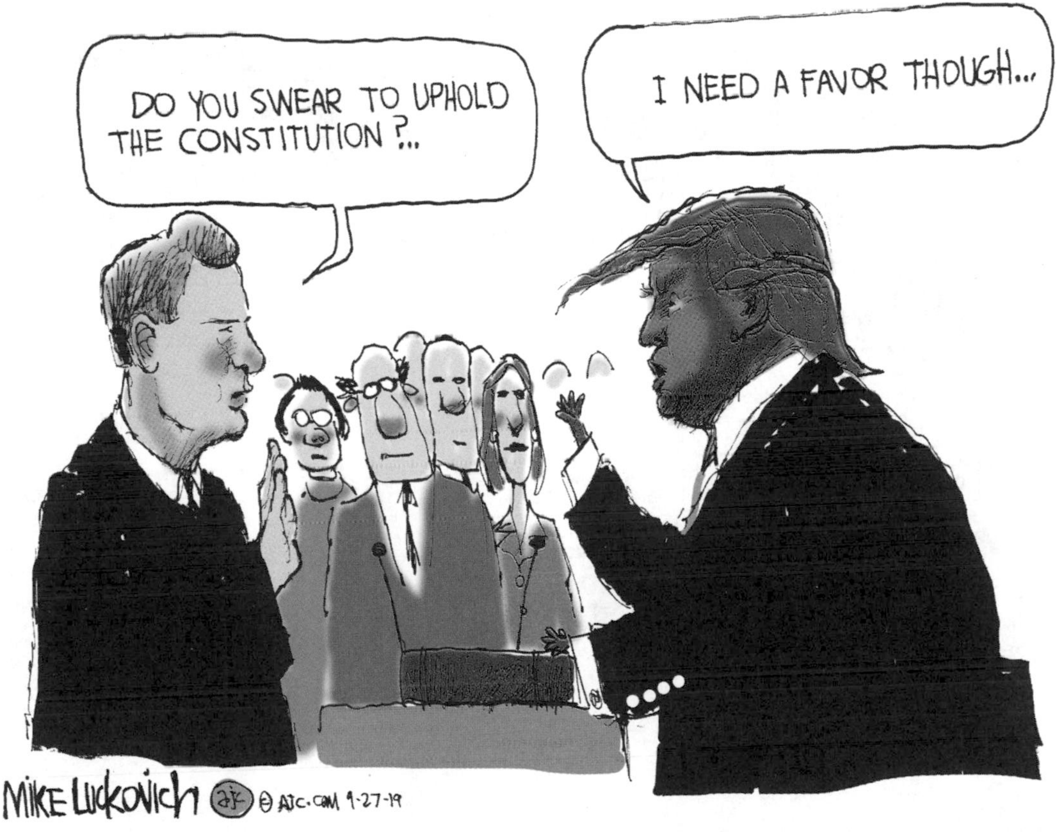
DO YOU SWEAR TO UPHOLD THE CONSTITUTION ?...
I NEED A FAVOR THOUGH...
MIKE LUCKOVICH
© AJC.COM 9-27-19

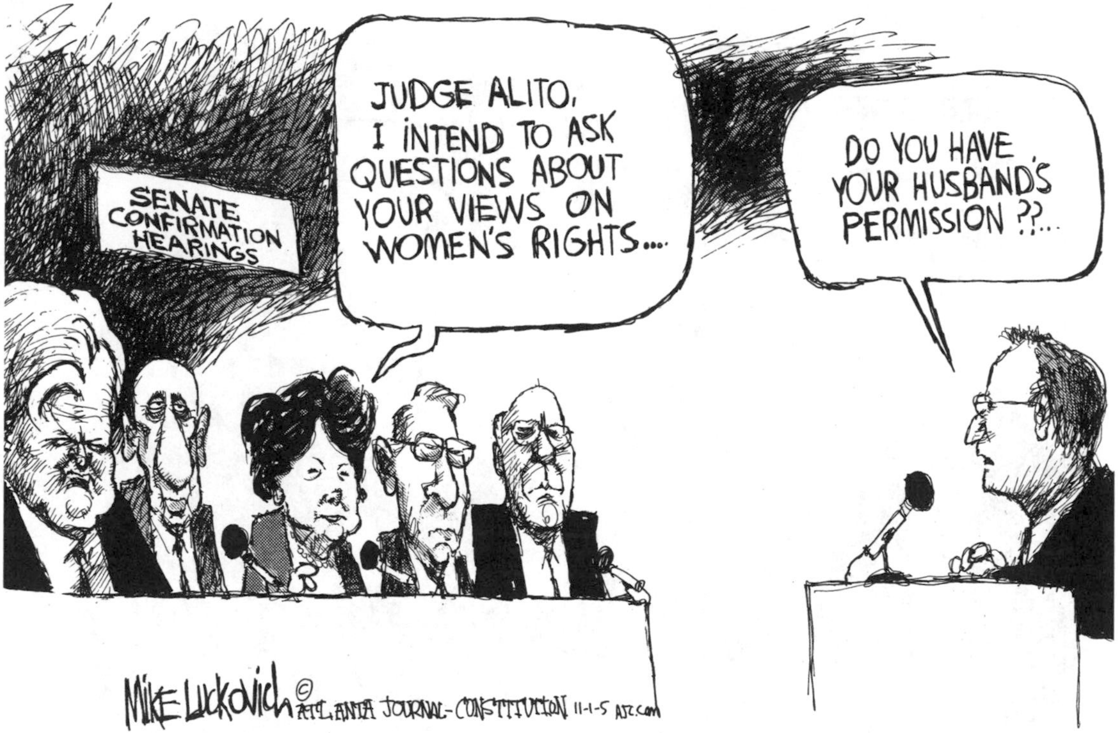
SENATE CONFIRMATION HEARINGS
JUDGE ALITO, I INTEND TO ASK QUESTIONS ABOUT YOUR VIEWS ON WOMEN'S RIGHTS....
DO YOU HAVE YOUR HUSBAND'S PERMISSION ??...
MIKE LUCKOVICH © ATLANTA JOURNAL-CONSTITUTION 11-1-5 AJC.com

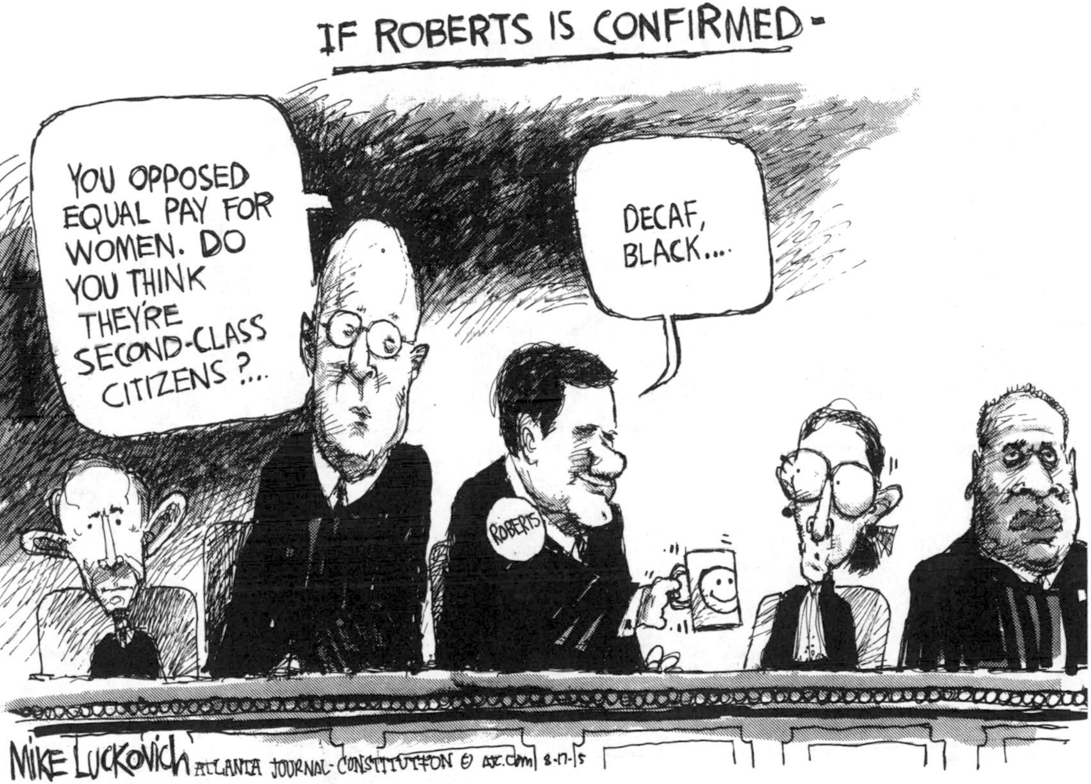
IF ROBERTS IS CONFIRMED-
YOU OPPOSED EQUAL PAY FOR WOMEN. DO YOU THINK THEY'RE SECOND-CLASS CITIZENS?...
DECAF, BLACK....
ROBERTS
MIKE LUCKOVICH ATLANTA JOURNAL-CONSTITUTION © AJC.com 8-17-5

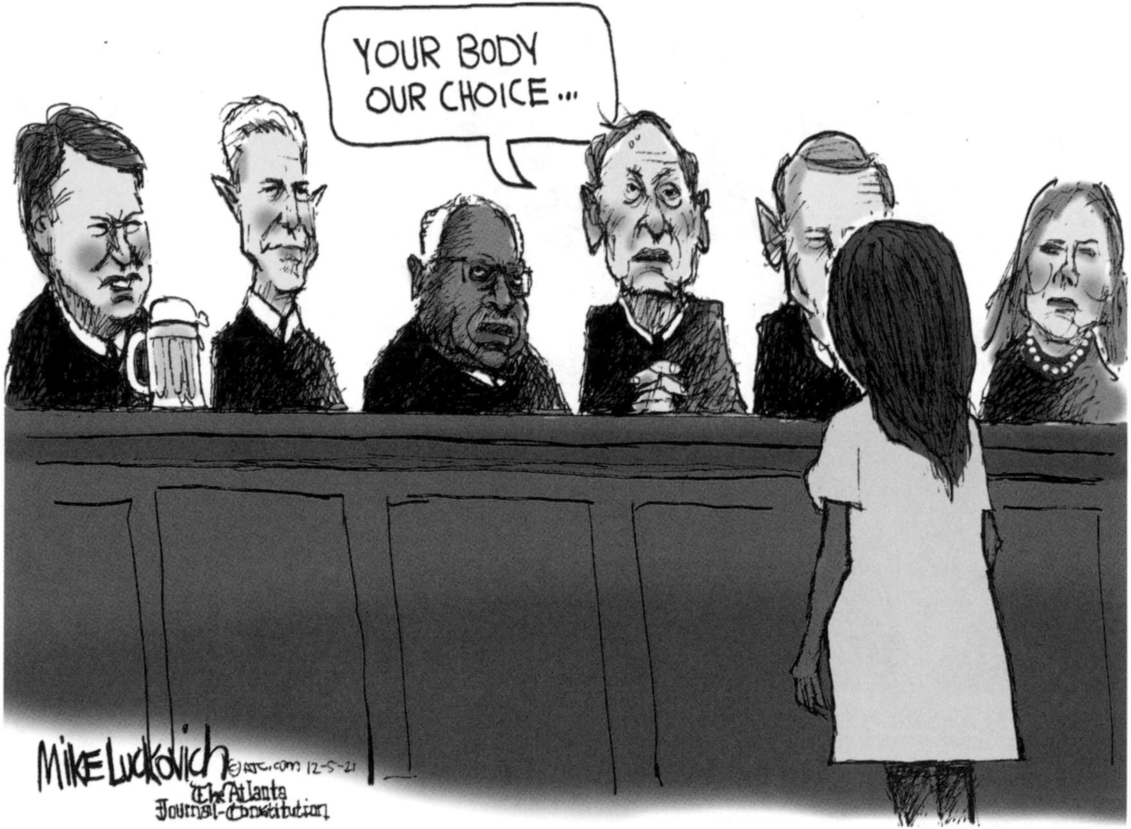
YOUR BODY OUR CHOICE...
MIKE LUCKOVICH ©AJC.com 12-5-21
The Atlanta Journal-Constitution

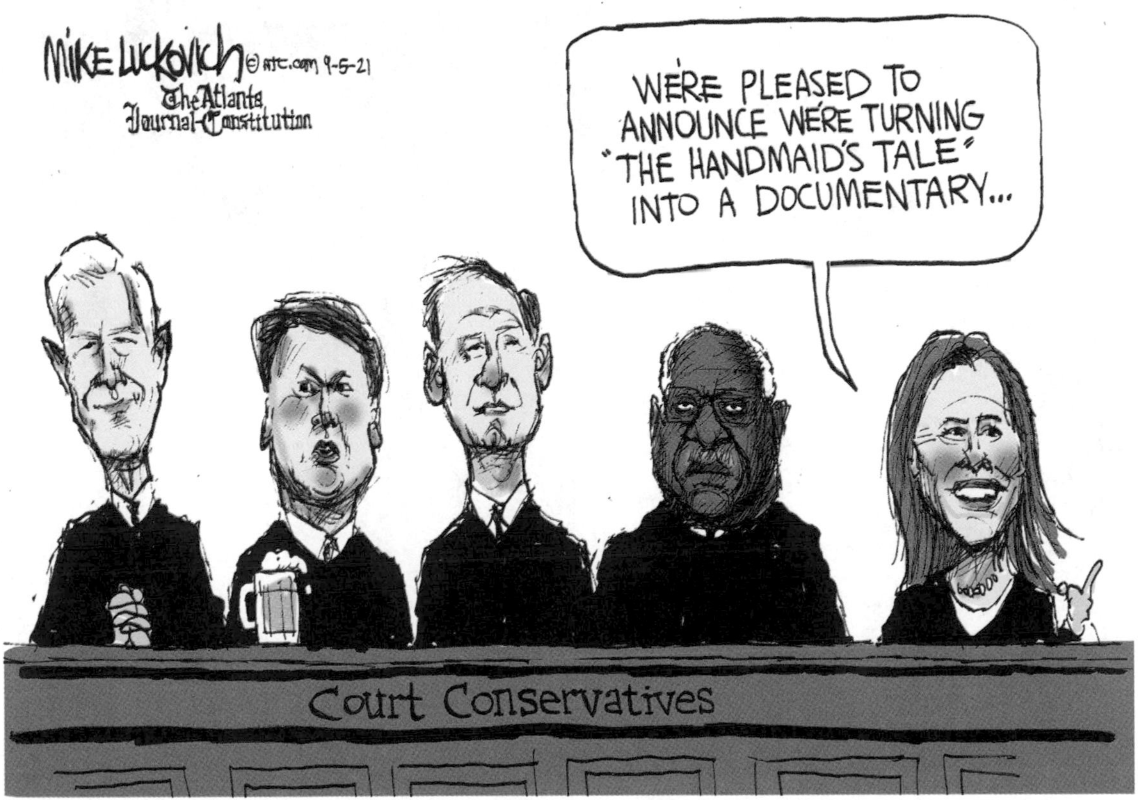
MIKE LUCKOVICH © ajc.com 9-5-21
The Atlanta Journal-Constitution
WE'RE PLEASED TO ANNOUNCE WE'RE TURNING "THE HANDMAID'S TALE" INTO A DOCUMENTARY...
Court Conservatives

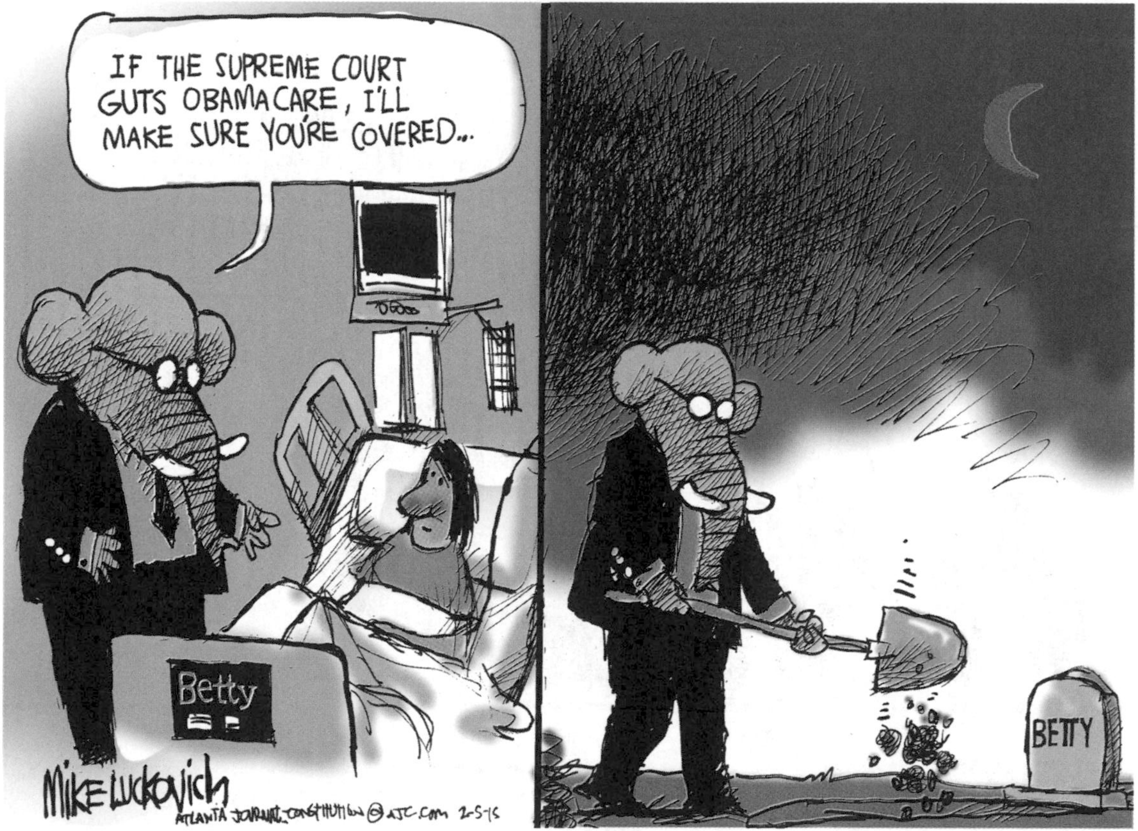
IF THE SUPREME COURT GUTS OBAMACARE, I'LL MAKE SURE YOU'RE COVERED...
Betty
MIKE LUCKOVICH
ATLANTA JOURNAL-CONSTITUTION @ AJC.COM 2-5-15
BETTY

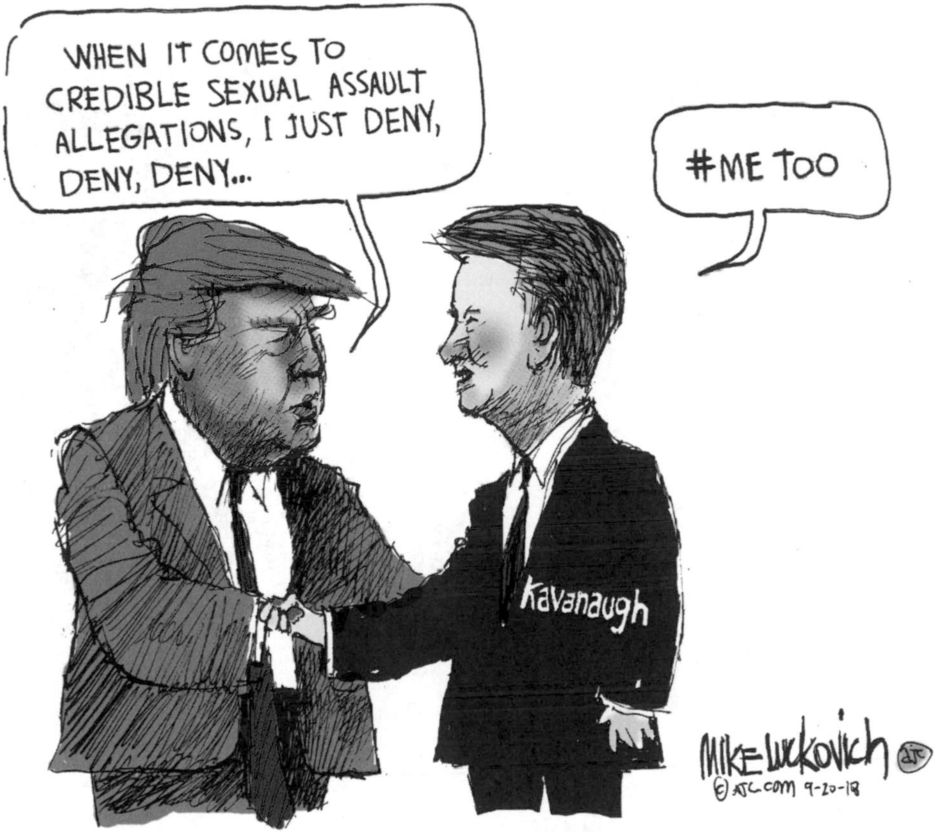
WHEN IT COMES TO CREDIBLE SEXUAL ASSAULT ALLEGATIONS, I JUST DENY, DENY, DENY...
#ME TOO
Kavanaugh
MIKE LUCKOVICH
© AJC.COM 9-20-18

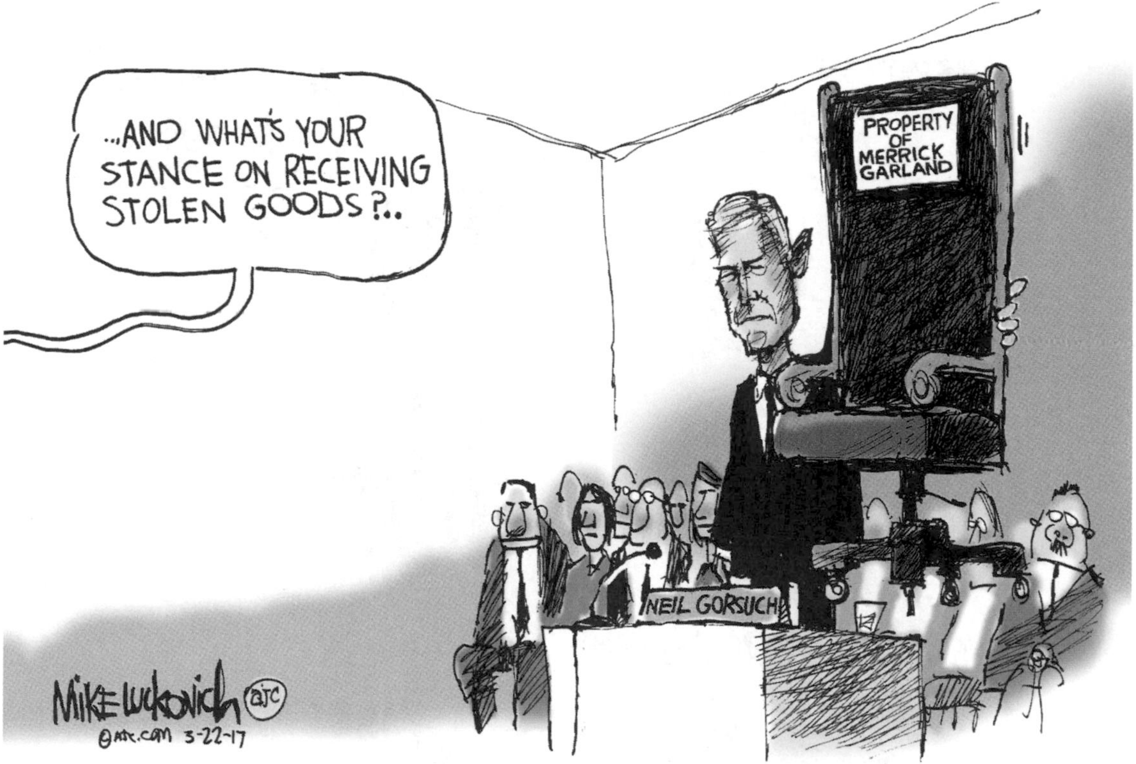
...AND WHAT'S YOUR STANCE ON RECEIVING STOLEN GOODS?..
PROPERTY OF MERRICK GARLAND
NEIL GORSUCH
MIKE LUCKOVICH
ajc
©ajc.com 3-22-17

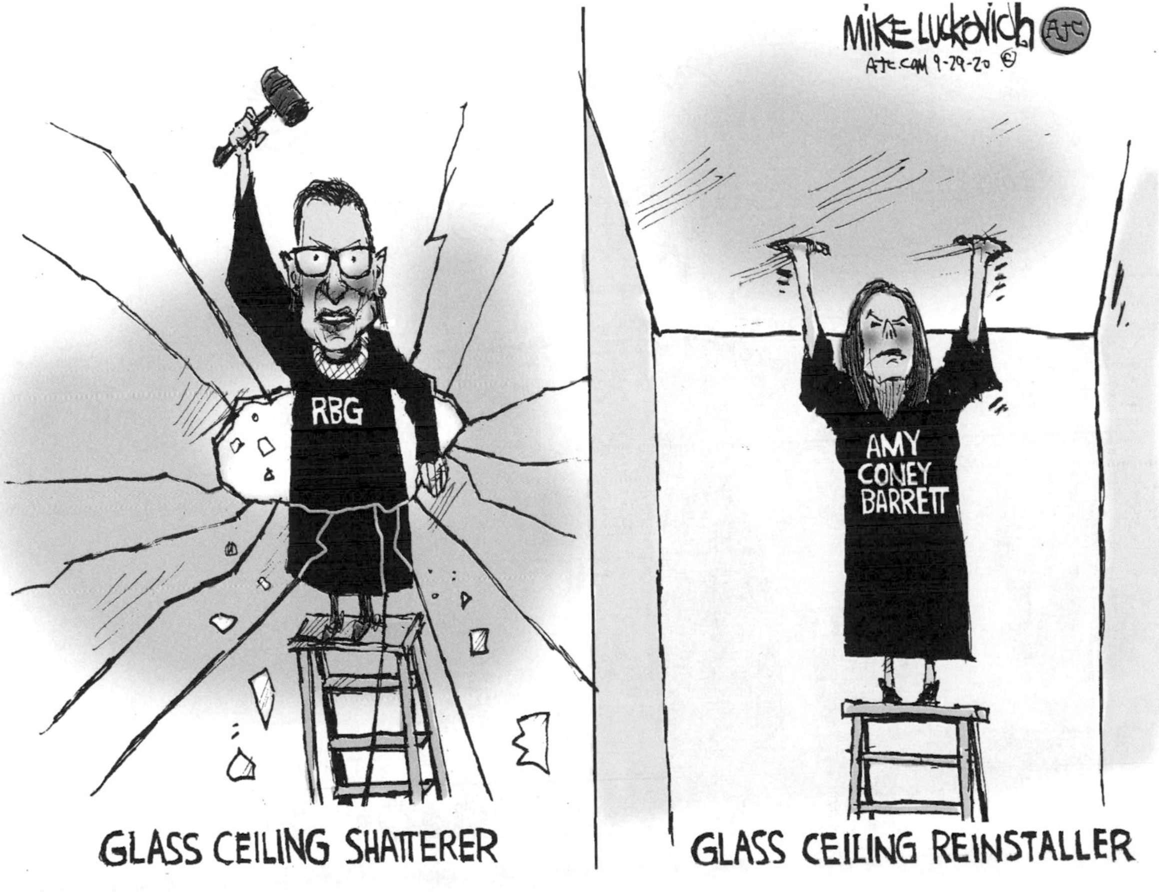
MIKE LUCKOVICH
AJC
AJC.COM 9-29-20 ©
RBG
GLASS CEILING SHATTERER
AMY
CONEY
BARRETT
GLASS CEILING REINSTALLER

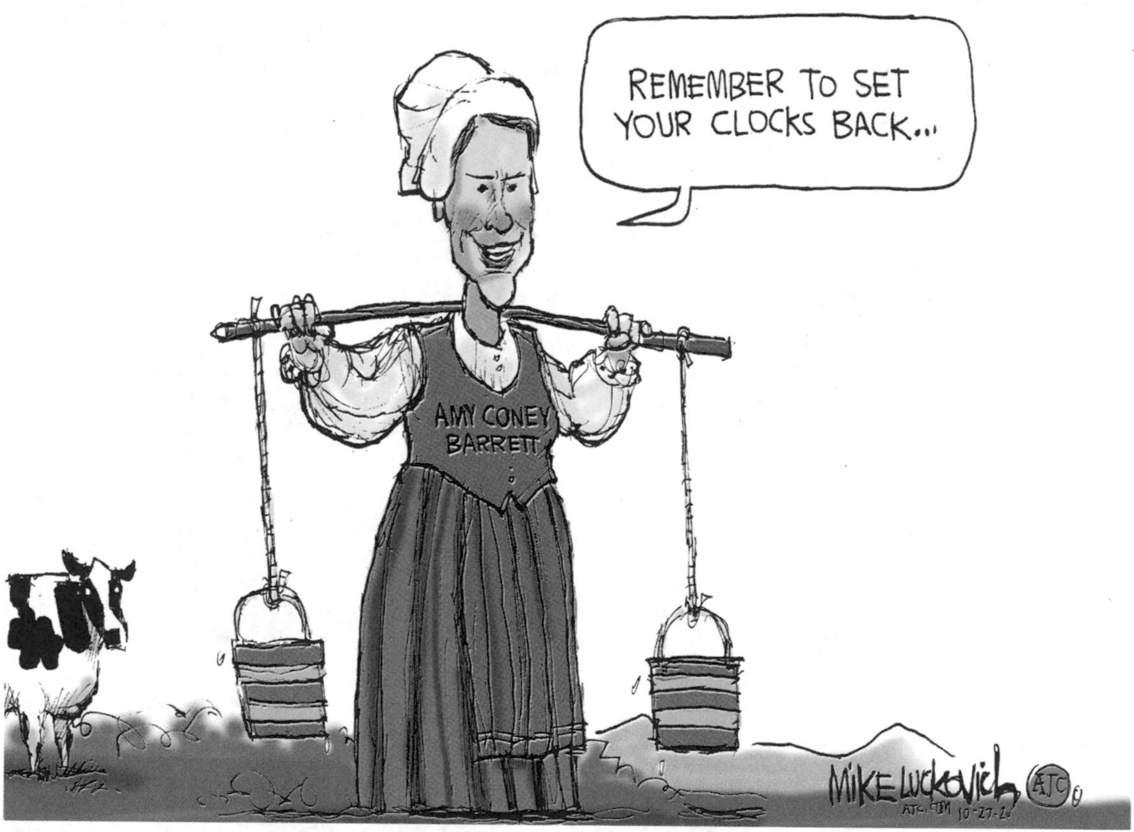
REMEMBER TO SET YOUR CLOCKS BACK...
AMY CONEY BARRETT
MIKE LUCKOVICH

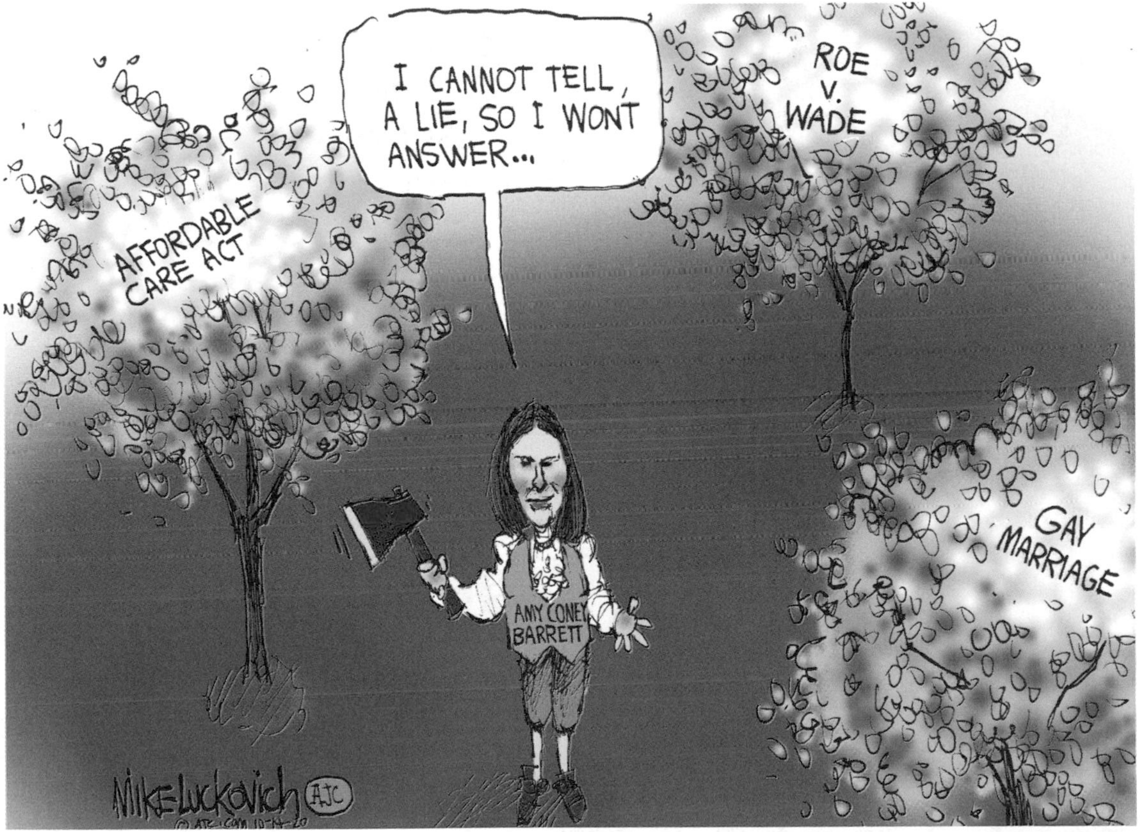
I CANNOT TELL, A LIE, SO I WON'T ANSWER...
AFFORDABLE CARE ACT
ROE V. WADE
GAY MARRIAGE
AMY CONEY BARRETT
MIKE LUCKOVICH
AJC

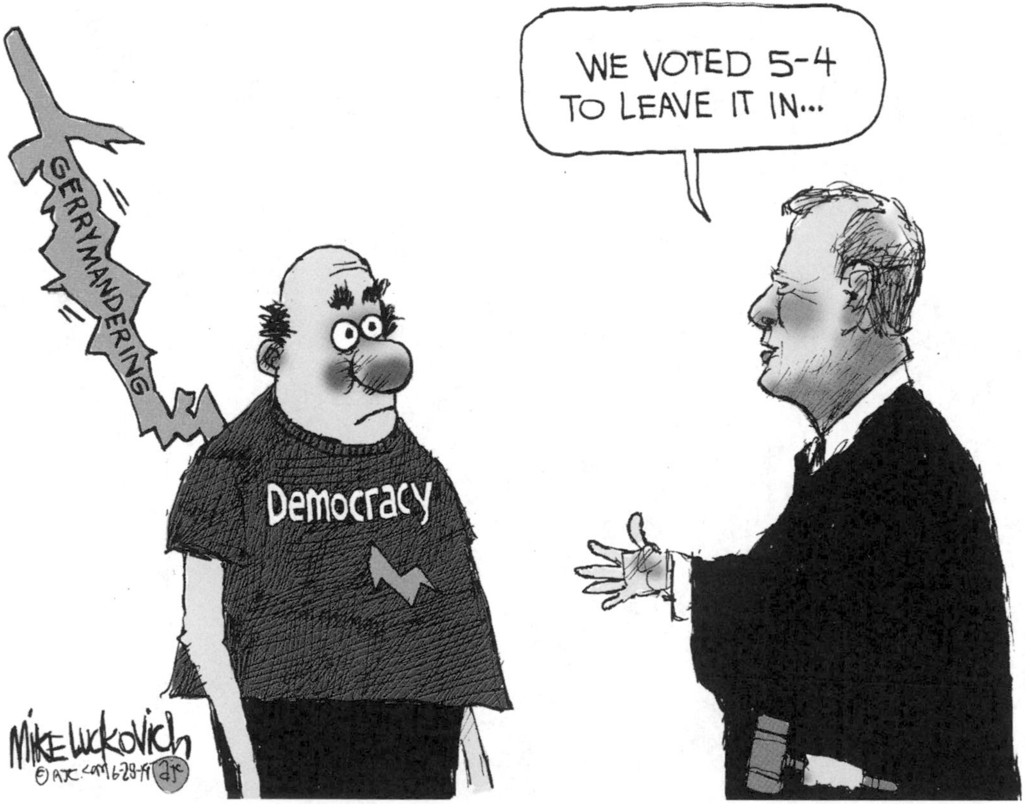
GERRYMANDERING
Democracy
WE VOTED 5-4 TO LEAVE IT IN...
MIKE LUCKOVICH

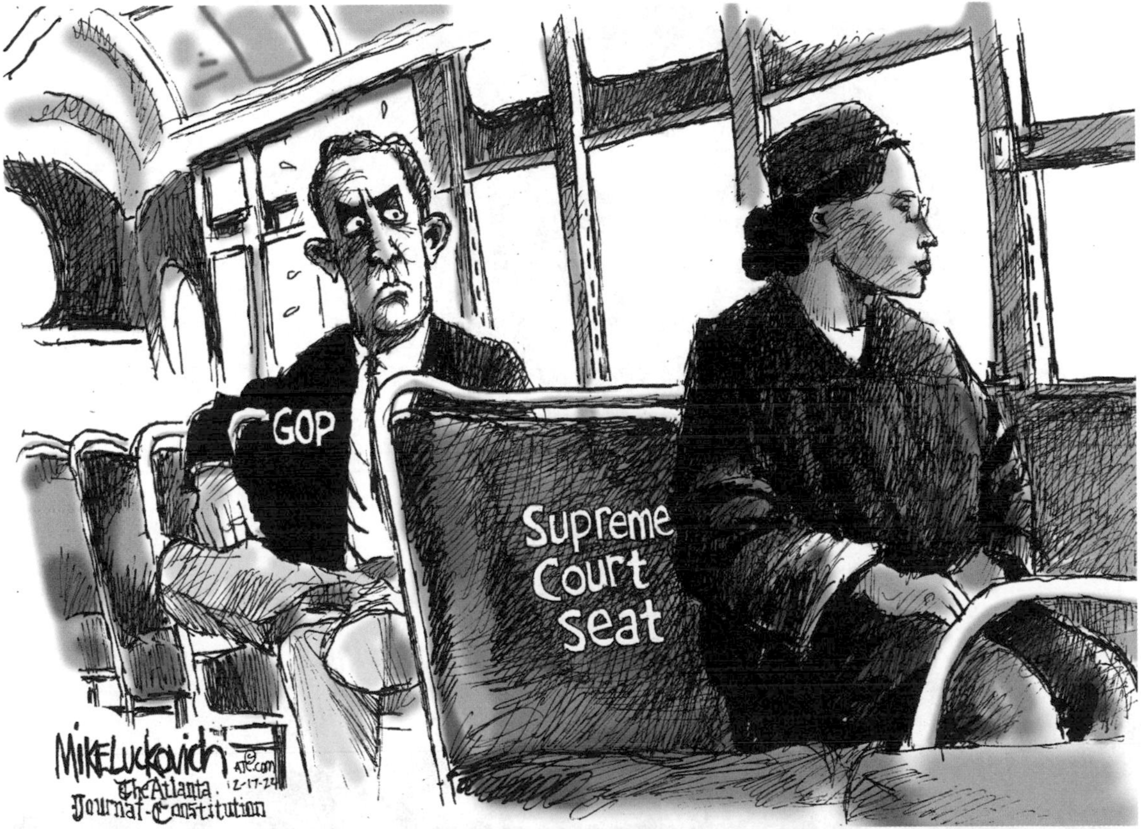
GOP
Supreme Court seat
MIKELUCKOVICH
AJC.com
The Atlanta Journal-Constitution

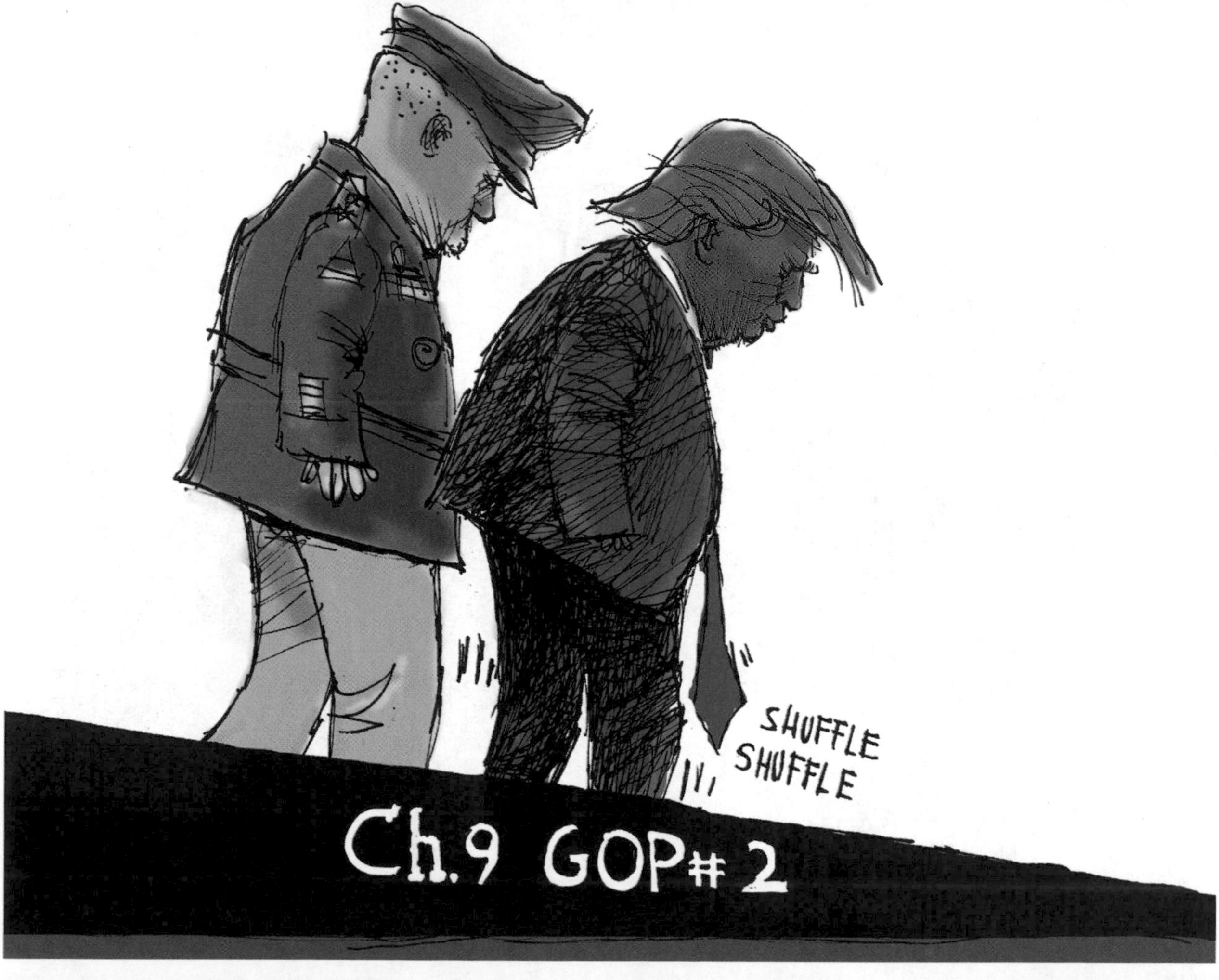
SHUFFLE
SHUFFLE
Ch.9 GOP#2

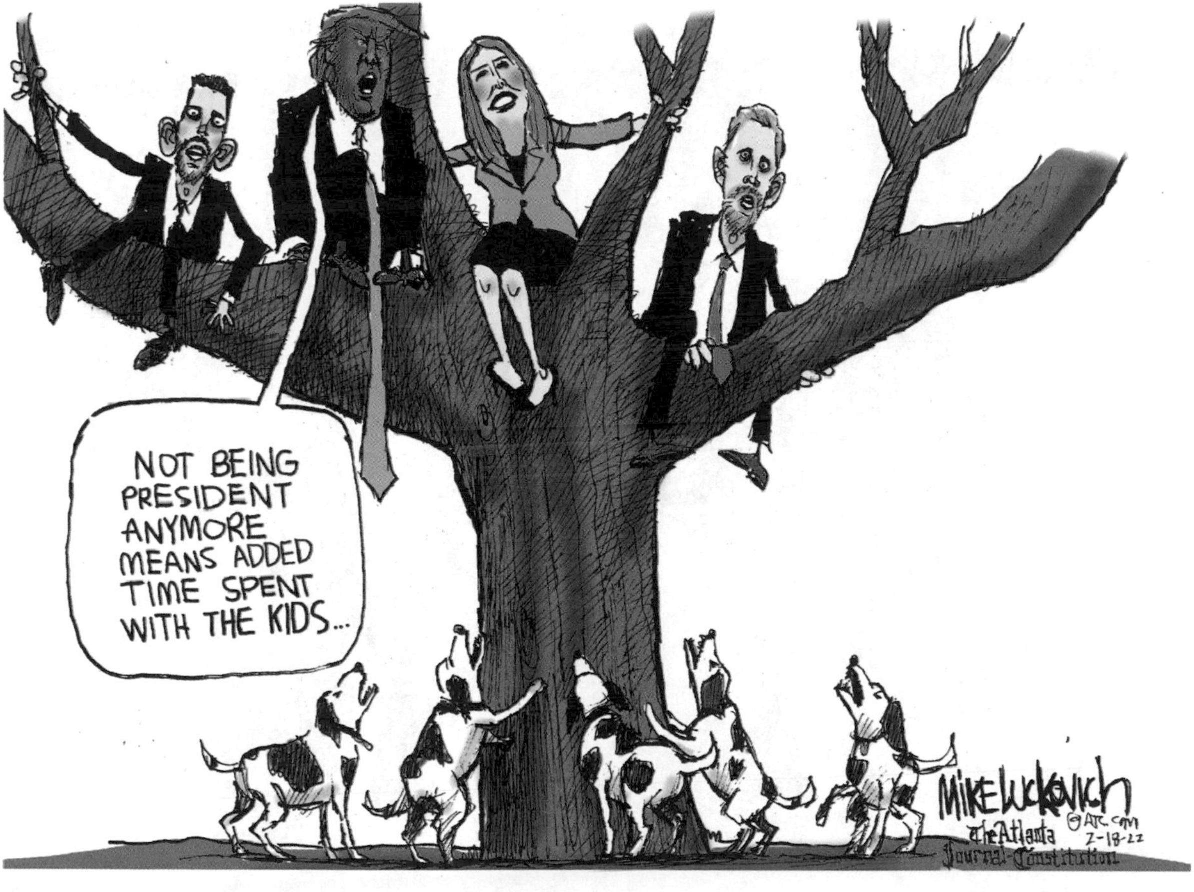
NOT BEING PRESIDENT ANYMORE MEANS ADDED TIME SPENT WITH THE KIDS...
MIKE LUCKOVICH
©AJC.com
The Atlanta Journal-Constitution
2-18-22

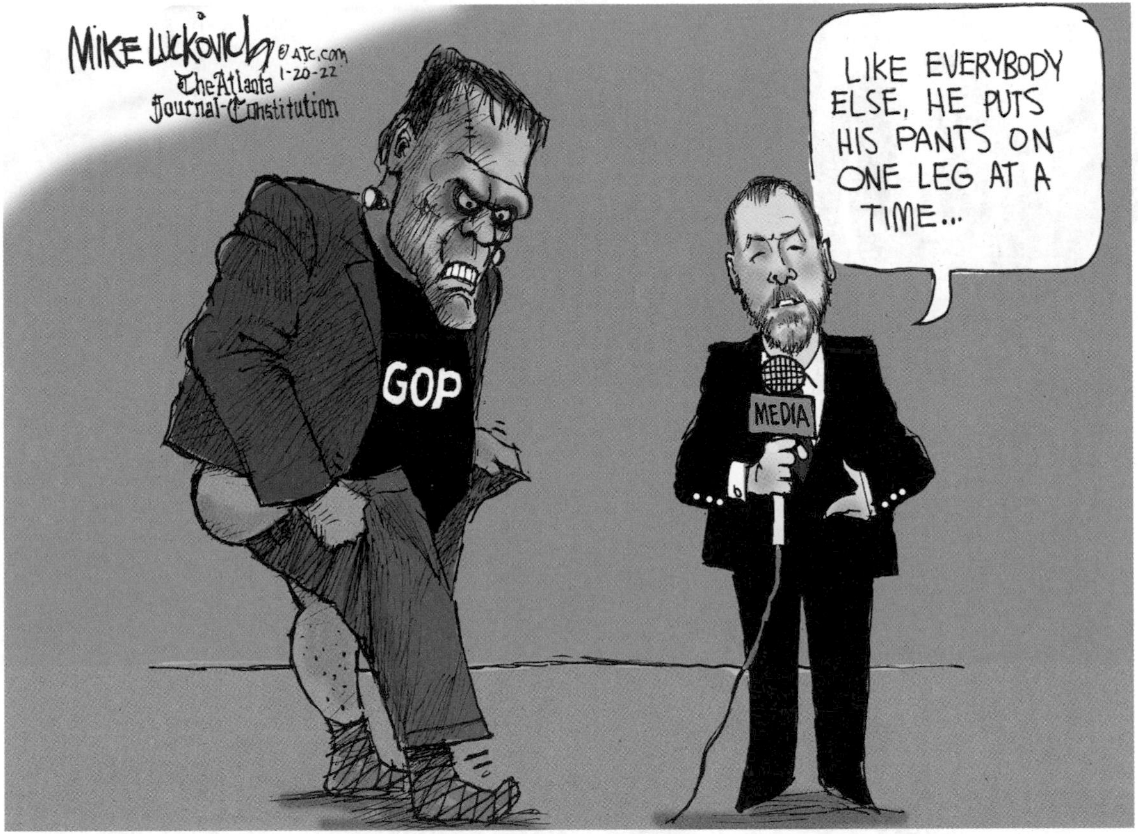
MIKE LUCKOVICH © AJC.com 1-20-22 The Atlanta Journal-Constitution
LIKE EVERYBODY ELSE, HE PUTS HIS PANTS ON ONE LEG AT A TIME...
GOP
MEDIA

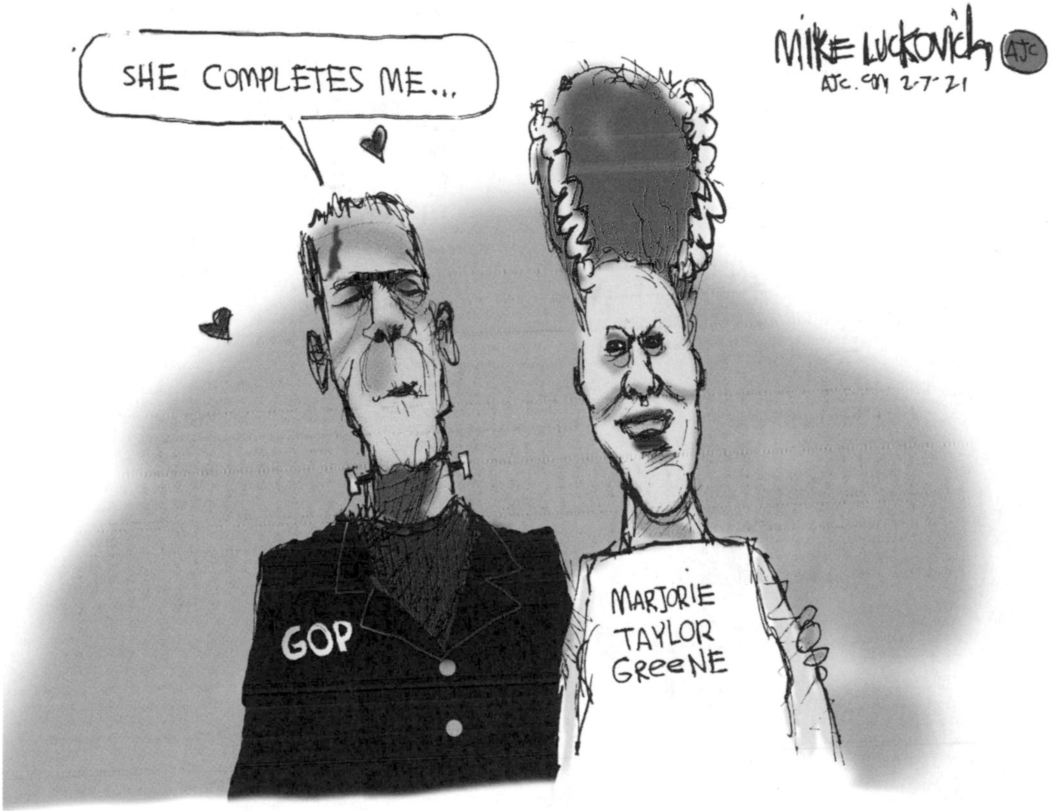
SHE COMPLETES ME...
MIKE LUCKOVICH AJC
AJC.com 2-7-21
GOP
MARJORIE TAYLOR GREENE

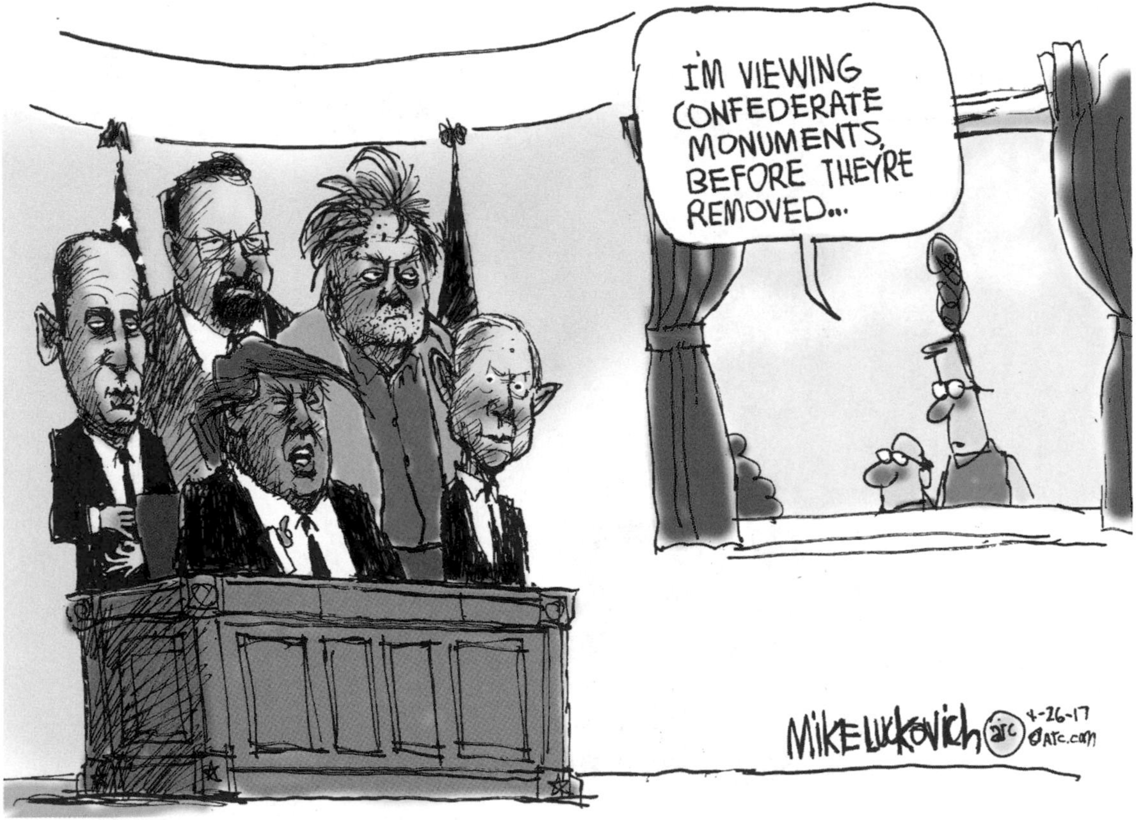
I'M VIEWING CONFEDERATE MONUMENTS, BEFORE THEYRE REMOVED...
MIKE LUCKOVICH
4-26-17
©arc.com

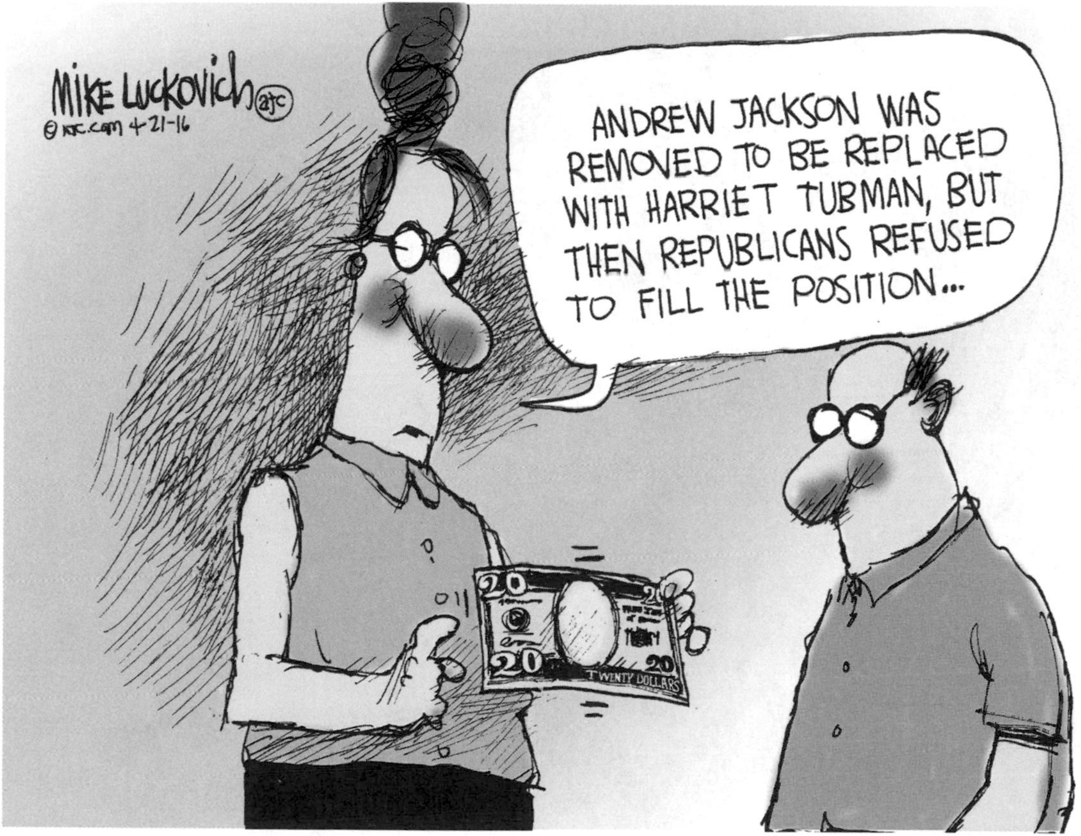
MIKE LUCKOVICH ajc
© ajc.com 4-21-16
ANDREW JACKSON WAS REMOVED TO BE REPLACED WITH HARRIET TUBMAN, BUT THEN REPUBLICANS REFUSED TO FILL THE POSITION...
20
TWENTY DOLLARS

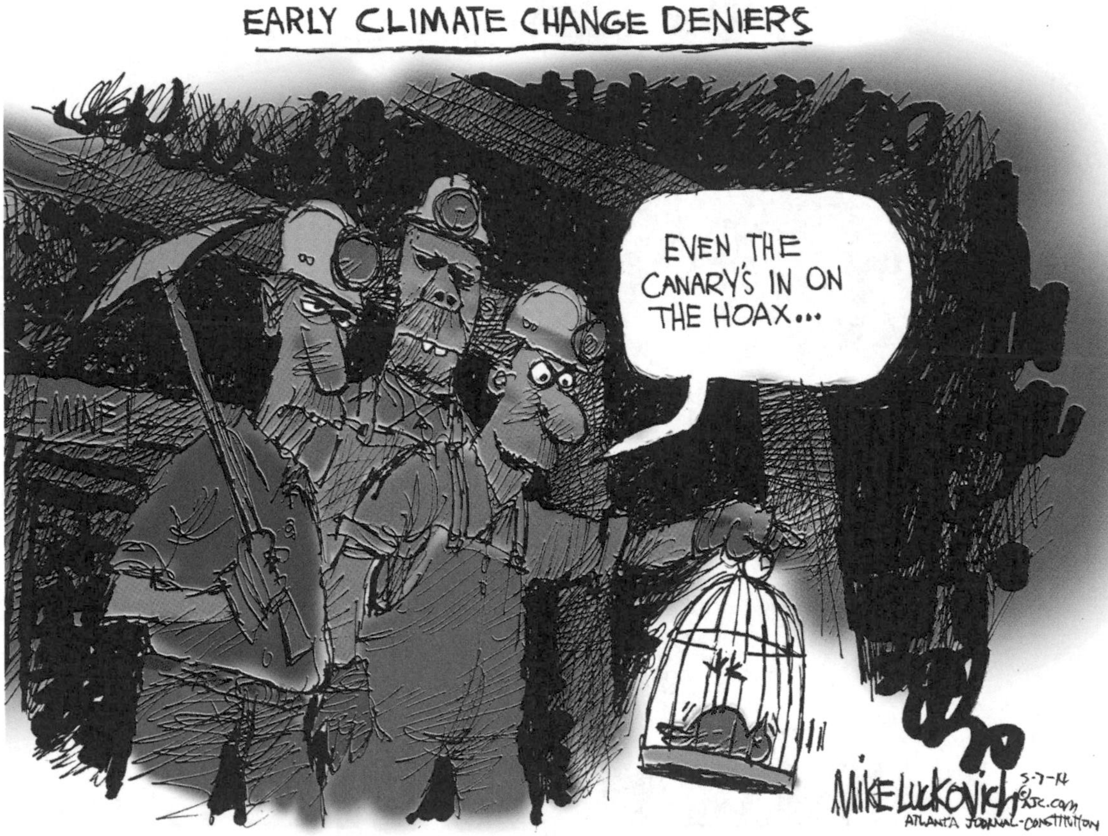
EARLY CLIMATE CHANGE DENIERS
EVEN THE CANARY'S IN ON THE HOAX...
MINE
MIKE LUCKOVICH 5-7-14 ©AJC.com
ATLANTA JOURNAL-CONSTITUTION

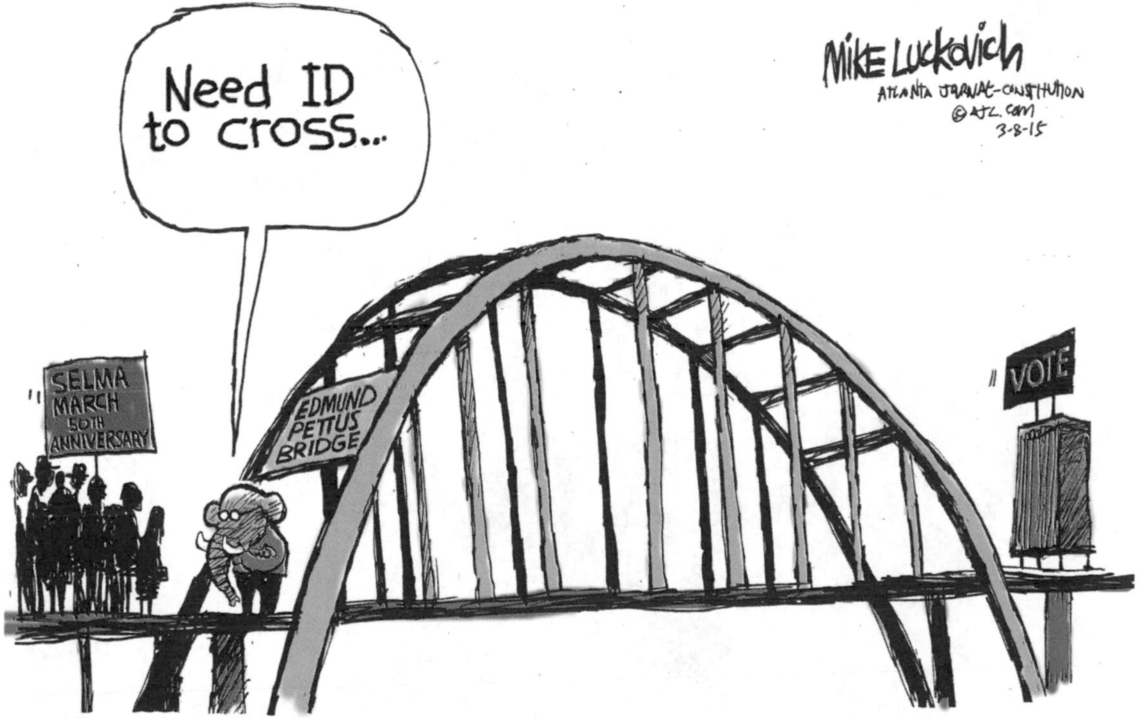
Need ID to cross...
MIKE LUCKOVICH
ATLANTA JOURNAL-CONSTITUTION
© AJC.com
3-8-15
SELMA MARCH 50TH ANNIVERSARY
EDMUND PETTUS BRIDGE
VOTE

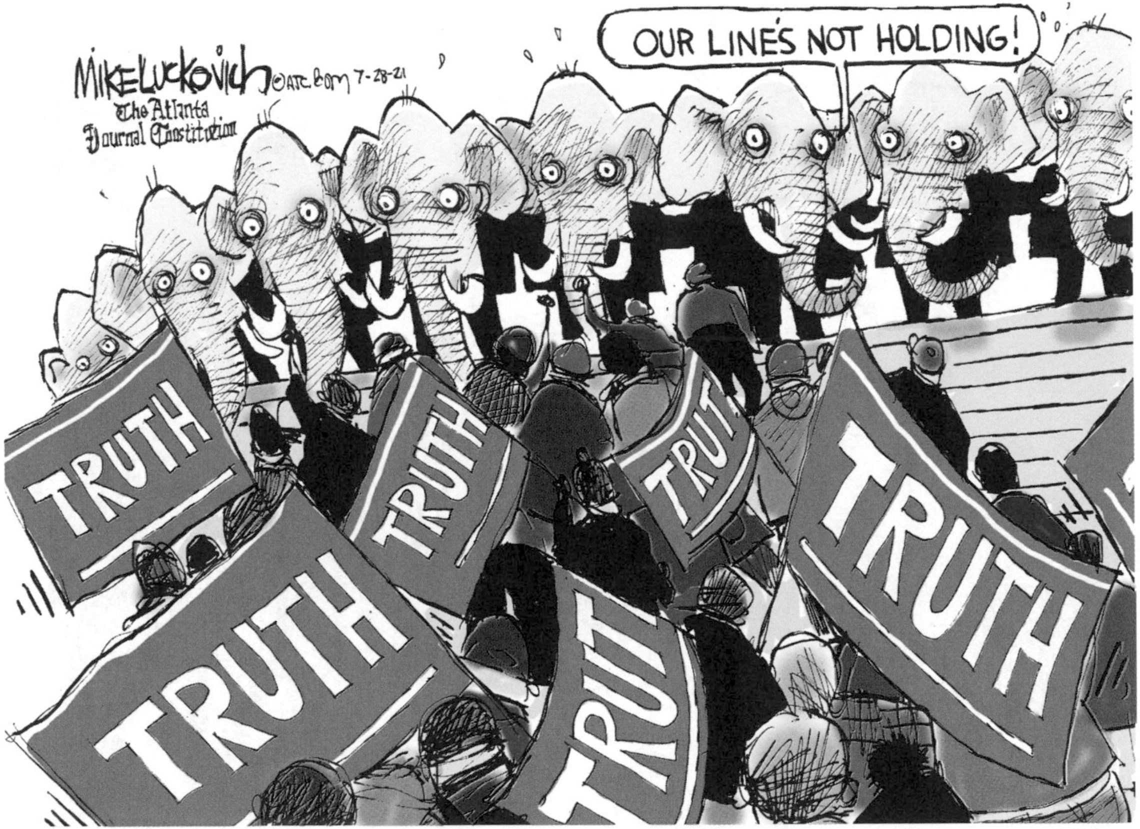
OUR LINE'S NOT HOLDING!
TRUTH
TRUTH
TRUTH
TRUT
TRUTH
TRUT
TRUTH
MIKE LUCKOVICH ©AJC.com 7-28-21
The Atlanta Journal Constitution

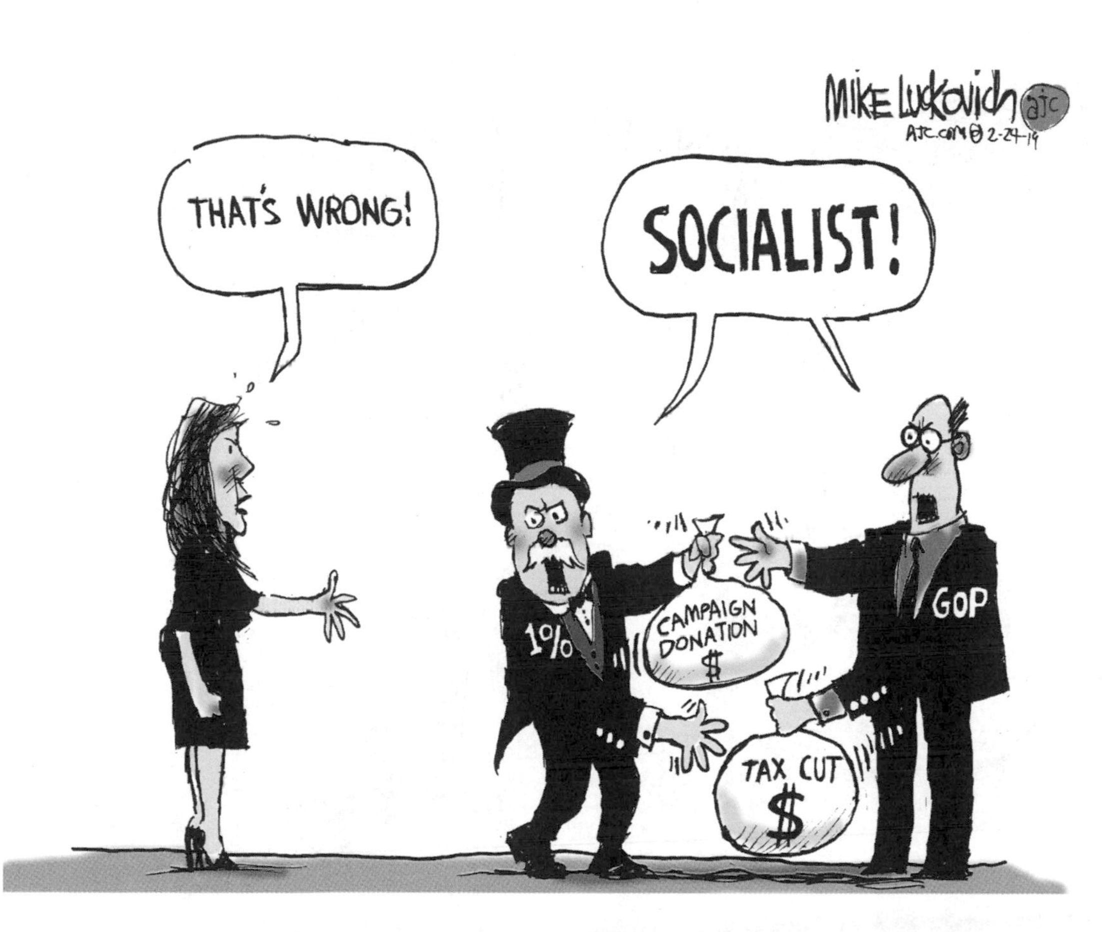
MIKE LUCKOVICH
AJC.COM © 2-24-19
THAT'S WRONG!
SOCIALIST!
1%
CAMPAIGN DONATION $
GOP
TAX CUT $

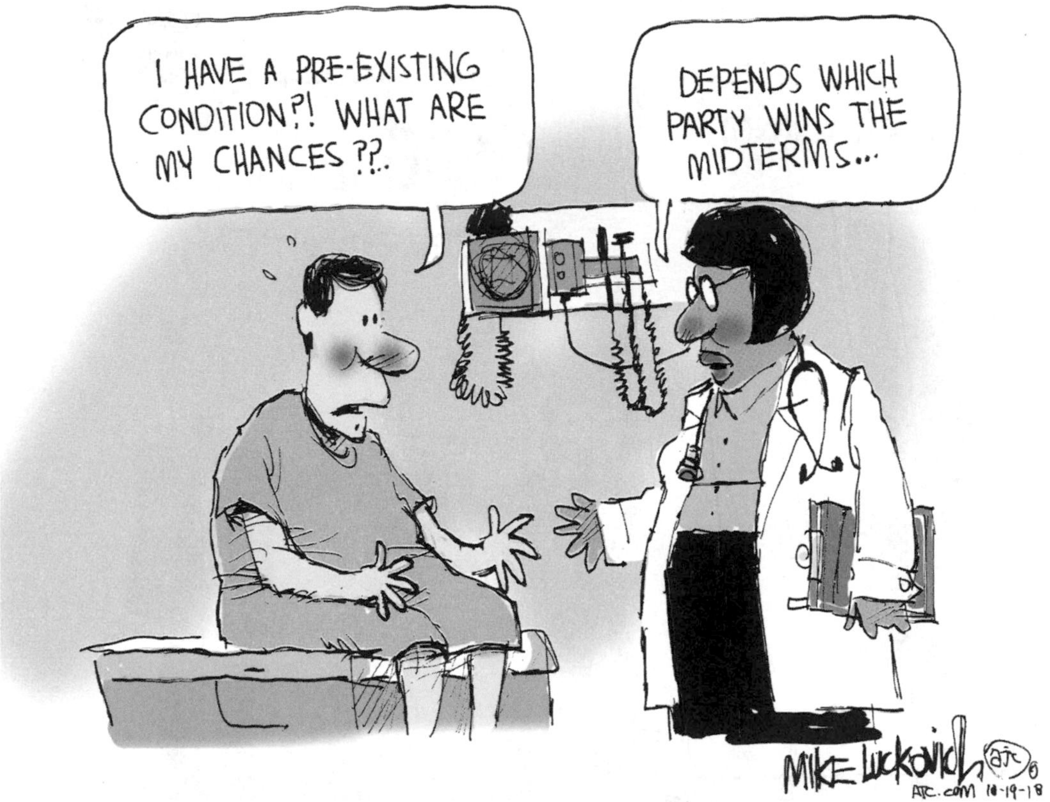
I HAVE A PRE-EXISTING CONDITION?! WHAT ARE MY CHANCES ??..
DEPENDS WHICH PARTY WINS THE MIDTERMS...
MIKE LUCKOVICH
AJC.com 10-19-18

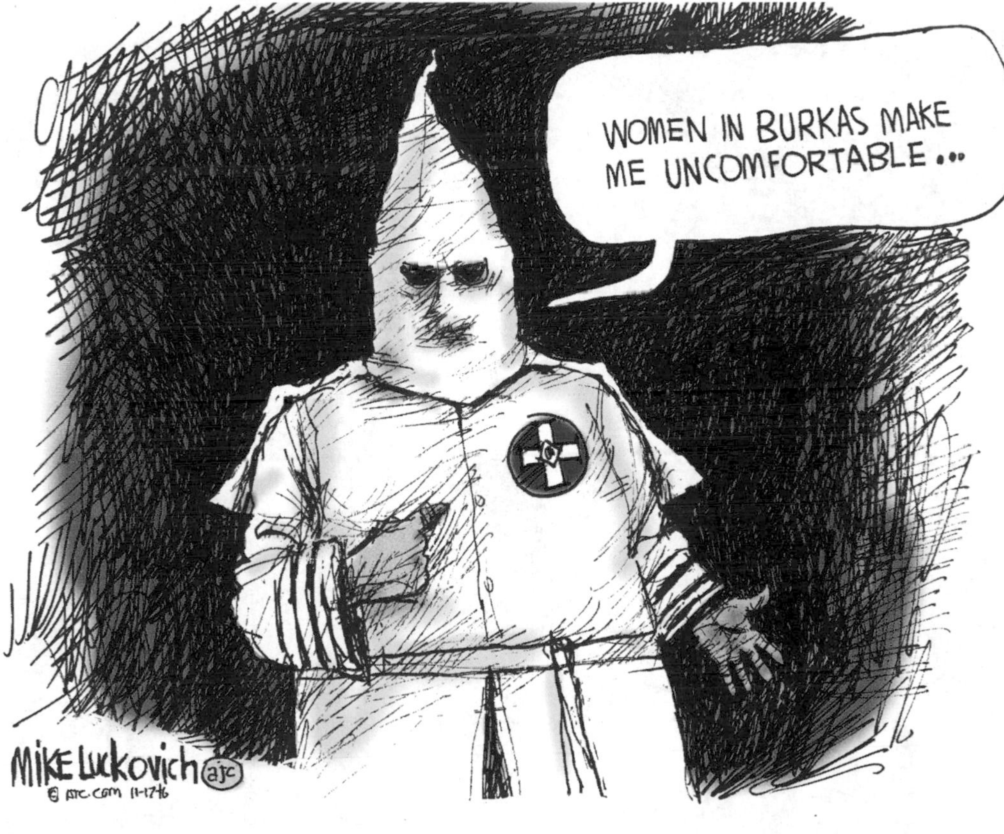
WOMEN IN BURKAS MAKE ME UNCOMFORTABLE...
MIKE LUCKOVICH ajc

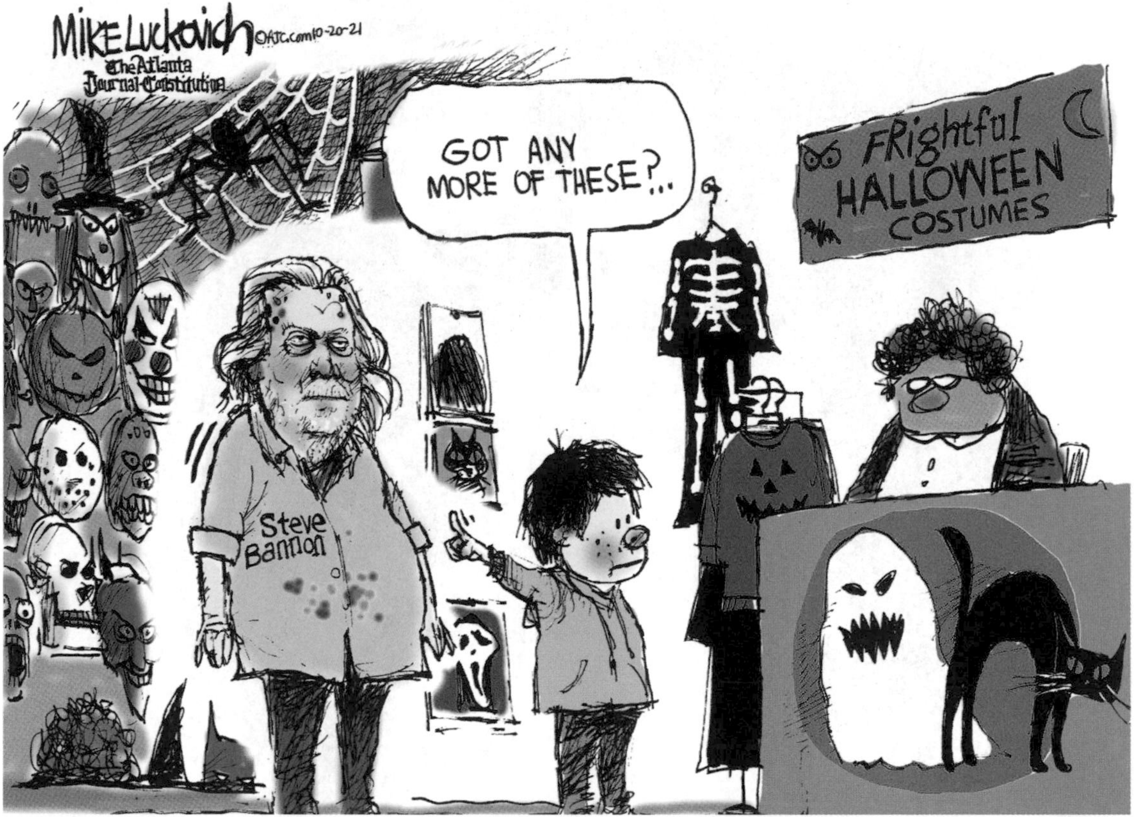
MIKE LUCKOVICH ©AJC.com 10-20-21
The Atlanta Journal-Constitution
GOT ANY MORE OF THESE?...
FRightful HALLOWEEN COSTUMES
Steve Bannon

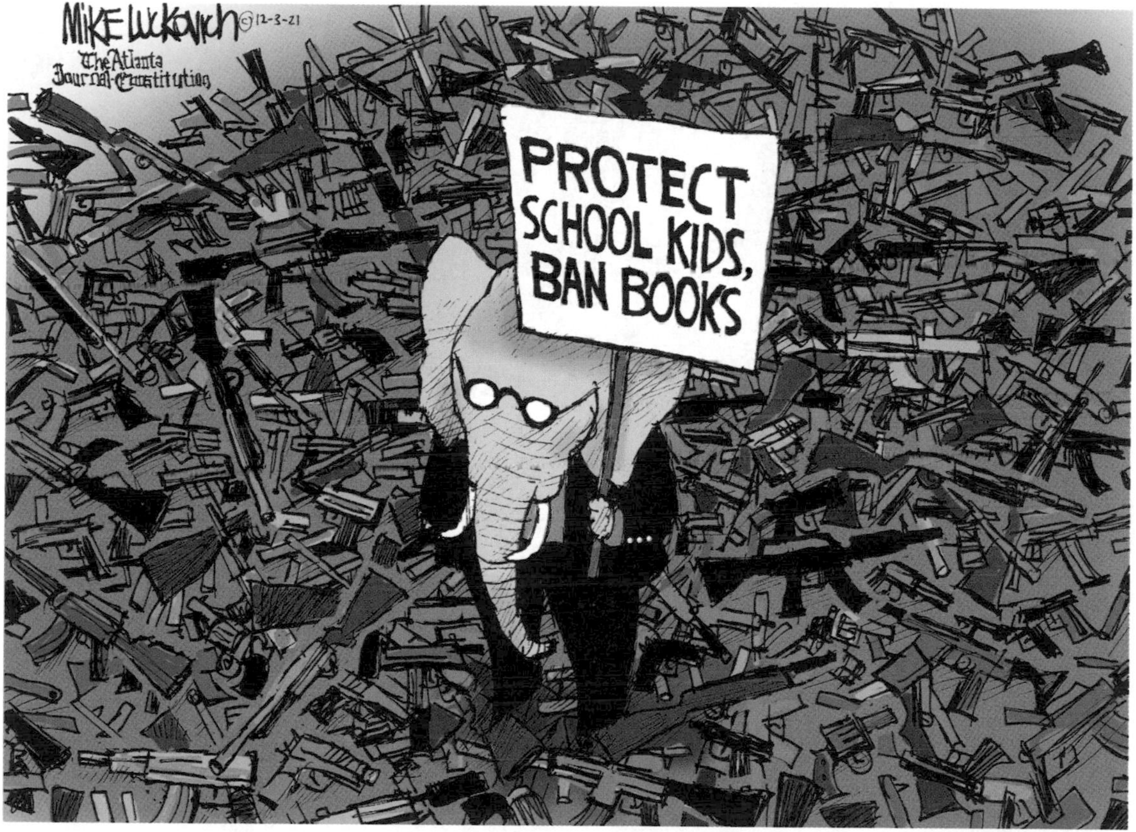
MIKE LUCKOVICH ©12-3-21
The Atlanta Journal-Constitution
PROTECT SCHOOL KIDS, BAN BOOKS

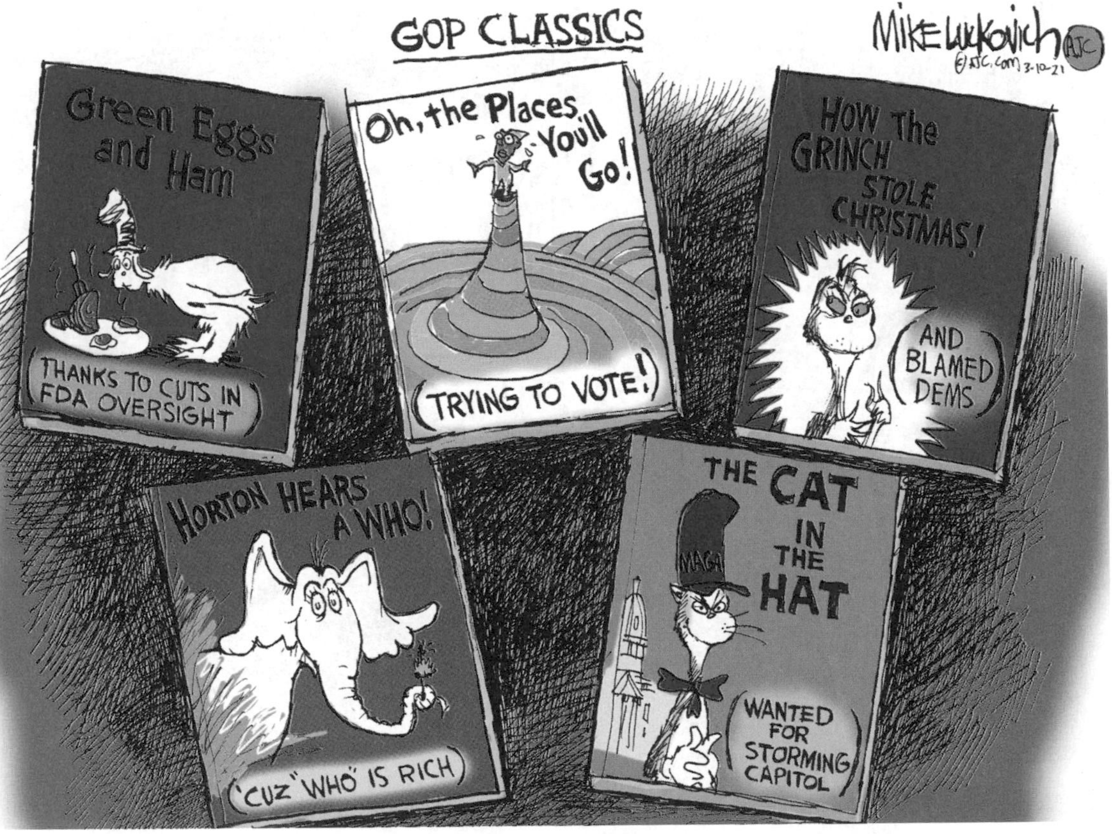
GOP CLASSICS
MIKE LUCKOVICH AJC
©AJC.com 3-10-21
Green Eggs and Ham
(THANKS TO CUTS IN FDA OVERSIGHT)
Oh, the Places You'll Go!
(TRYING TO VOTE!)
HOW THE GRINCH STOLE CHRISTMAS!
(AND BLAMED DEMS)
HORTON HEARS A WHO!
('CUZ "WHO" IS RICH)
THE CAT IN THE HAT
MAGA
(WANTED FOR STORMING CAPITOL)

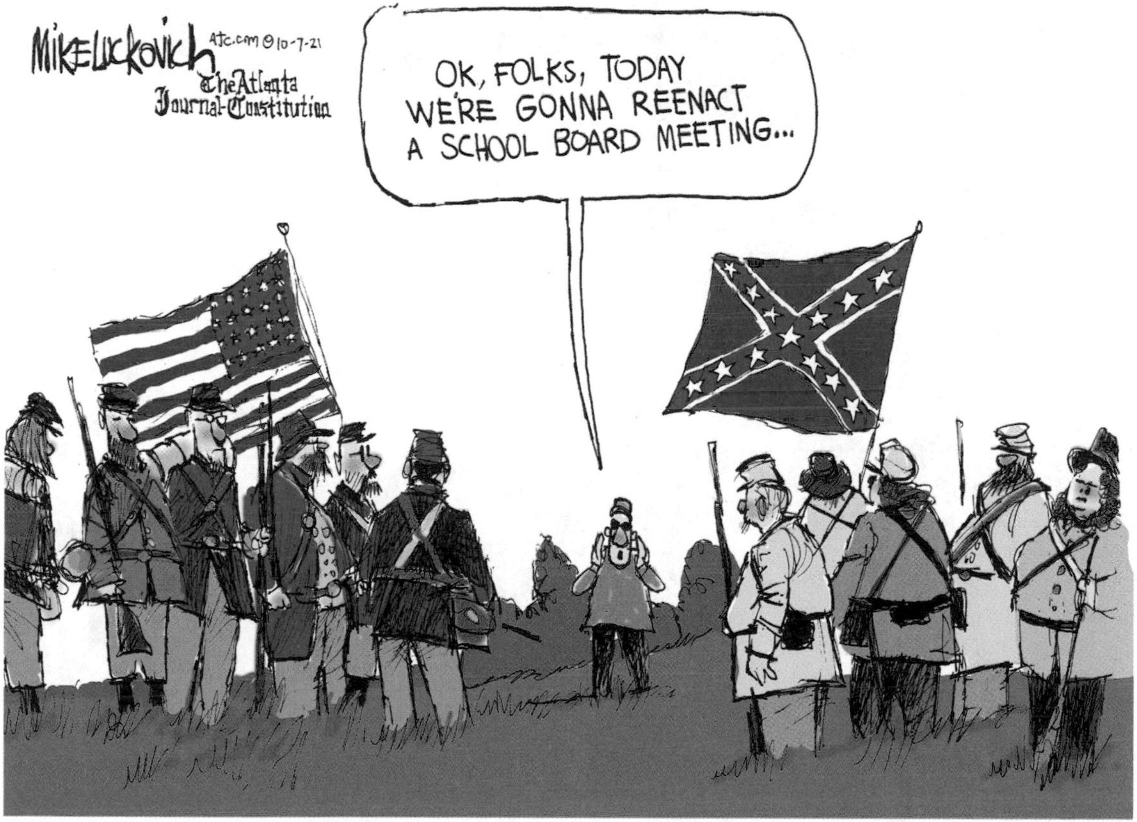
MIKELUCKOVICH
AJC.com ©10-7-21
The Atlanta Journal-Constitution
OK, FOLKS, TODAY WE'RE GONNA REENACT A SCHOOL BOARD MEETING...

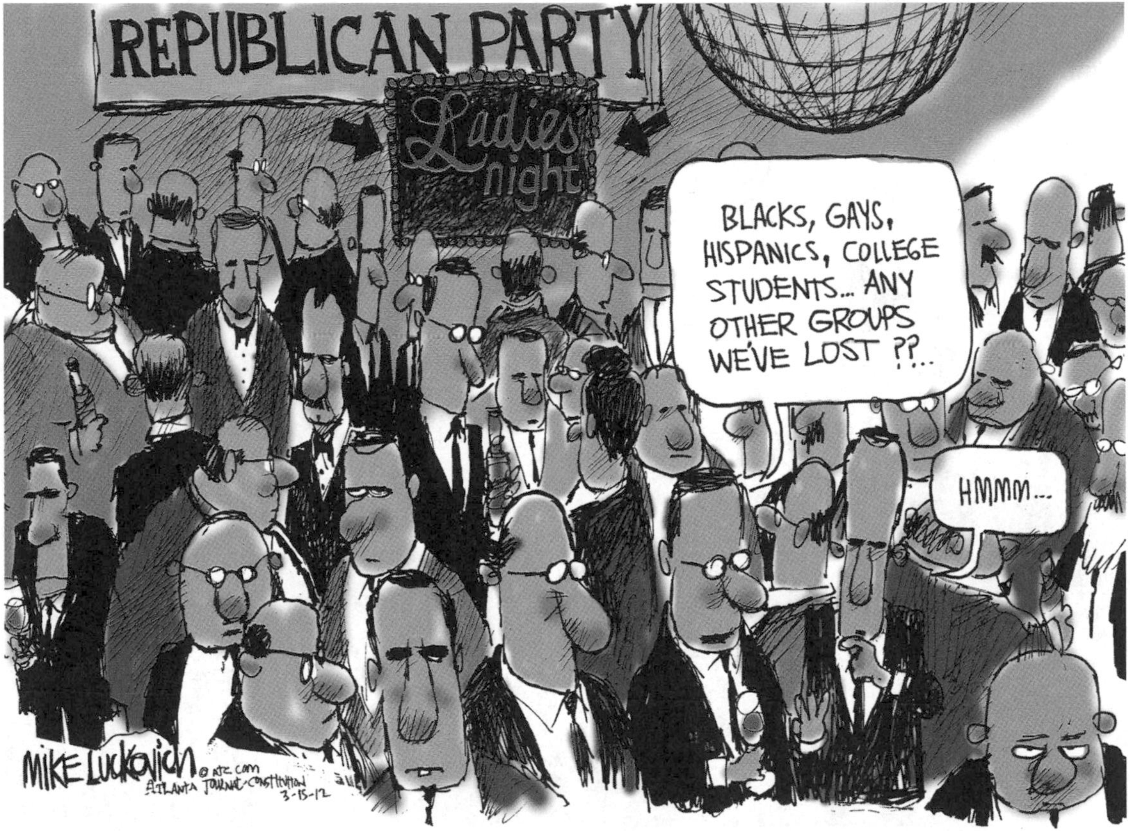
REPUBLICAN PARTY
Ladies' night
BLACKS, GAYS, HISPANICS, COLLEGE STUDENTS... ANY OTHER GROUPS WE'VE LOST ??...
HMMM...
MIKE LUCKOVICH
© AJC.com ATLANTA JOURNAL-CONSTITUTION 3-15-12

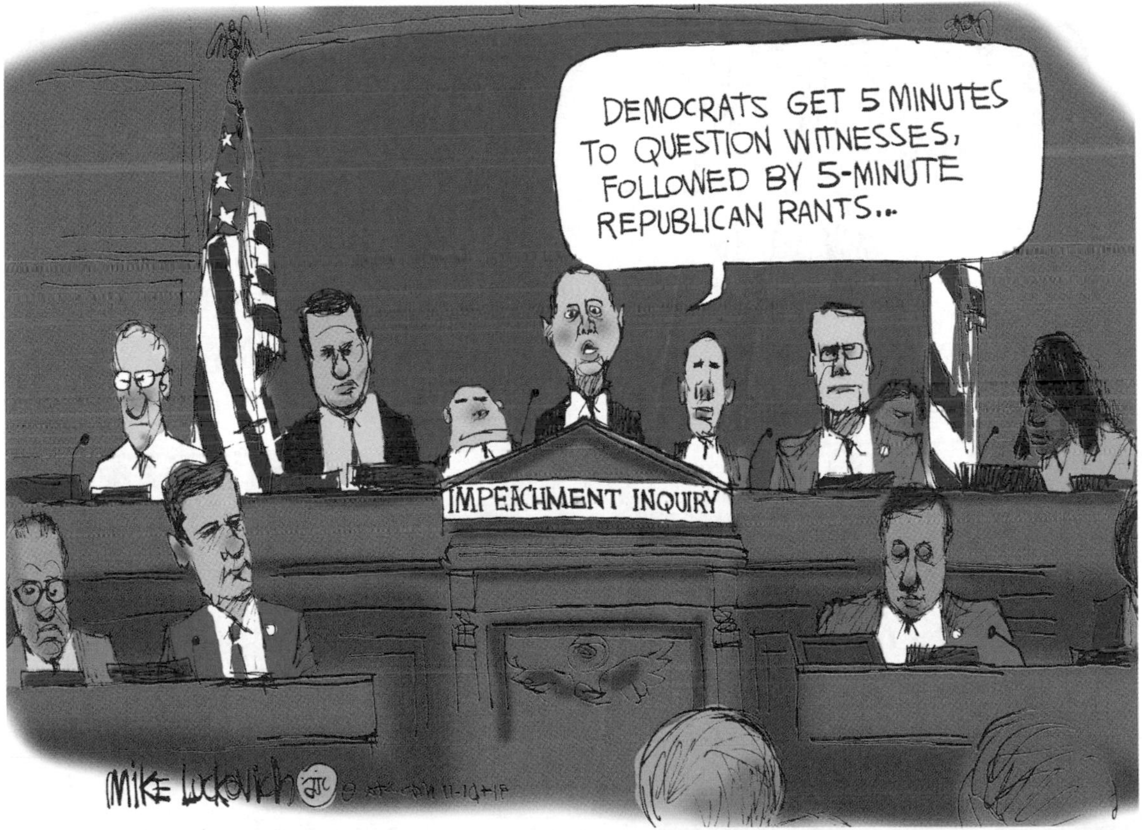
DEMOCRATS GET 5 MINUTES TO QUESTION WITNESSES, FOLLOWED BY 5-MINUTE REPUBLICAN RANTS...
IMPEACHMENT INQUIRY
MIKE LUCKOVICH

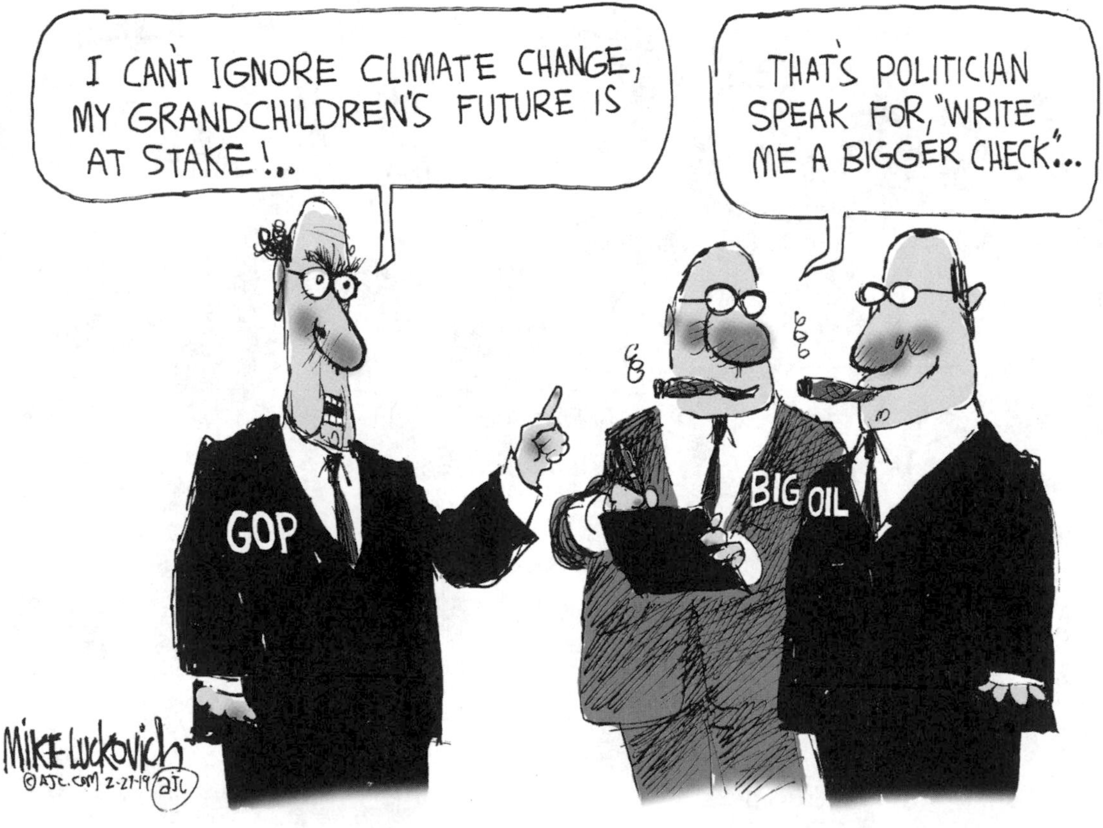
I CAN'T IGNORE CLIMATE CHANGE, MY GRANDCHILDREN'S FUTURE IS AT STAKE!..
THAT'S POLITICIAN SPEAK FOR, "WRITE ME A BIGGER CHECK."...
GOP
BIG OIL
MIKE LUCKOVICH
©AJC.COM 2-27-19

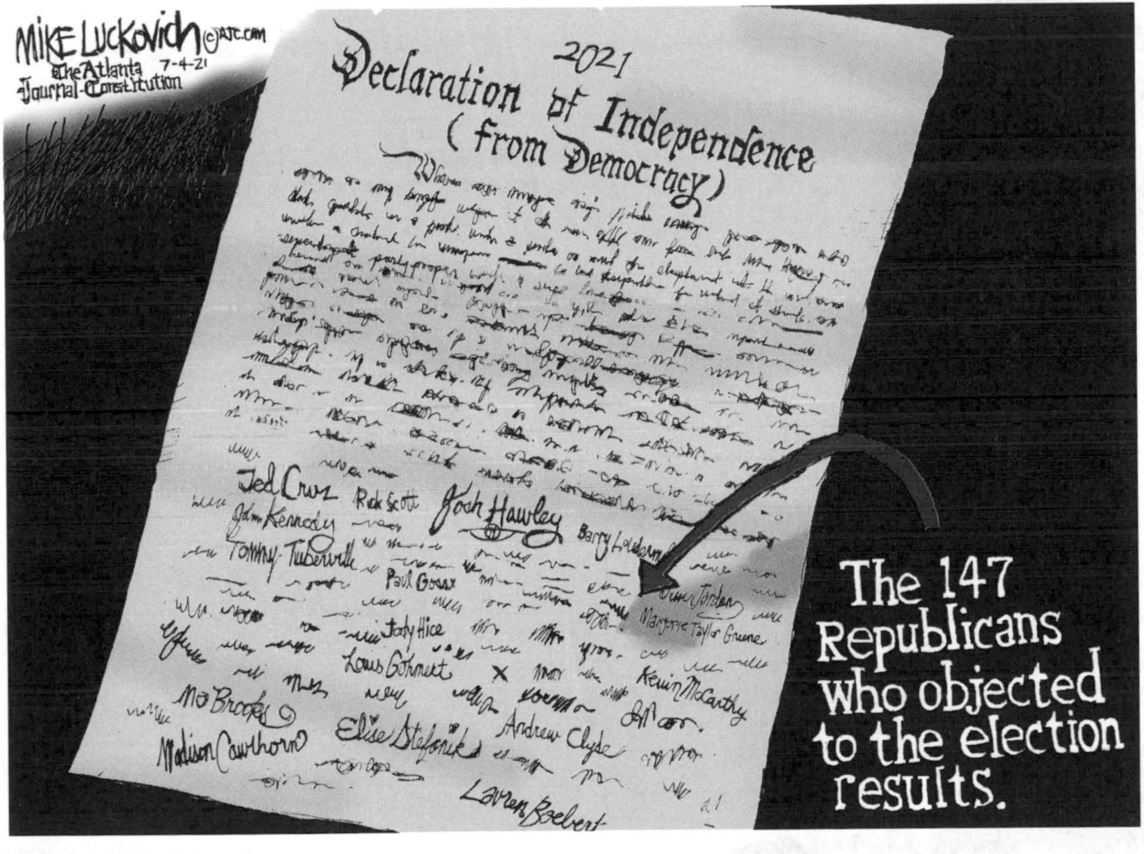
MIKE LUCKOVICH ©AJC.COM
The Atlanta Journal-Constitution 7-4-21
2021
Declaration of Independence
(from Democracy)
Ted Cruz
Rick Scott
Josh Hawley
John Kennedy
Tommy Tuberville
Paul Gosar
Jody Hice
Louis Gohmert
Mo Brooks
Madison Cawthorn
Elise Stefanik
Andrew Clyde
Kevin McCarthy
Marjorie Taylor Greene
Lauren Boebert
The 147 Republicans who objected to the election results.

Ch.10 Fox

In America, there are facts, and then there is Fox News, which many old white people view as truth. I sadly have members of my own family who trust Fox News, and there's nothing I can say that will convince them otherwise. They want to believe what Fox News tells them, that scary brown and Black people are threats to them, while COVID-19, which has literally killed over a million Americans, gets downplayed. Fox News is leading a third of Americans deeper and deeper into Trumpist madness.

ECLIPSE

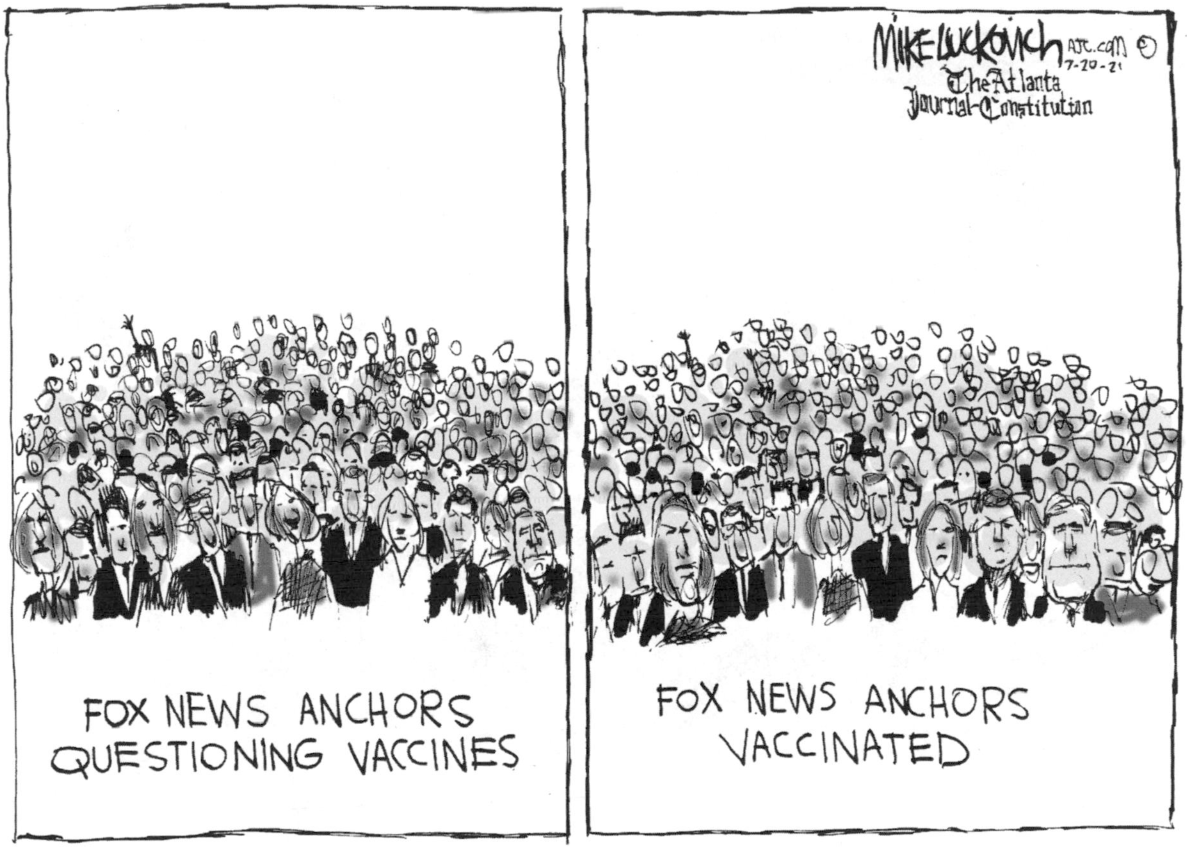
MIKE LUCKOVICH AJC.com ©
7-20-21
The Atlanta Journal-Constitution
FOX NEWS ANCHORS QUESTIONING VACCINES
FOX NEWS ANCHORS VACCINATED

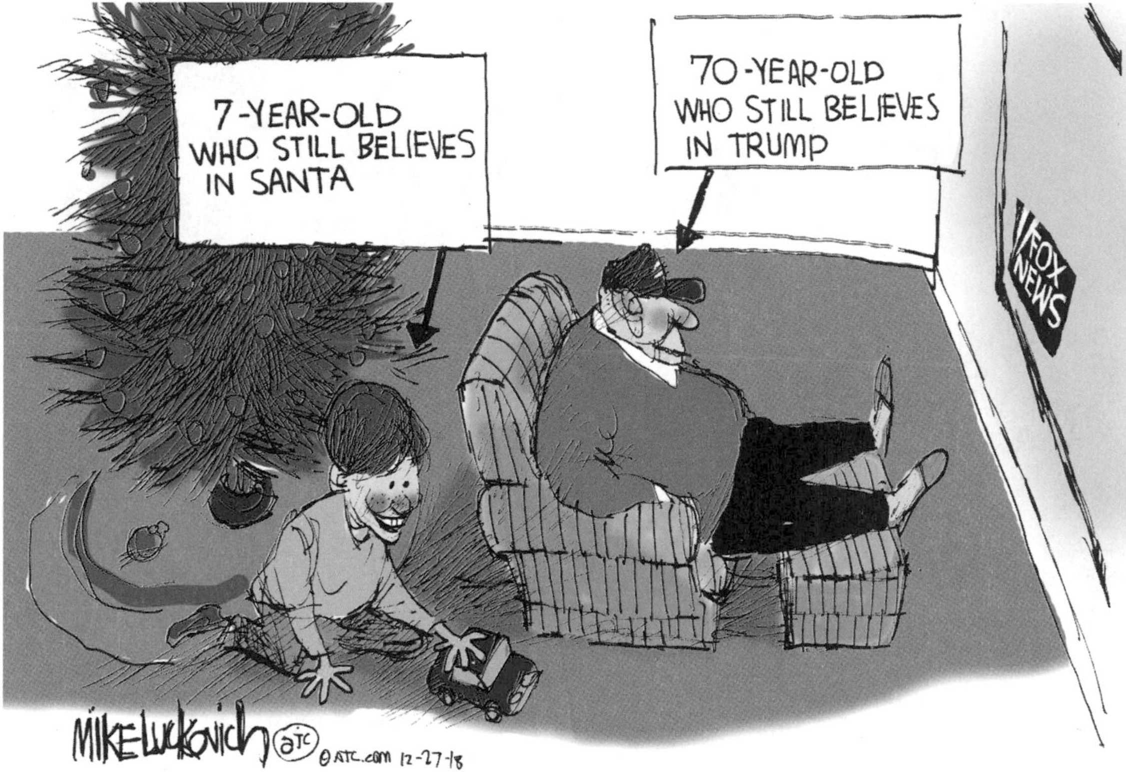
7-YEAR-OLD
WHO STILL BELIEVES
IN SANTA
70-YEAR-OLD
WHO STILL BELIEVES
IN TRUMP
FOX NEWS
MIKE LUCKOVICH
AJC
©AJC.com 12-27-18

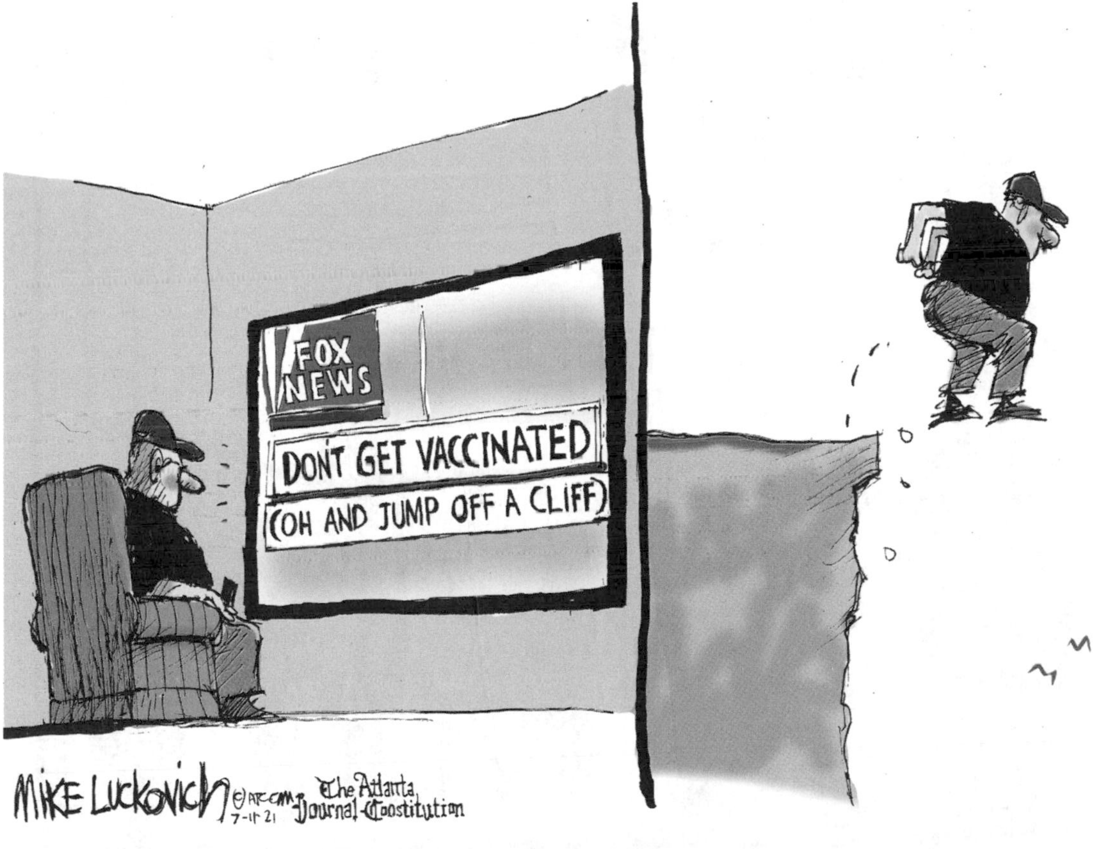
FOX NEWS
DON'T GET VACCINATED
(OH AND JUMP OFF A CLIFF)
MIKE LUCKOVICH
The Atlanta Journal-Constitution
7-11-21

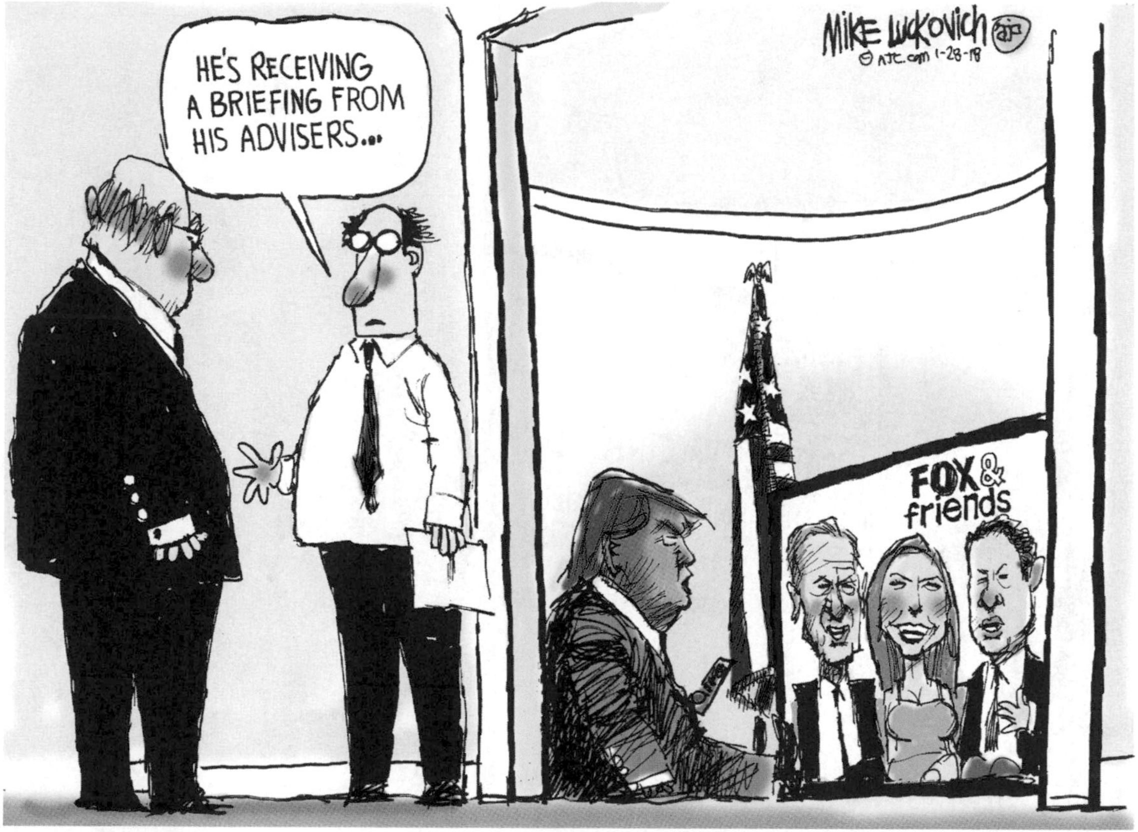
HE'S RECEIVING A BRIEFING FROM HIS ADVISERS...
MIKE LUCKOVICH
FOX & friends

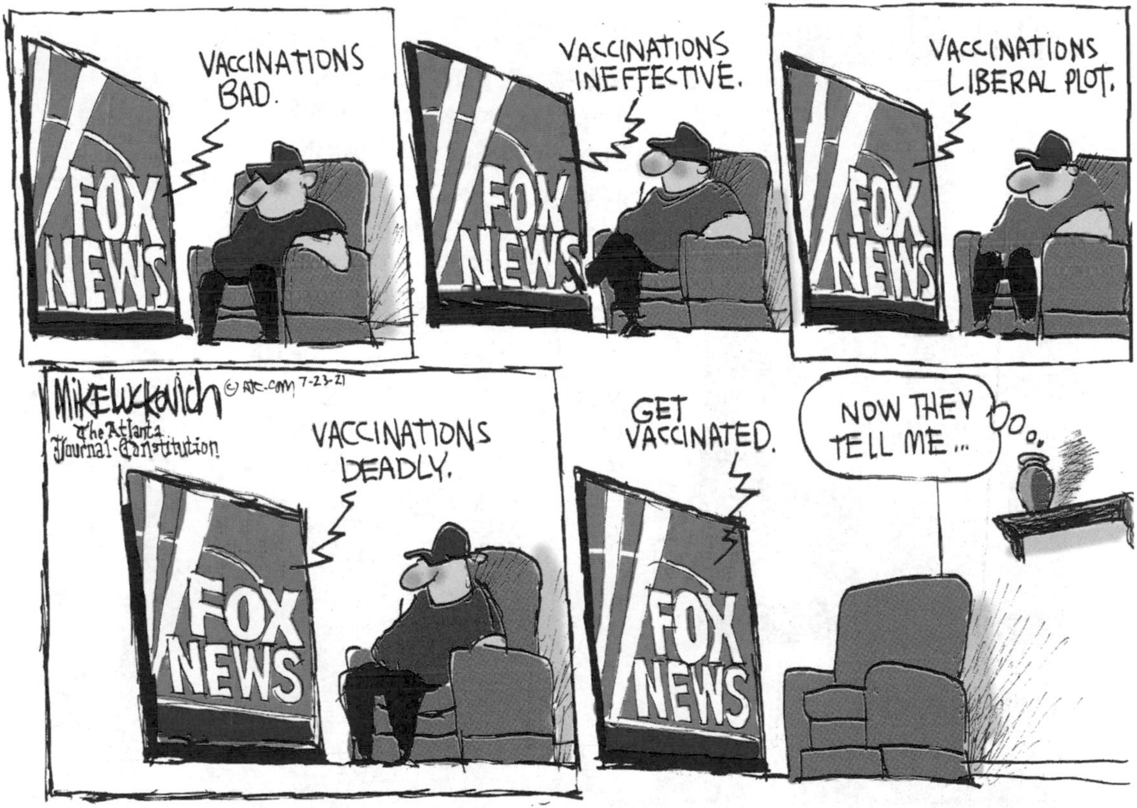
VACCINATIONS BAD.
FOX NEWS
VACCINATIONS INEFFECTIVE.
FOX NEWS
VACCINATIONS LIBERAL PLOT.
FOX NEWS
MIKE LUCKOVICH © AJC.COM 7-23-21
The Atlanta Journal-Constitution
VACCINATIONS DEADLY.
FOX NEWS
GET VACCINATED.
FOX NEWS
NOW THEY TELL ME...

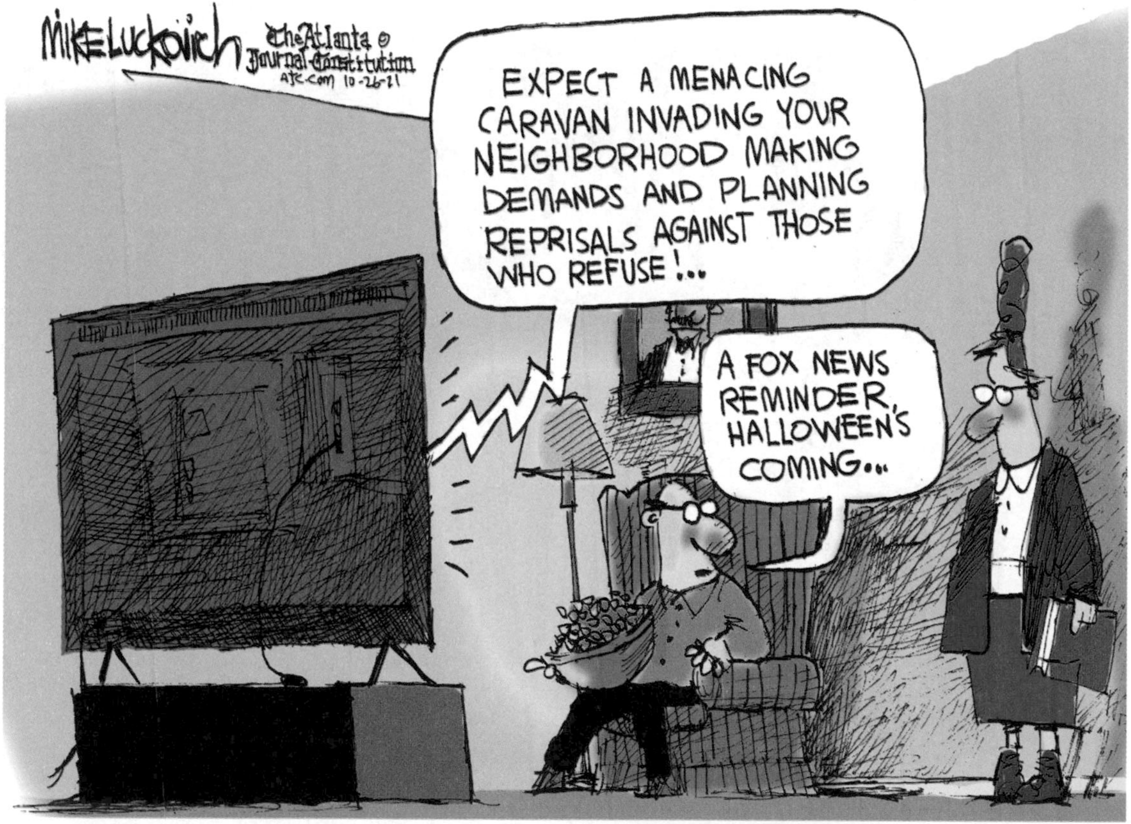
MIKE LUCKOVICH The Atlanta Journal-Constitution ajc.com 10-26-21
EXPECT A MENACING CARAVAN INVADING YOUR NEIGHBORHOOD MAKING DEMANDS AND PLANNING REPRISALS AGAINST THOSE WHO REFUSE!...
A FOX NEWS REMINDER, HALLOWEEN'S COMING...

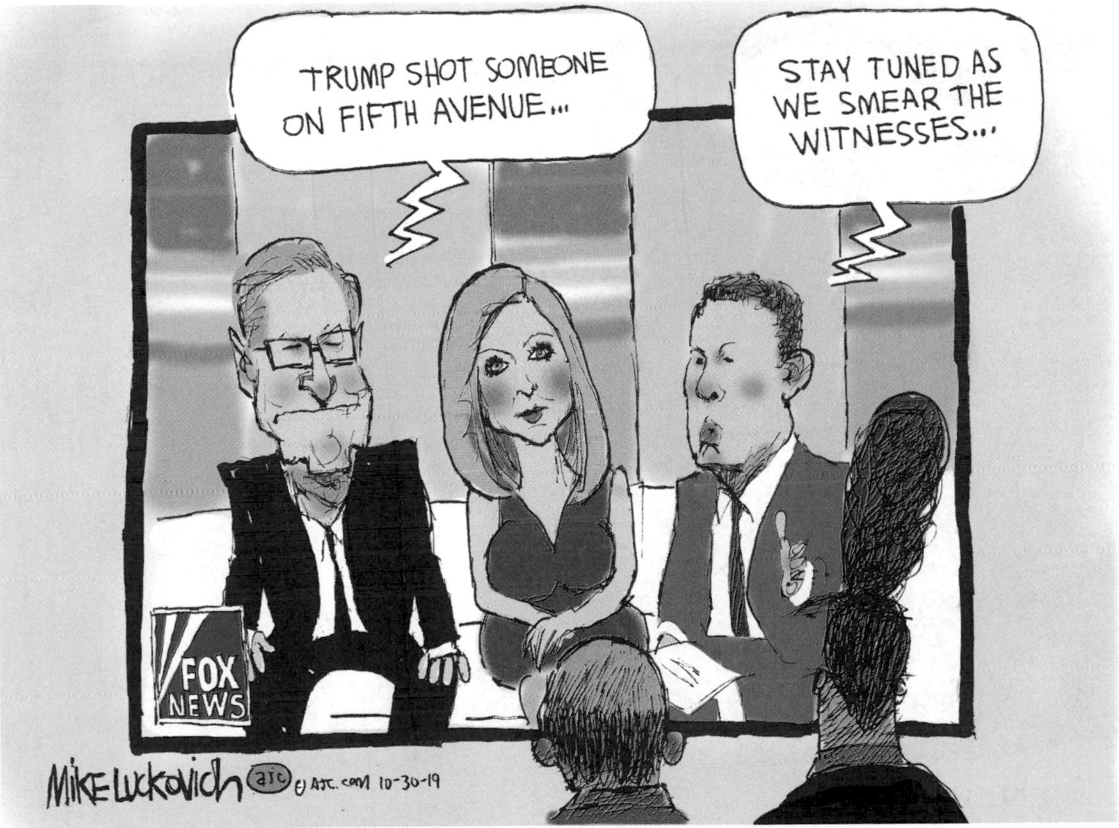
TRUMP SHOT SOMEONE ON FIFTH AVENUE...
STAY TUNED AS WE SMEAR THE WITNESSES...
FOX NEWS
MIKE LUCKOVICH ajc ©AJC.com 10-30-19

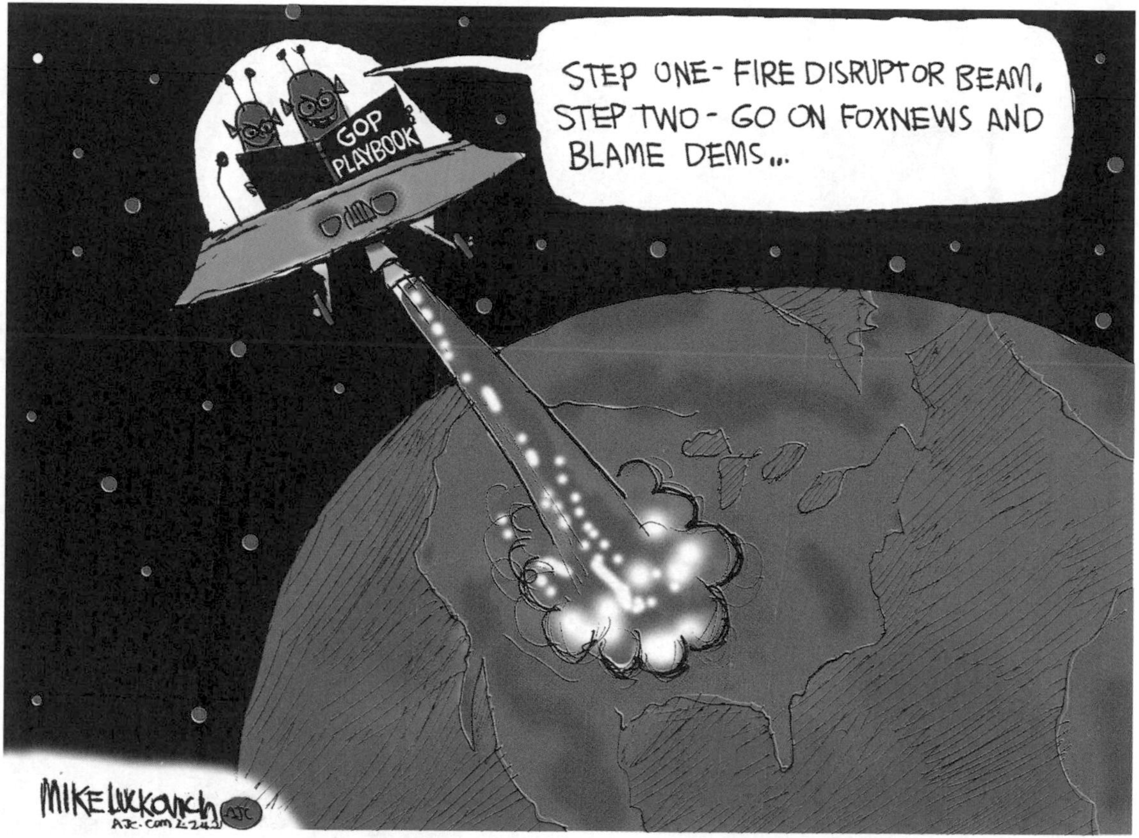
GOP PLAYBOOK
STEP ONE - FIRE DISRUPTOR BEAM. STEP TWO - GO ON FOXNEWS AND BLAME DEMS...
MIKE LUCKOVICH
AJC.com 2-24-21
AJC

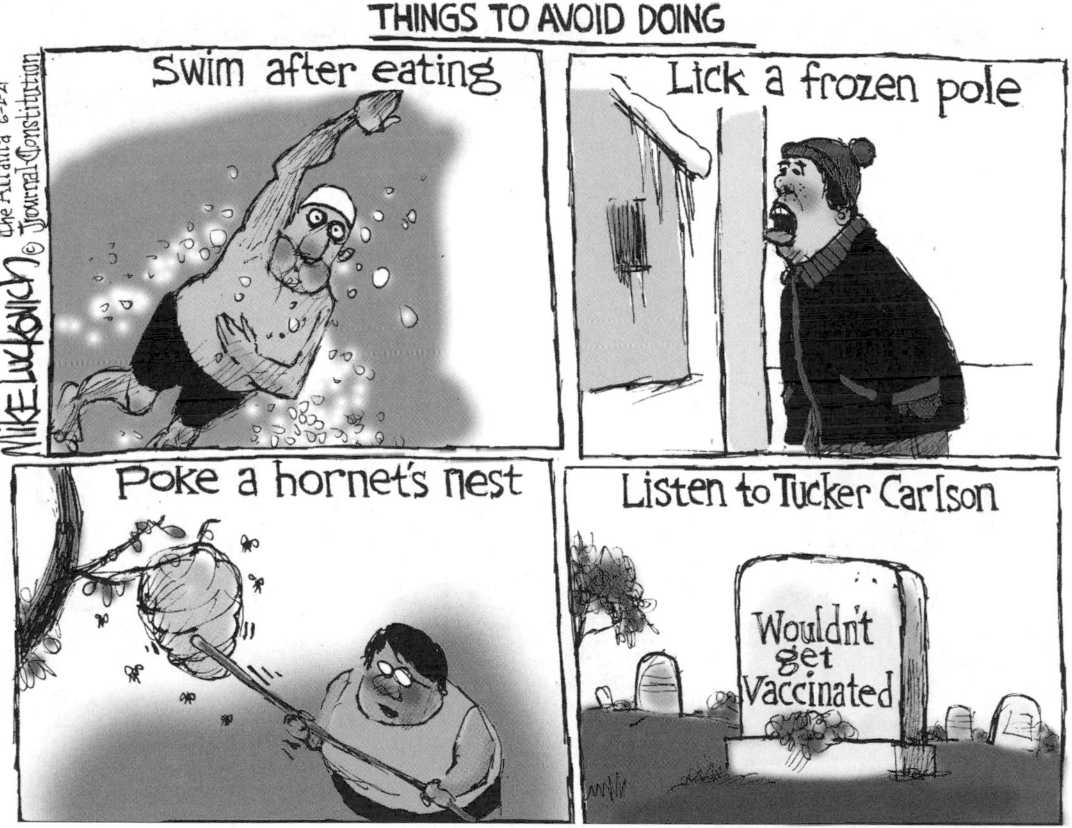
THINGS TO AVOID DOING
Swim after eating
Lick a frozen pole
Poke a hornet's nest
Listen to Tucker Carlson
Wouldn't get Vaccinated
MIKE LUCKOVICH
The Atlanta Journal-Constitution ©
6-2-21

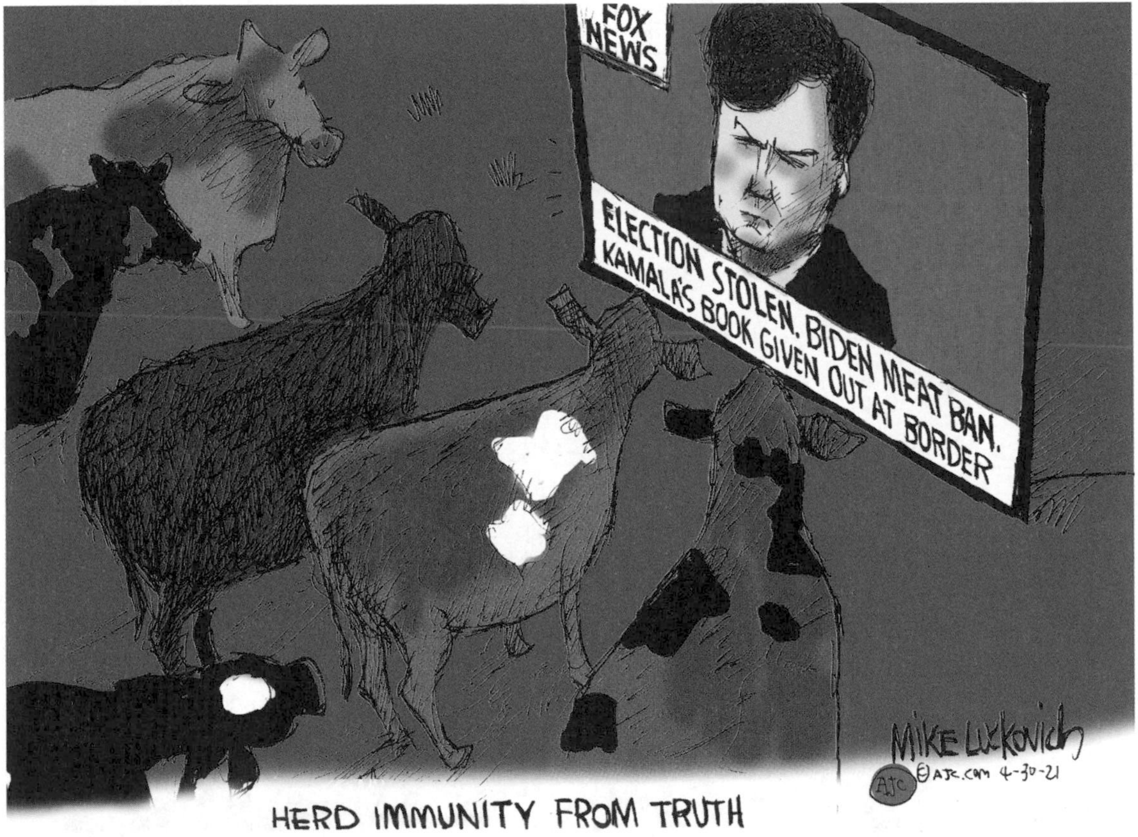
FOX NEWS
ELECTION STOLEN. BIDEN MEAT BAN. KAMALA'S BOOK GIVEN OUT AT BORDER
MIKE LUCKOVICH
©AJC.com 4-30-21
AJC
HERD IMMUNITY FROM TRUTH

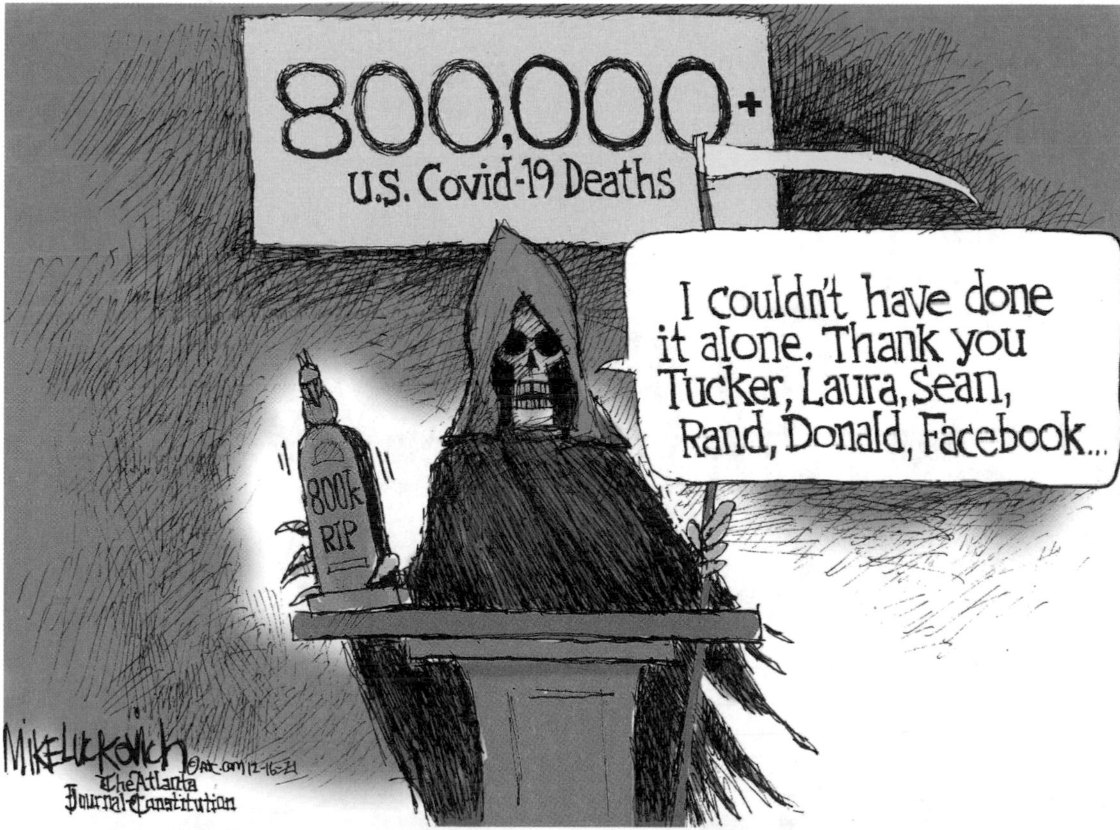
800,000+
U.S. Covid-19 Deaths
I couldn't have done it alone. Thank you Tucker, Laura, Sean, Rand, Donald, Facebook...
800K RIP
MIKE LUCKOVICH
The Atlanta Journal-Constitution

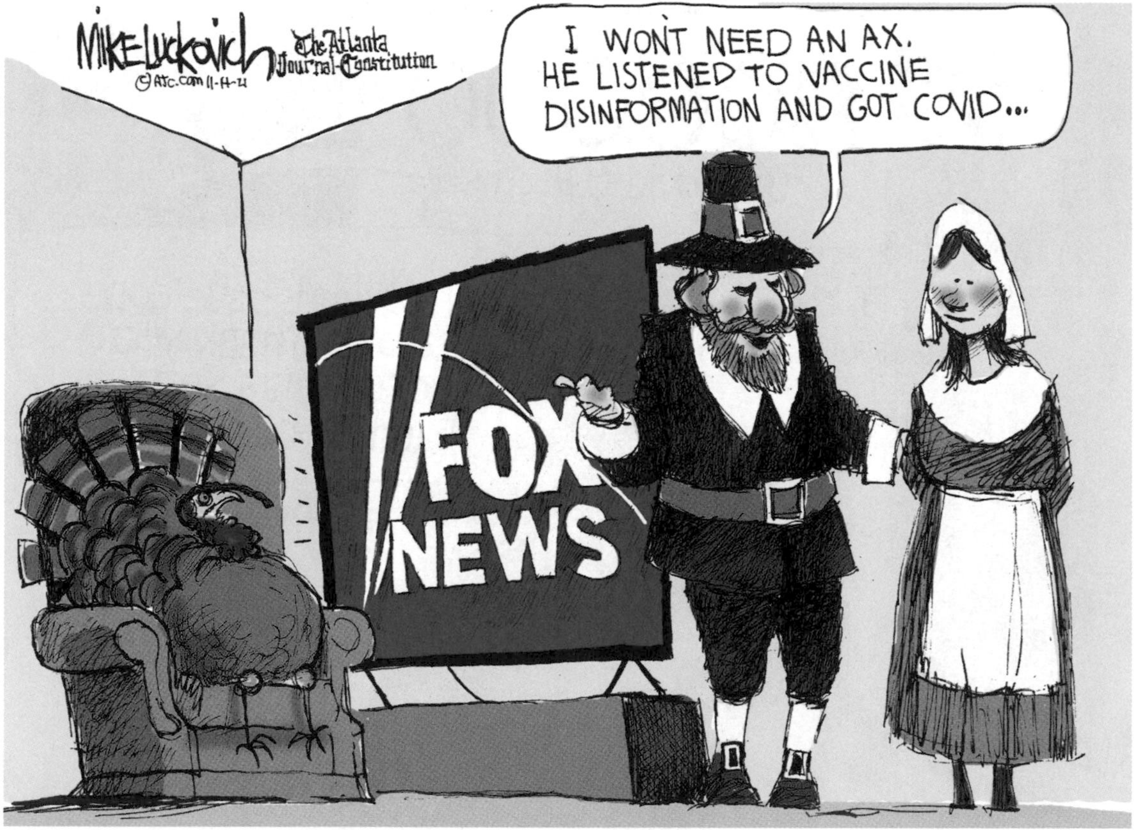
MIKE LUCKOVICH The Atlanta Journal-Constitution
©AJC.com 11-14-21
I WON'T NEED AN AX. HE LISTENED TO VACCINE DISINFORMATION AND GOT COVID...
FOX NEWS

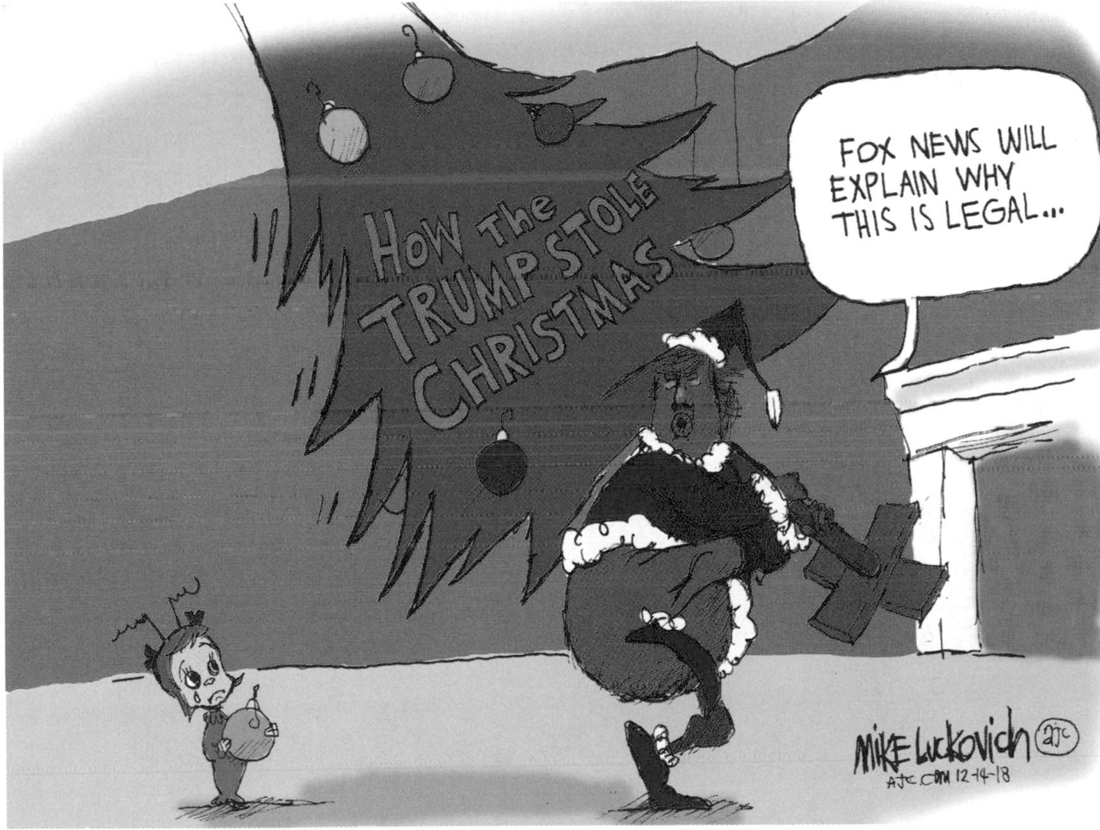
FOX NEWS WILL EXPLAIN WHY THIS IS LEGAL...
HOW THE TRUMP STOLE CHRISTMAS
MIKE LUCKOVICH
AJC.COM 12-14-18

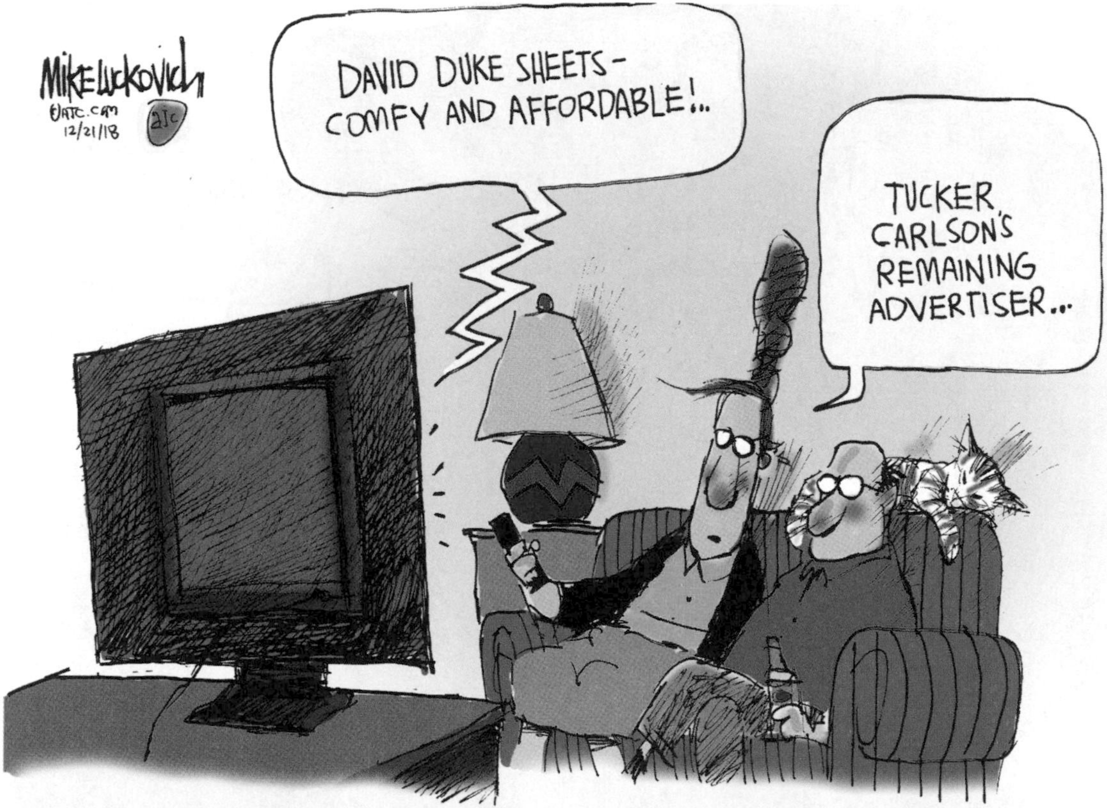
MIKE LUCKOVICH
©AJC.com
12/21/18
ajc
DAVID DUKE SHEETS - COMFY AND AFFORDABLE!..
TUCKER CARLSON'S REMAINING ADVERTISER...

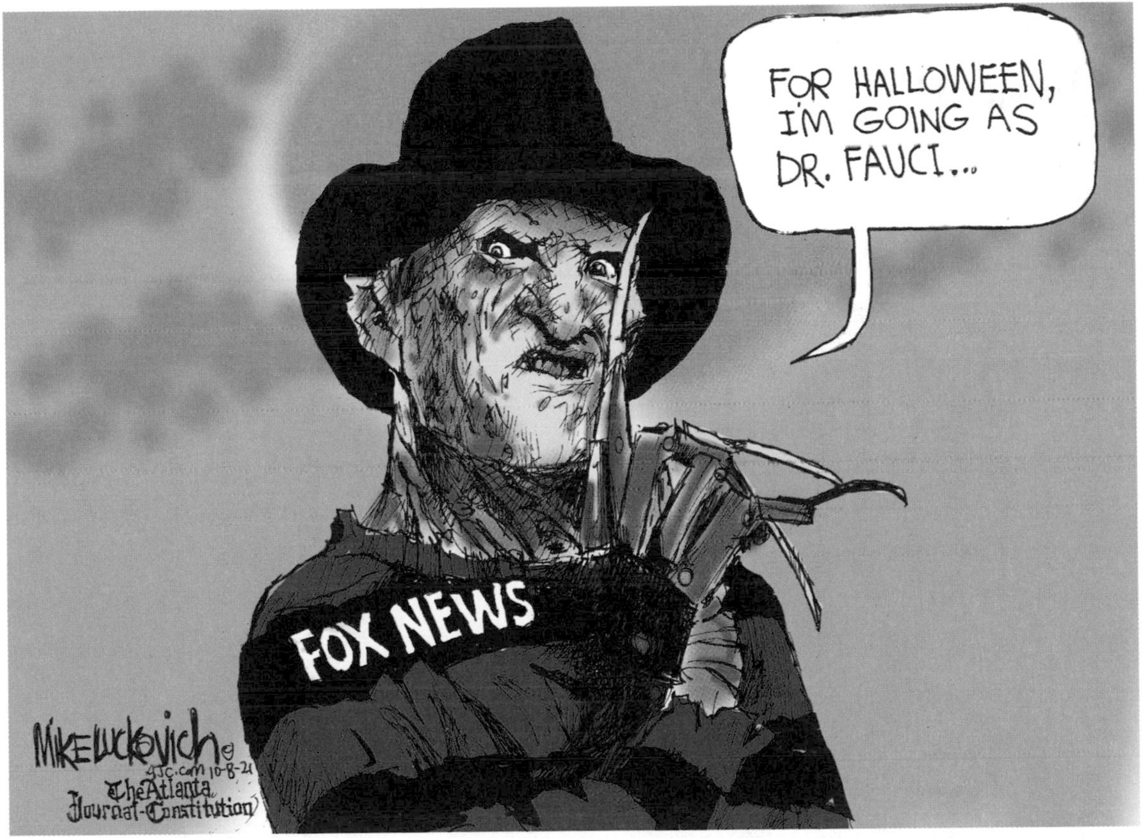
FOR HALLOWEEN, I'M GOING AS DR. FAUCI...
FOX NEWS
MIKELUCKOVICH
AJC.com 10-8-21
The Atlanta Journal-Constitution

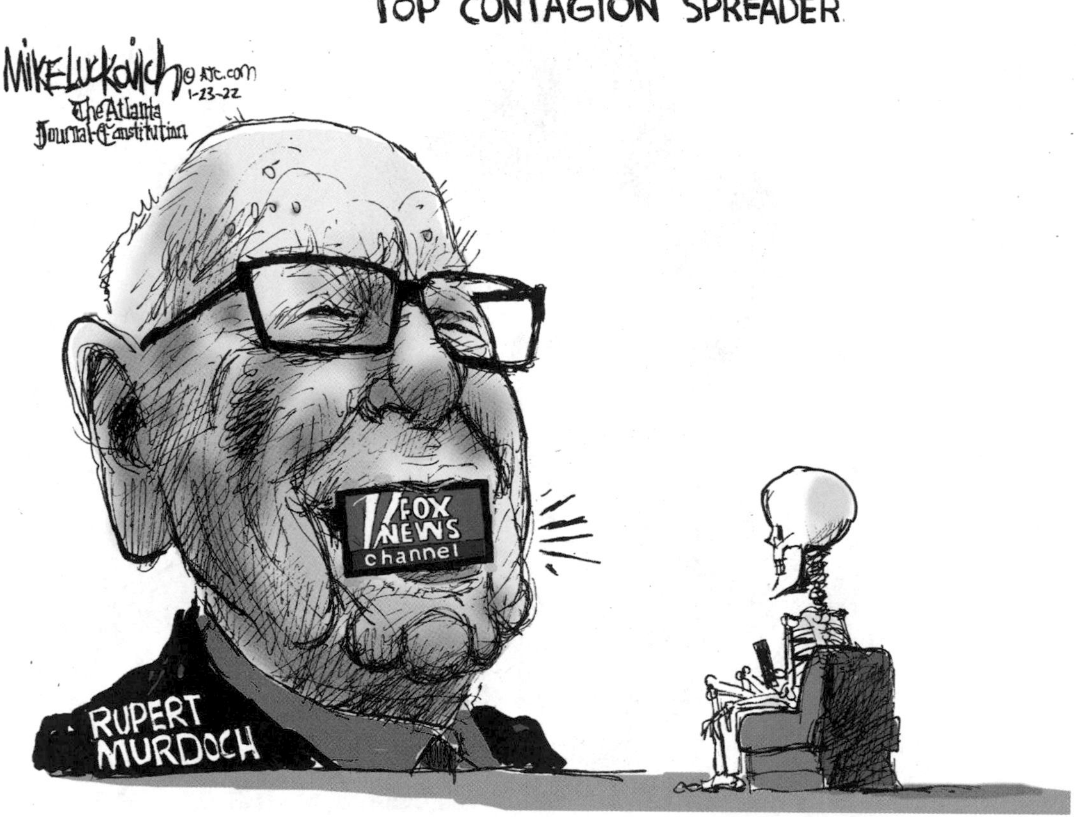
TOP CONTAGION SPREADER
MIKE LUCKOVICH © AJC.com 1-23-22
The Atlanta Journal-Constitution
FOX NEWS channel
RUPERT MURDOCH

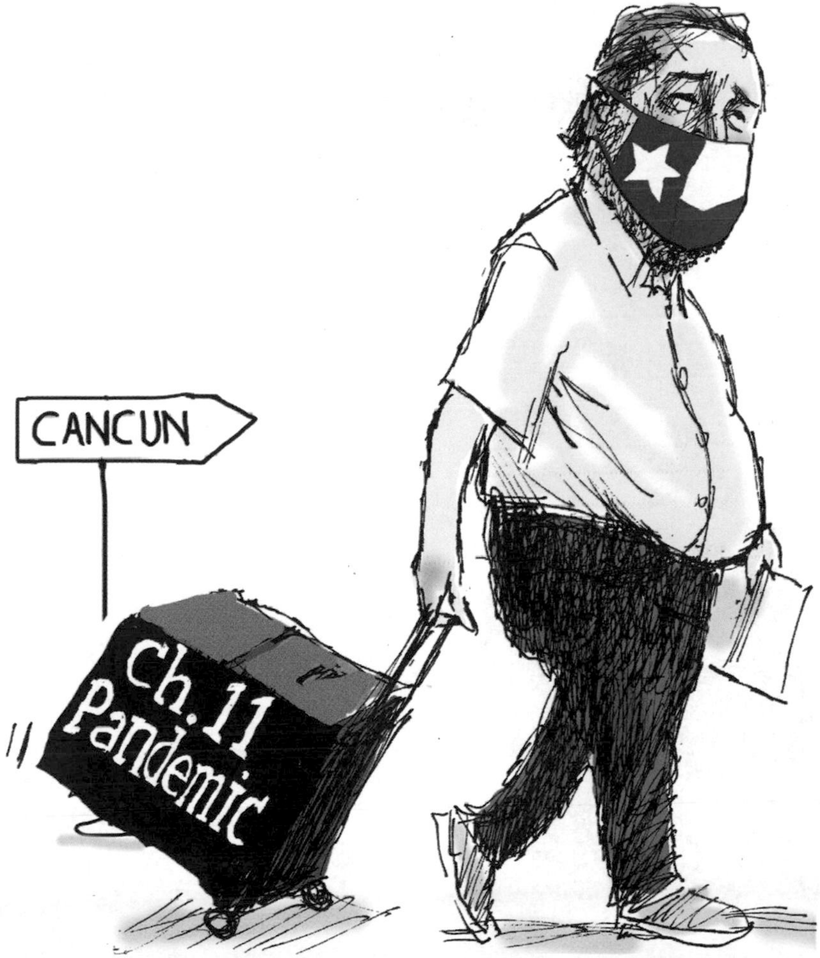
CANCUN
Ch. 11
Pandemic

Polarization is so strong in America that even a deadly pandemic gets politicized. Republican governors keep their voters riled up by making Dr. Fauci an enemy, and precautions against COVID-19 (masks, vaccinations, mandates) seem like assaults on their supporters' freedoms. While feeding their base's anger helps a Republican politician's election chances, a side-effect these politicians willingly accept is that some of their followers die.

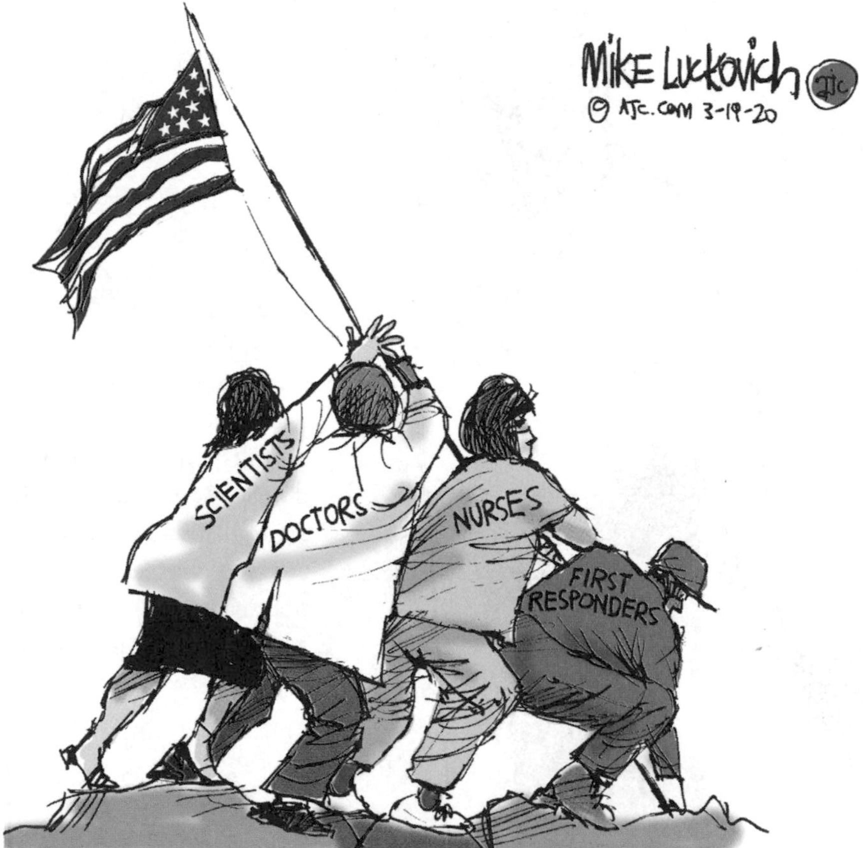
MIKE LUCKOVICH
© AJC.COM 3-19-20
SCIENTISTS
DOCTORS
NURSES
FIRST RESPONDERS

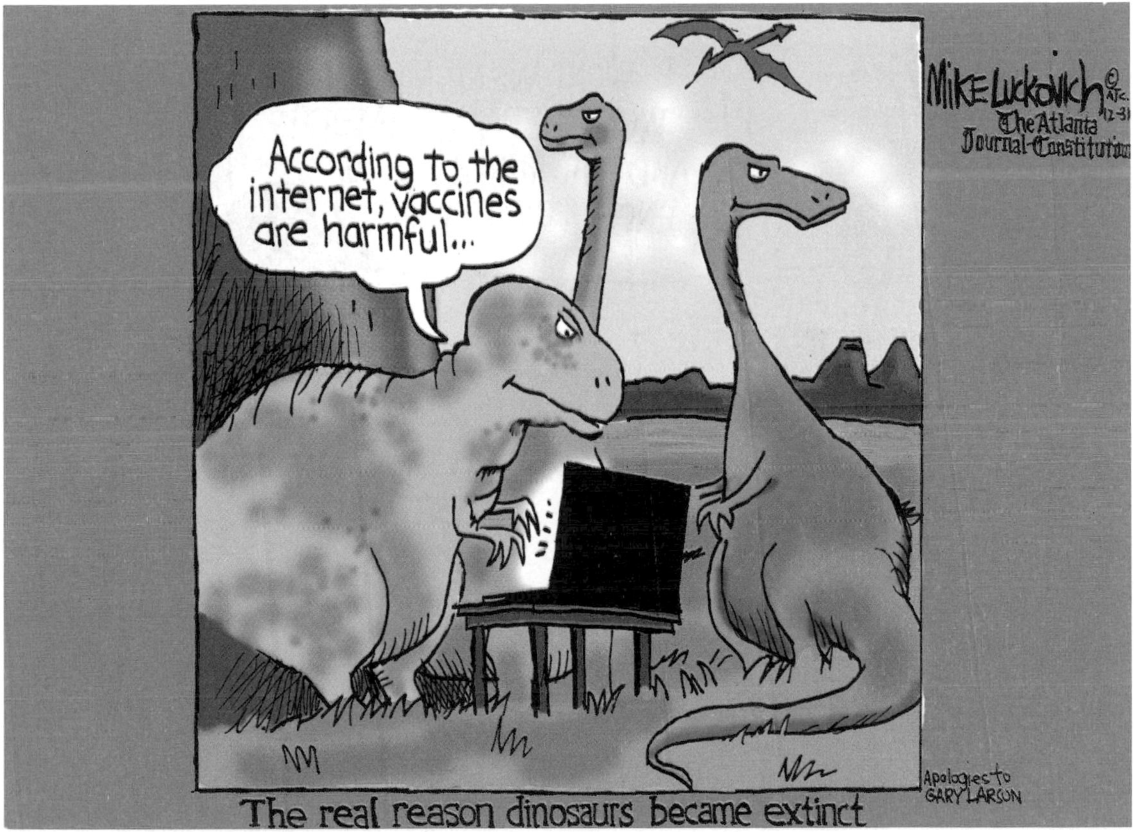
According to the internet, vaccines are harmful...
MIKE LUCKOVICH © AJC 12-31
The Atlanta Journal-Constitution
Apologies to GARY LARSON
The real reason dinosaurs became extinct

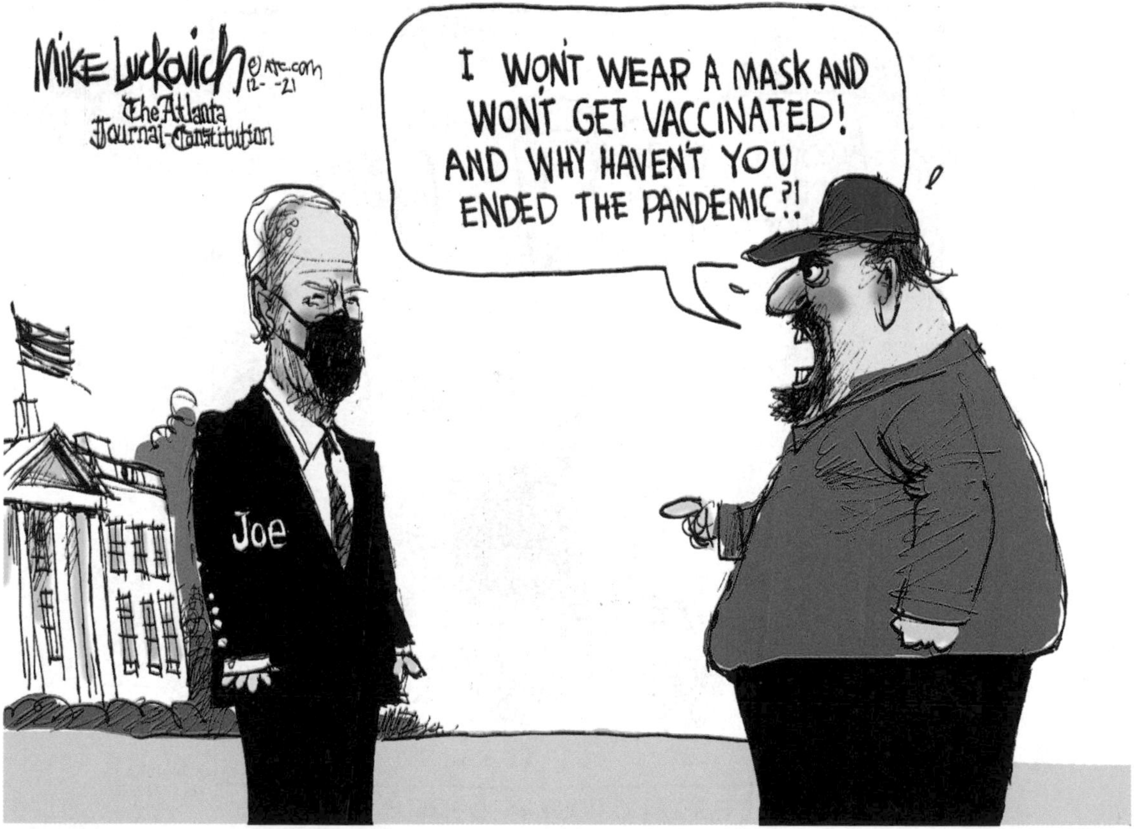
MIKE LUCKOVICH © AJC.com 12- -21
The Atlanta Journal-Constitution
I WON'T WEAR A MASK AND WON'T GET VACCINATED! AND WHY HAVEN'T YOU ENDED THE PANDEMIC?!
Joe

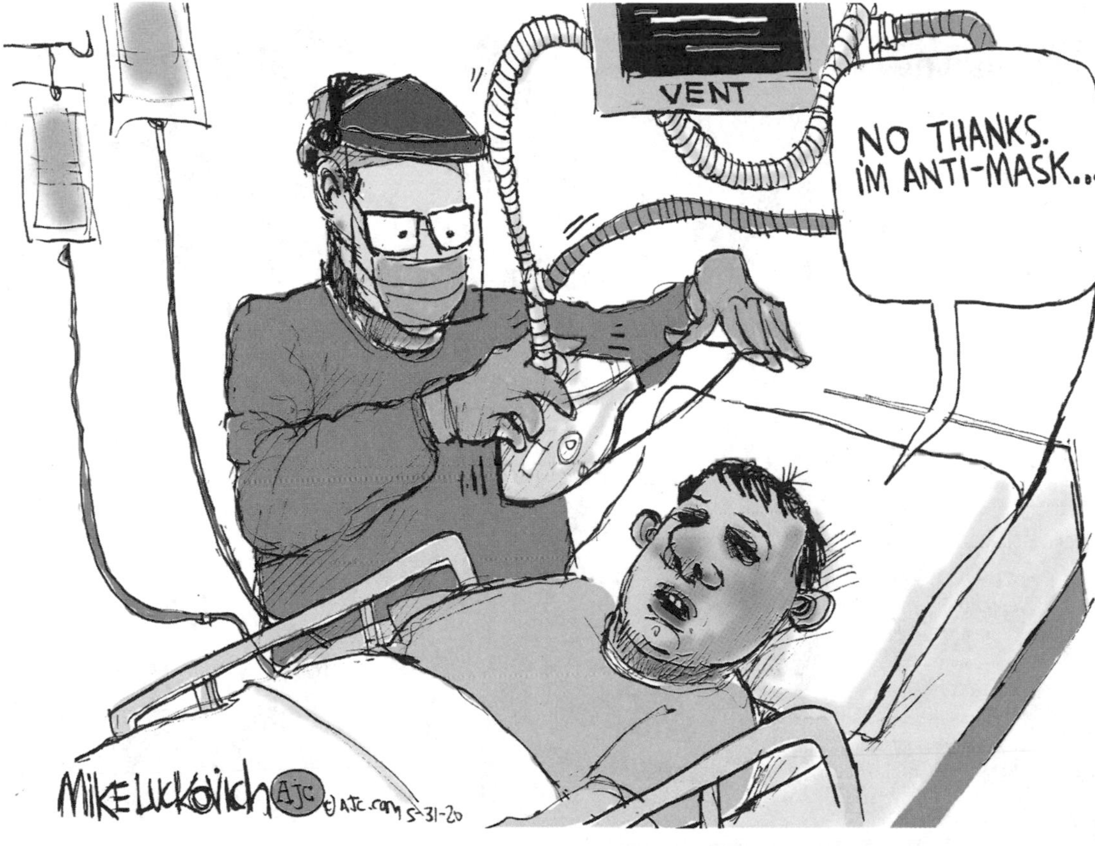
VENT
NO THANKS. IM ANTI-MASK...
MIKE LUCKOVICH AJC ©AJC.com 5-31-20

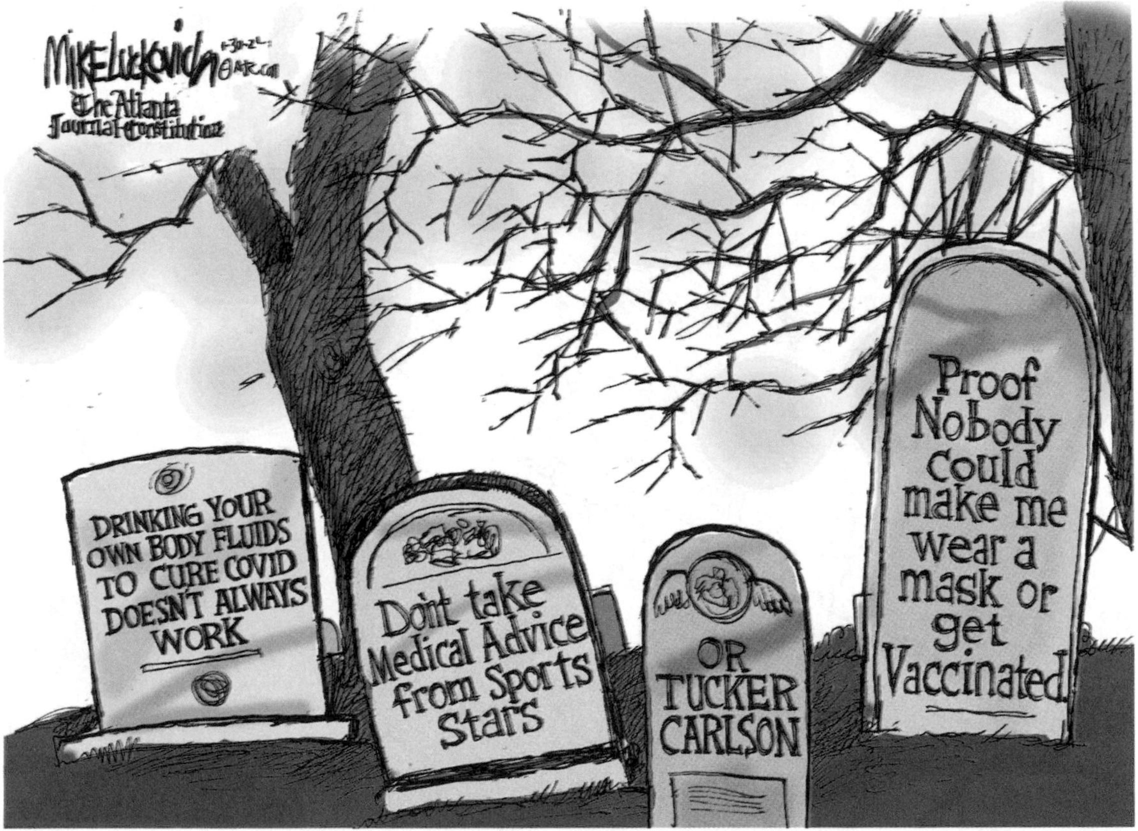
MIKE LUCKOVICH
The Atlanta Journal-Constitution
DRINKING YOUR OWN BODY FLUIDS TO CURE COVID DOESN'T ALWAYS WORK
Don't take Medical Advice from Sports Stars
OR TUCKER CARLSON
Proof Nobody could make me wear a mask or get Vaccinated!

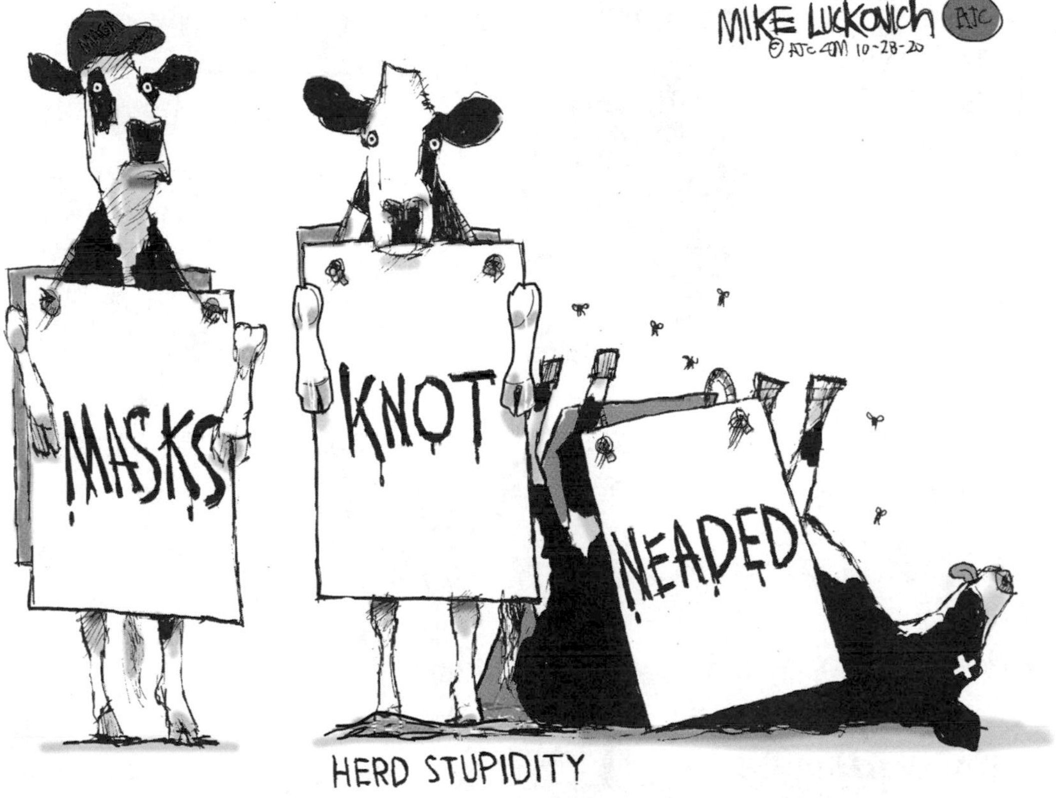
MIKE LUCKOVICH
AJC
© AJC.COM 10-28-20
MASKS
KNOT
NEADED
HERD STUPIDITY

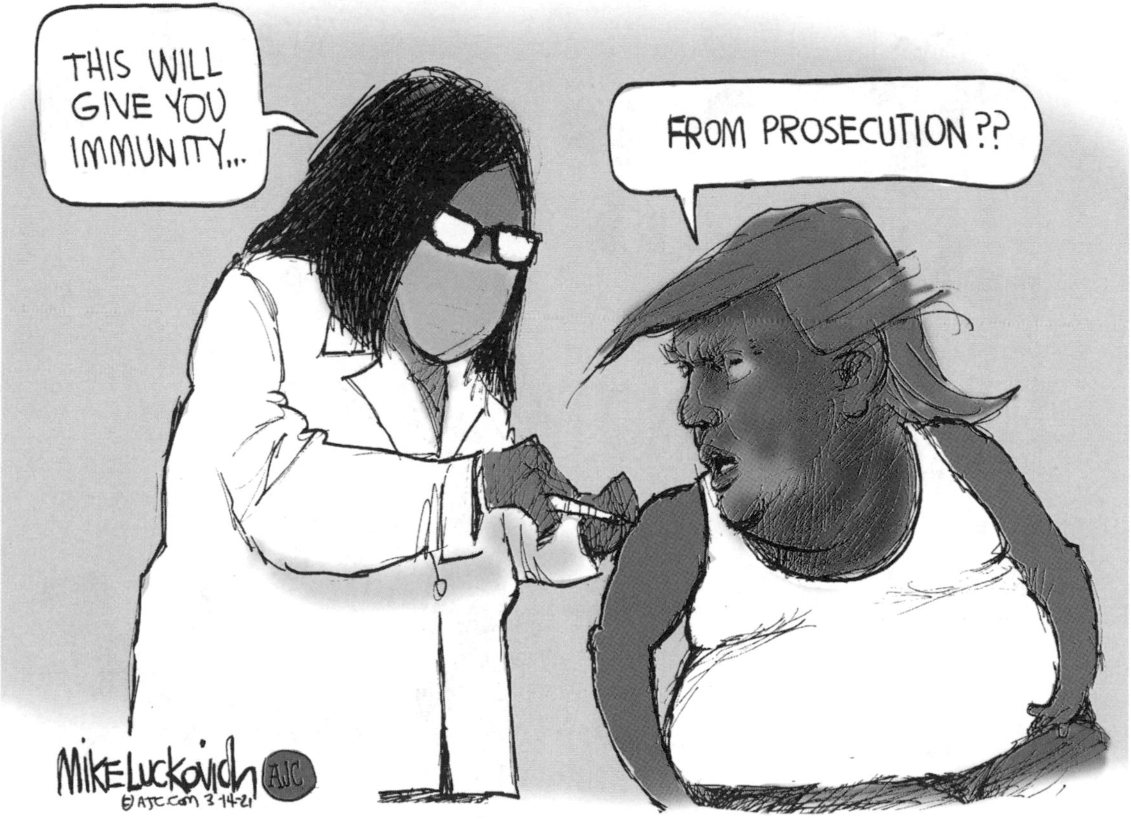
THIS WILL GIVE YOU IMMUNITY...
FROM PROSECUTION??
MIKELUCKOVICH
AJC
©AJC.com 3-14-21

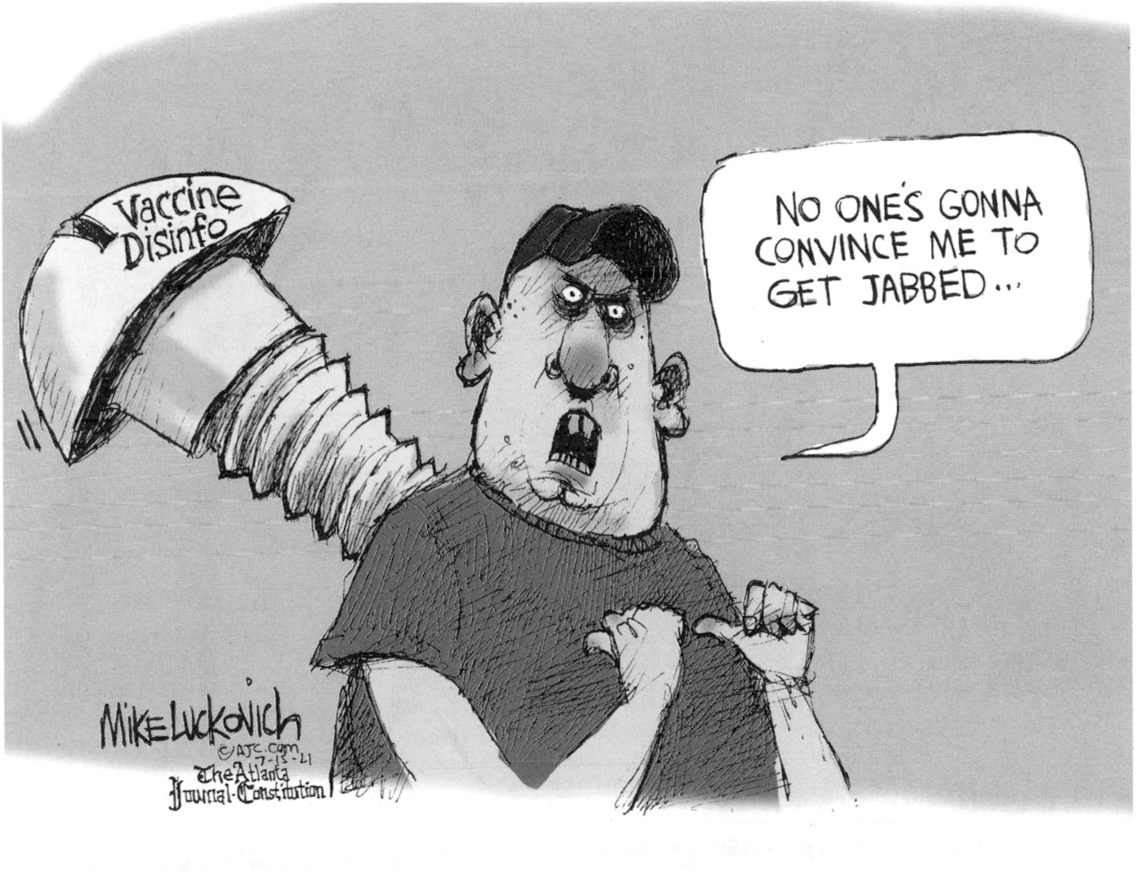
Vaccine Disinfo
NO ONE'S GONNA CONVINCE ME TO GET JABBED...
MIKE LUCKOVICH
©AJC.com 7-15-21
The Atlanta Journal-Constitution

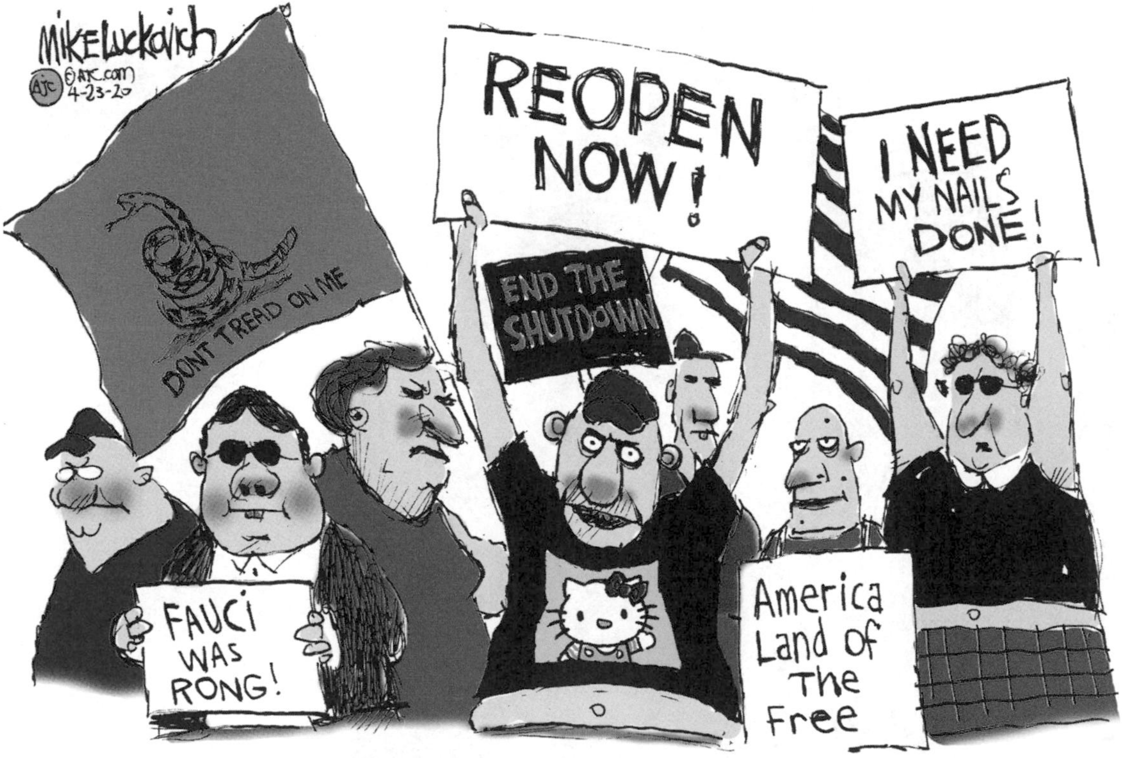
MIKE LUCKOVICH
AJC ©AJC.com 4-23-20
DONT TREAD ON ME
REOPEN NOW!
END THE SHUTDOWN
I NEED MY NAILS DONE!
FAUCI WAS RONG!
America Land of The Free

CORONAVIRUS TASK FORCE ADVISING SOUTHERN GOVERNORS

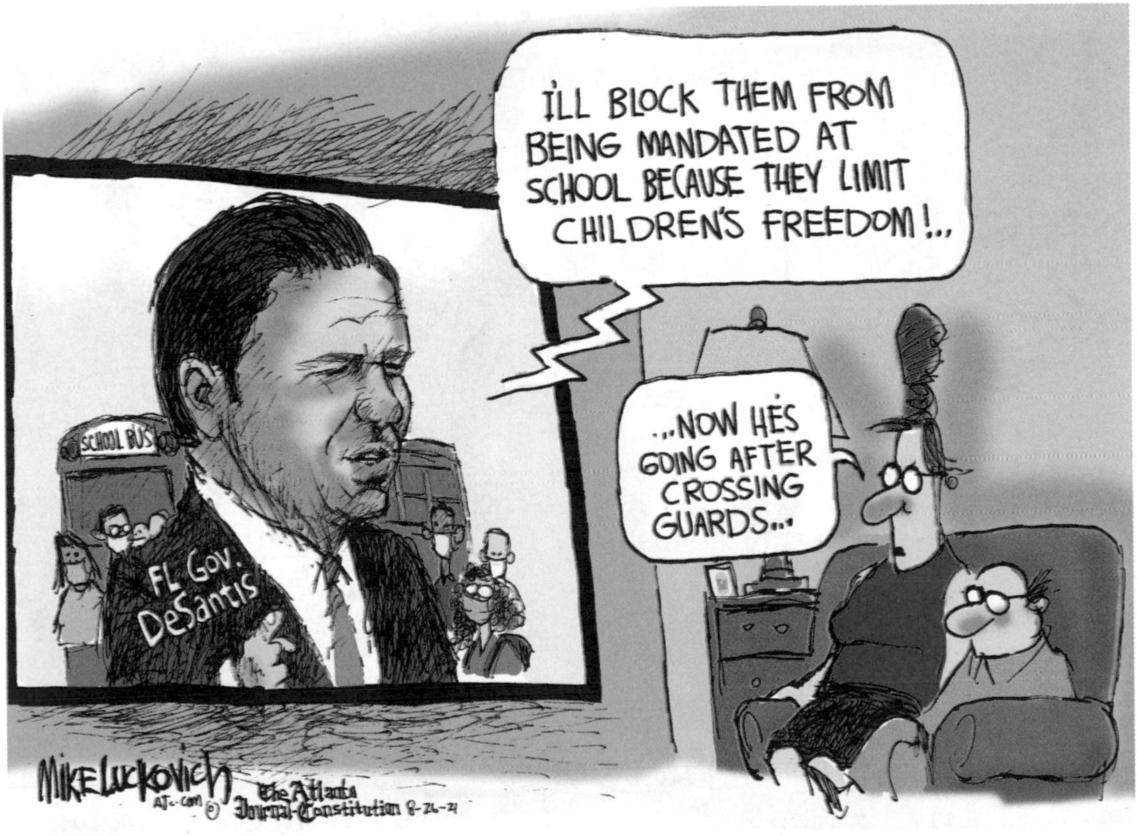
I'LL BLOCK THEM FROM BEING MANDATED AT SCHOOL BECAUSE THEY LIMIT CHILDREN'S FREEDOM!..
...NOW HE'S GOING AFTER CROSSING GUARDS...
SCHOOL BUS
FL Gov. DeSantis
MIKE LUCKOVICH
AJC.com ©
The Atlanta Journal-Constitution 8-26-21

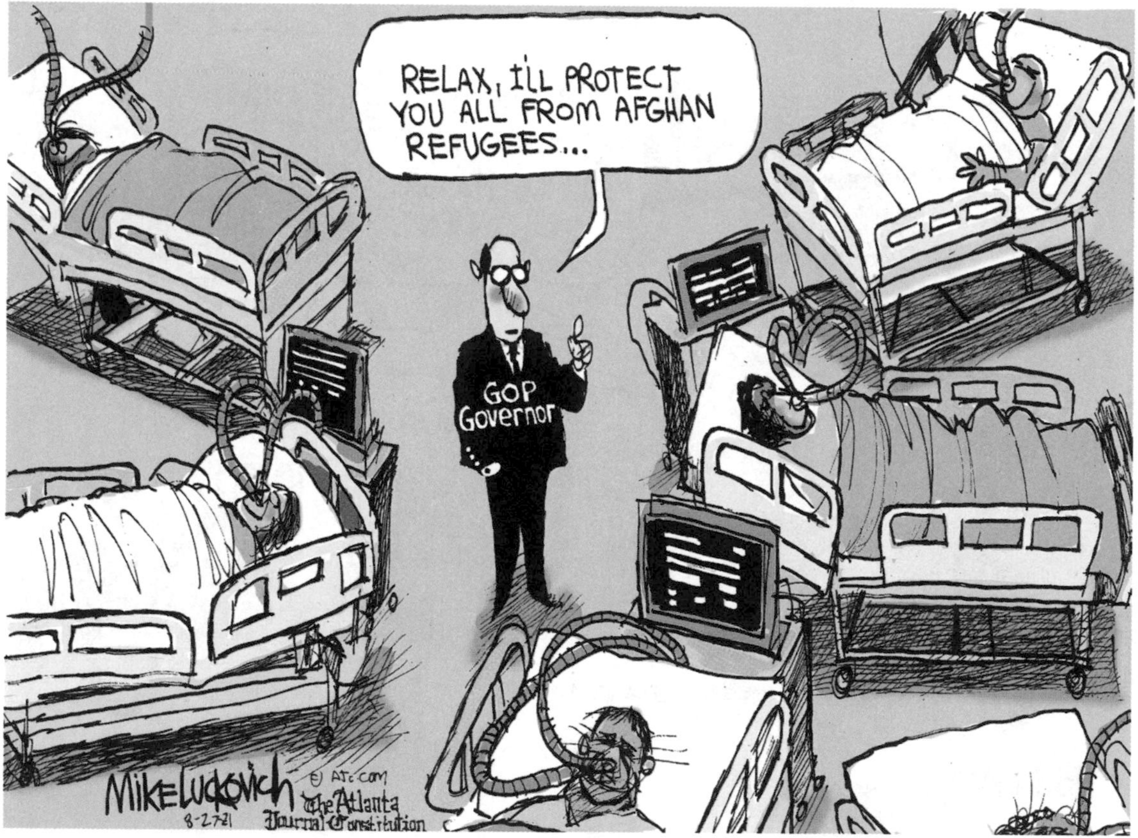
RELAX, I'LL PROTECT YOU ALL FROM AFGHAN REFUGEES...
GOP Governor
MIKE LUCKOVICH
© AJC.COM
The Atlanta Journal-Constitution
8-27-21

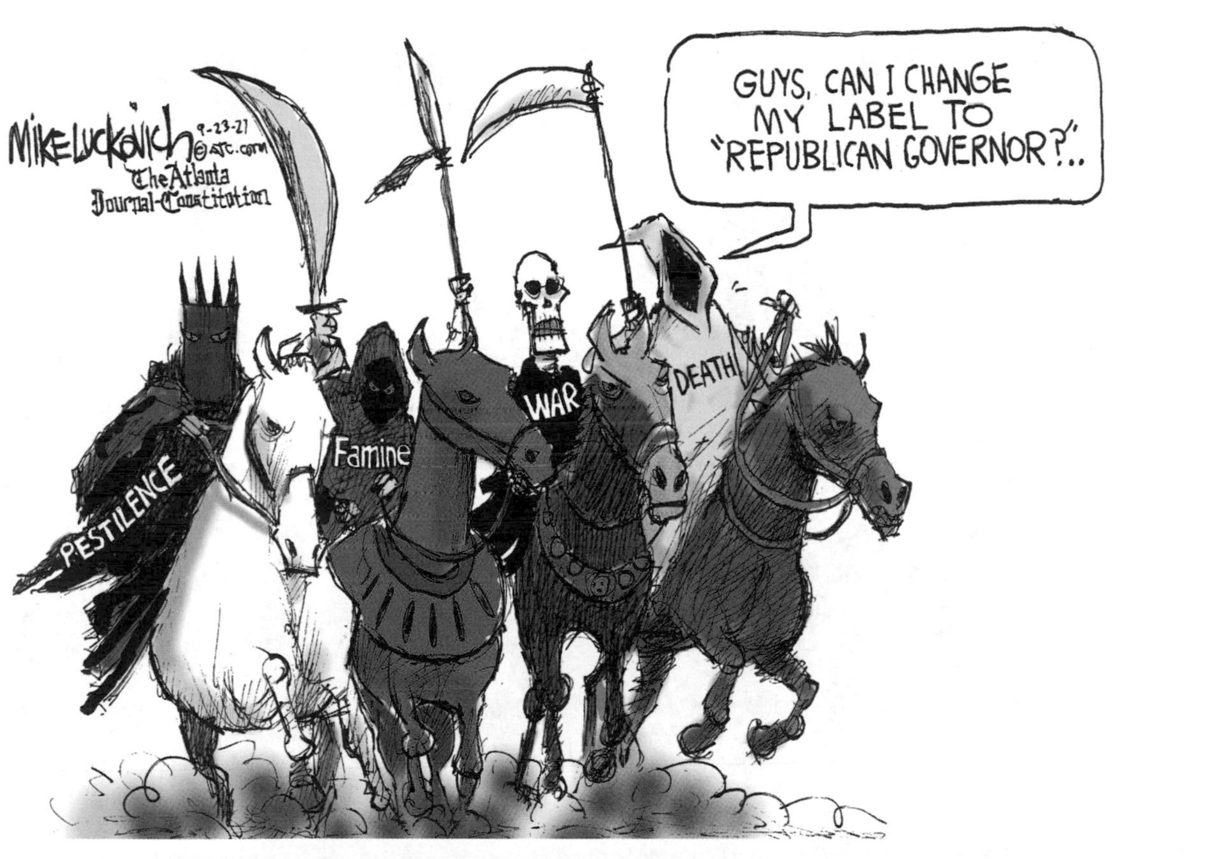
MIKE LUCKOVICH 9-23-21 ©AJC.com The Atlanta Journal-Constitution
GUYS, CAN I CHANGE MY LABEL TO "REPUBLICAN GOVERNOR?"..
PESTILENCE
Famine
WAR
DEATH

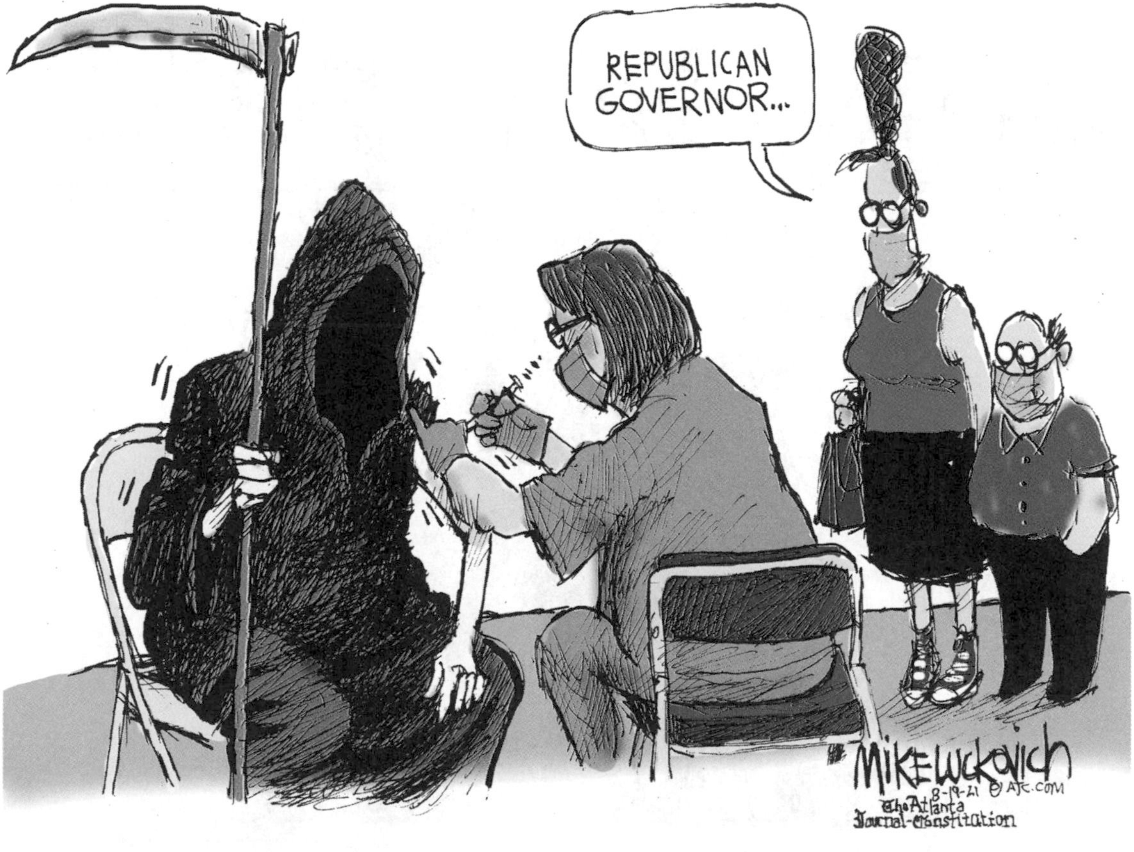
REPUBLICAN GOVERNOR...
MIKE LUCKOVICH
8-19-21 © AJC.COM
The Atlanta Journal-Constitution

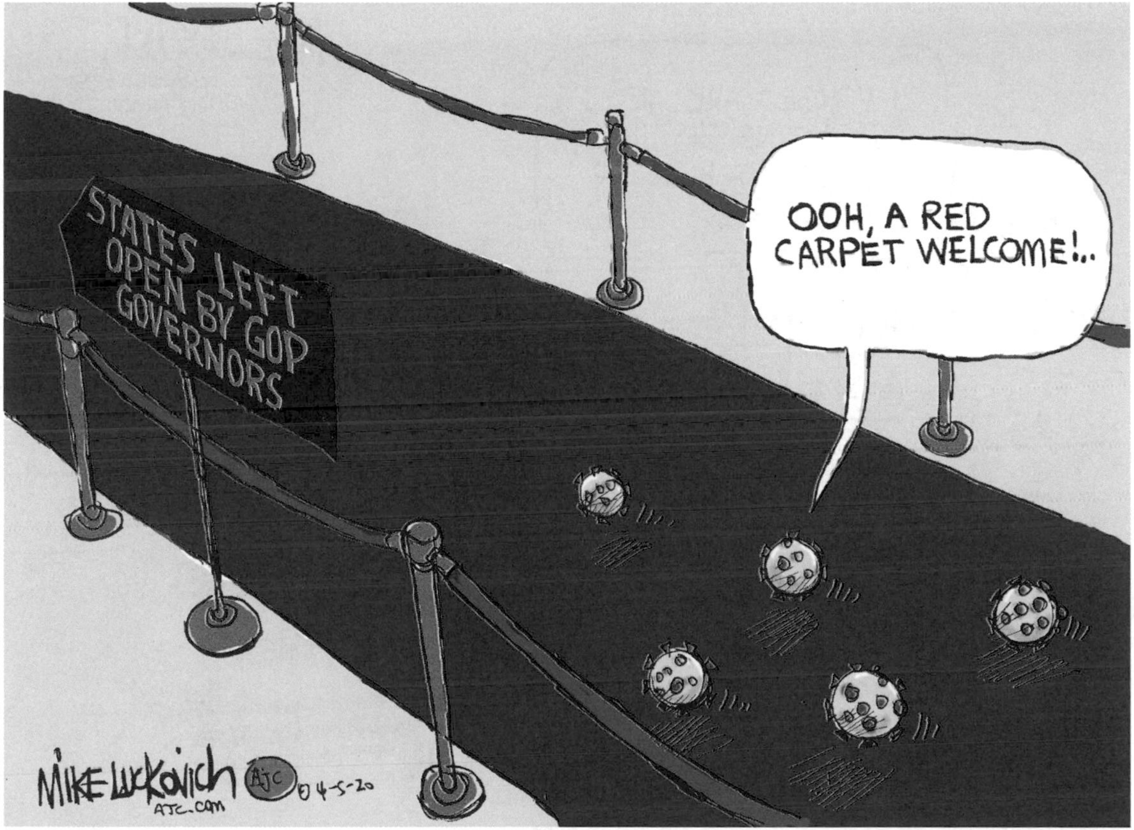
STATES LEFT OPEN BY GOP GOVERNORS
OOH, A RED CARPET WELCOME!..
MIKE LUCKOVICH AJC.com
AJC
© 4-5-20

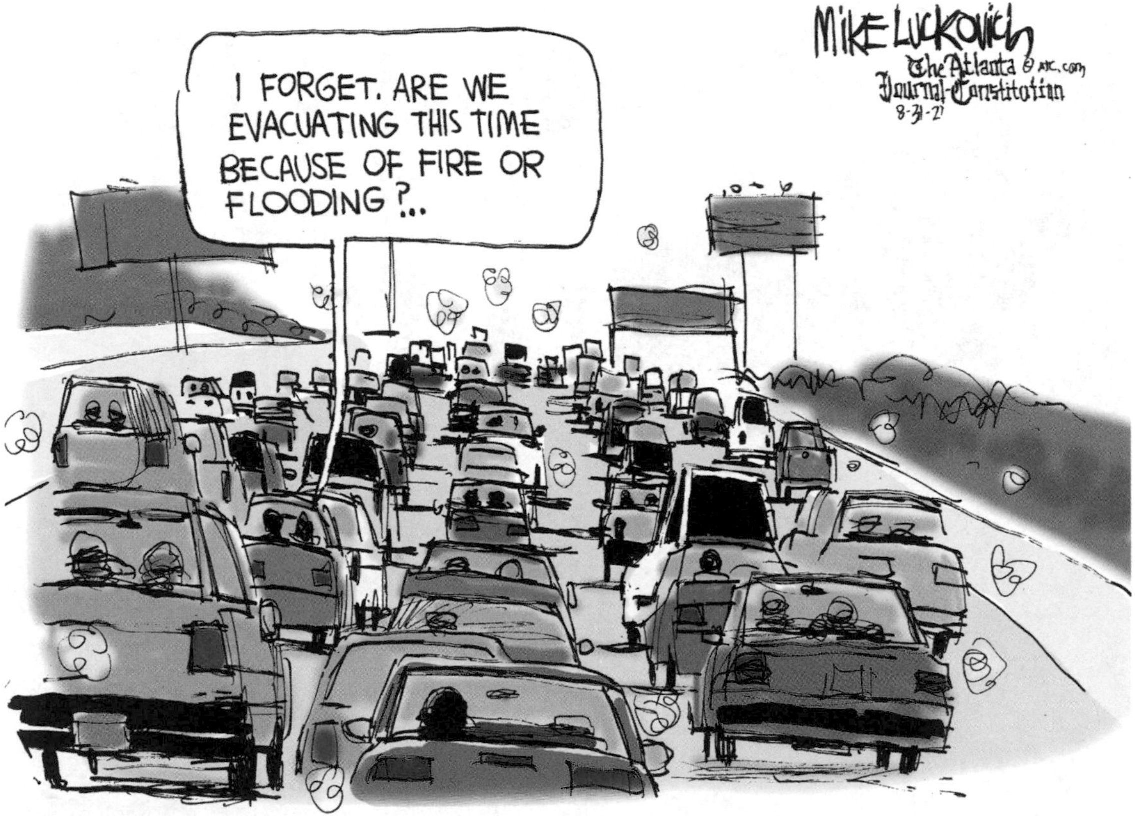
I FORGET. ARE WE EVACUATING THIS TIME BECAUSE OF FIRE OR FLOODING?...
MIKE LUCKOVICH
The Atlanta Journal-Constitution
8-31-21

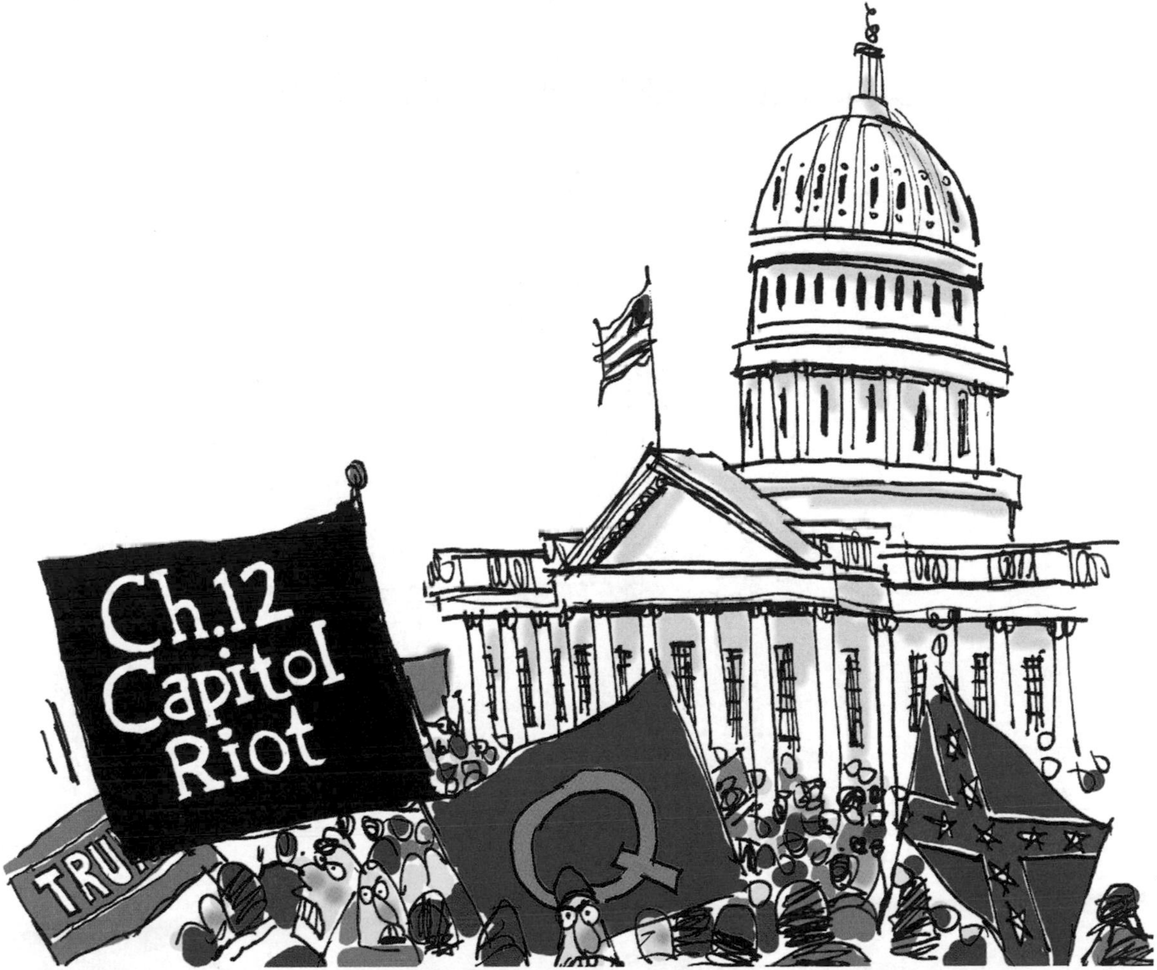
Ch.12
Capitol
Riot
TRU
Q

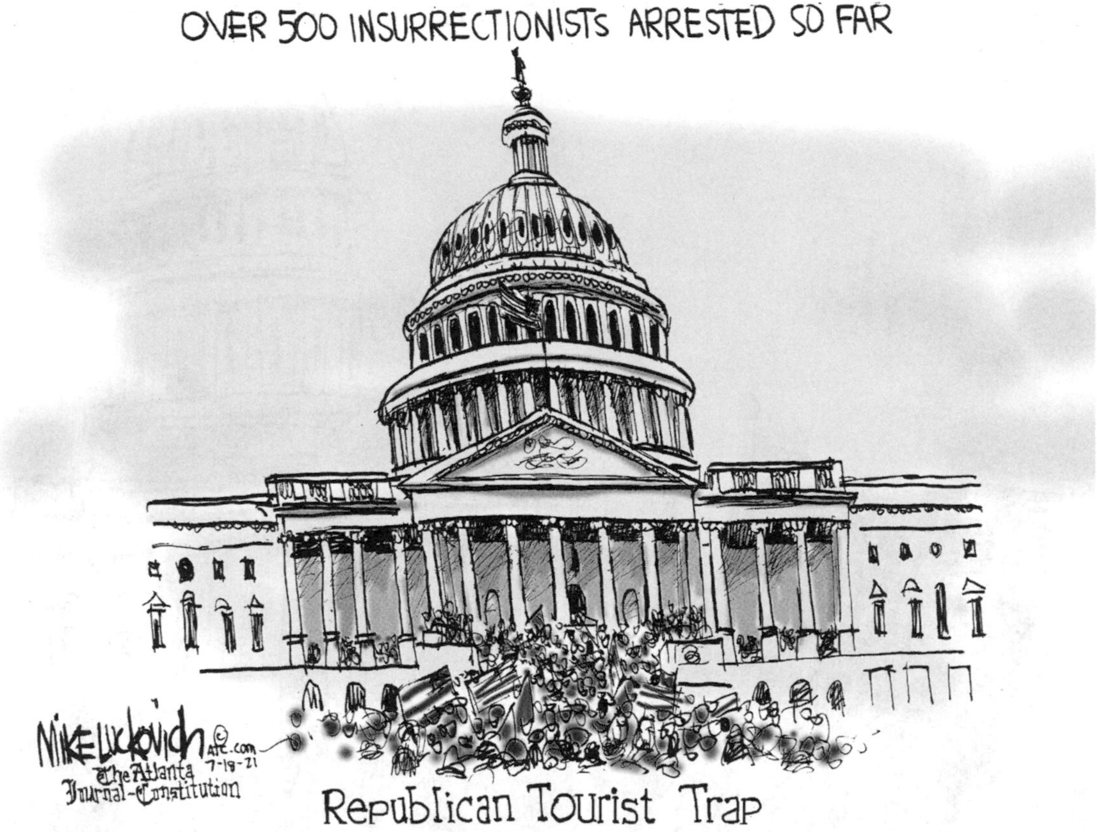
OVER 500 INSURRECTIONISTS ARRESTED SO FAR
NIKE LUCKOVICH ©
AJC.com
The Atlanta Journal-Constitution
7-18-21
Republican Tourist Trap

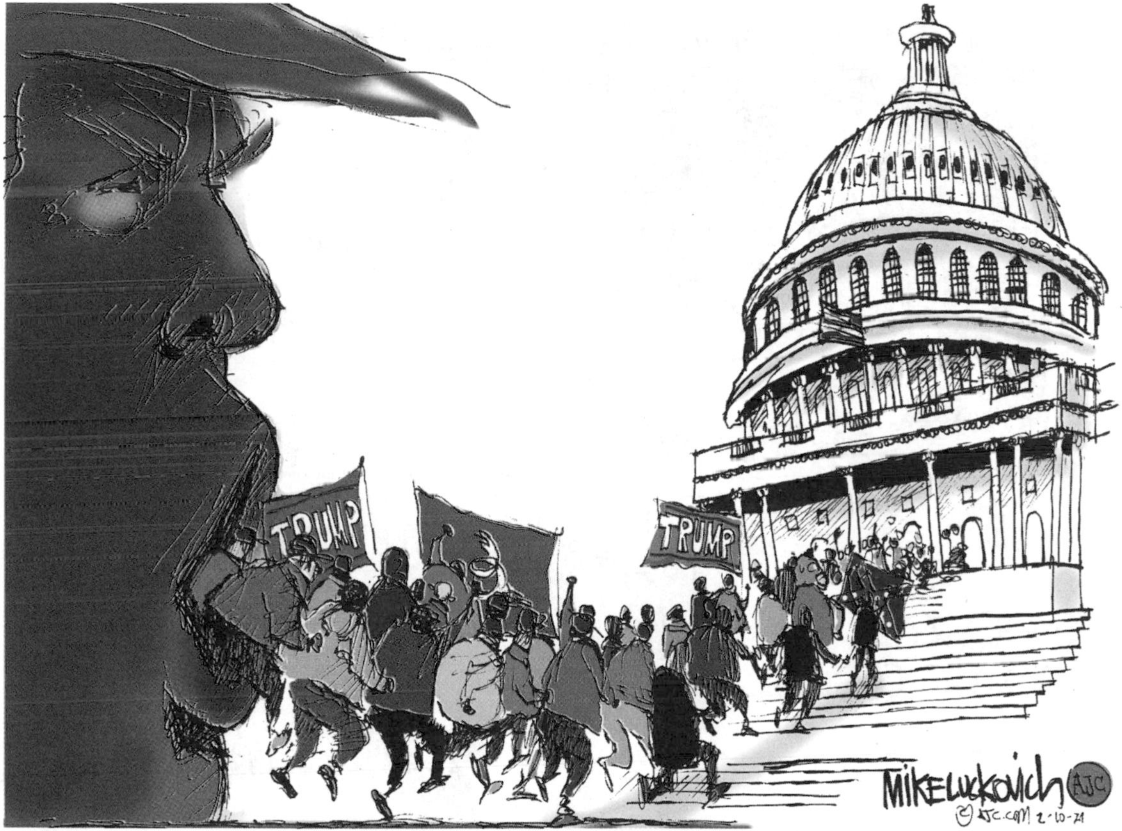
TRUMP
TRUMP
MIKELUCKOVICH
AJC
©AJC.COM 2-10-21

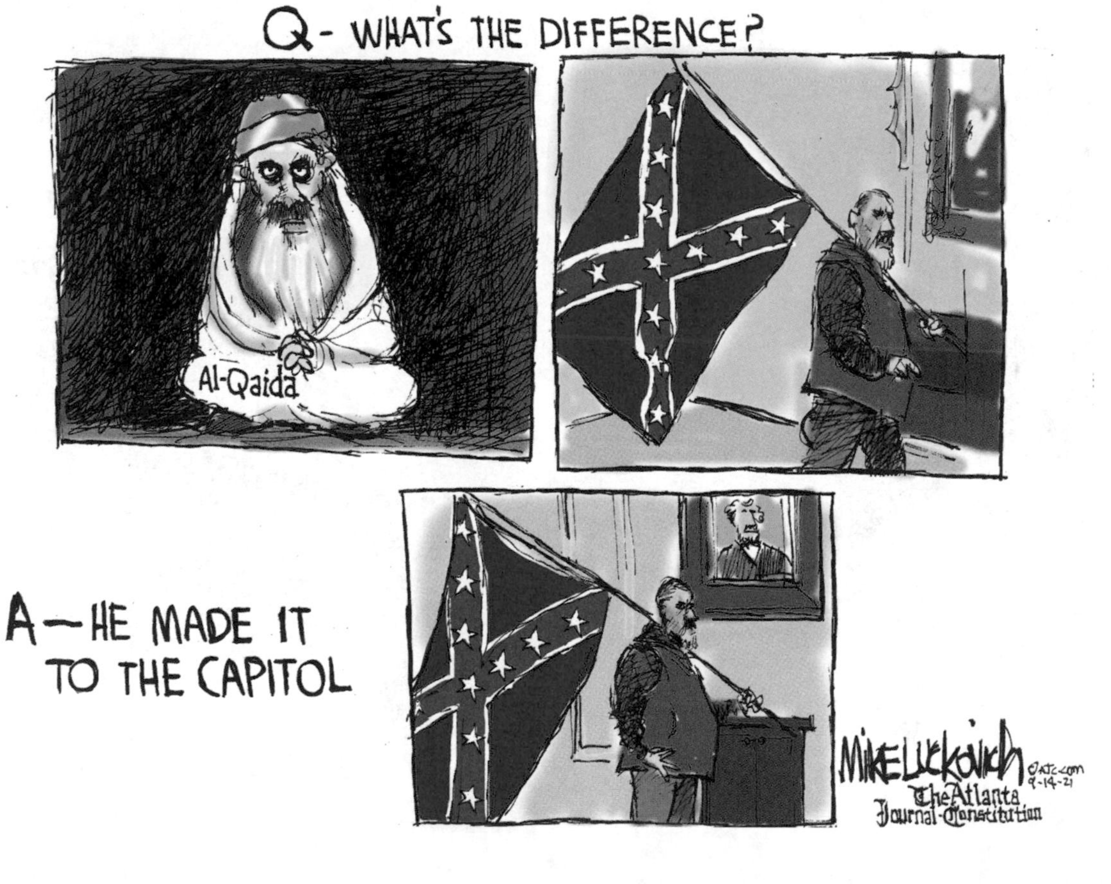
Q- WHAT'S THE DIFFERENCE?
Al-Qaida
A— HE MADE IT TO THE CAPITOL
MIKE LUCKOVICH
©AJC.com 9-14-21
The Atlanta Journal-Constitution

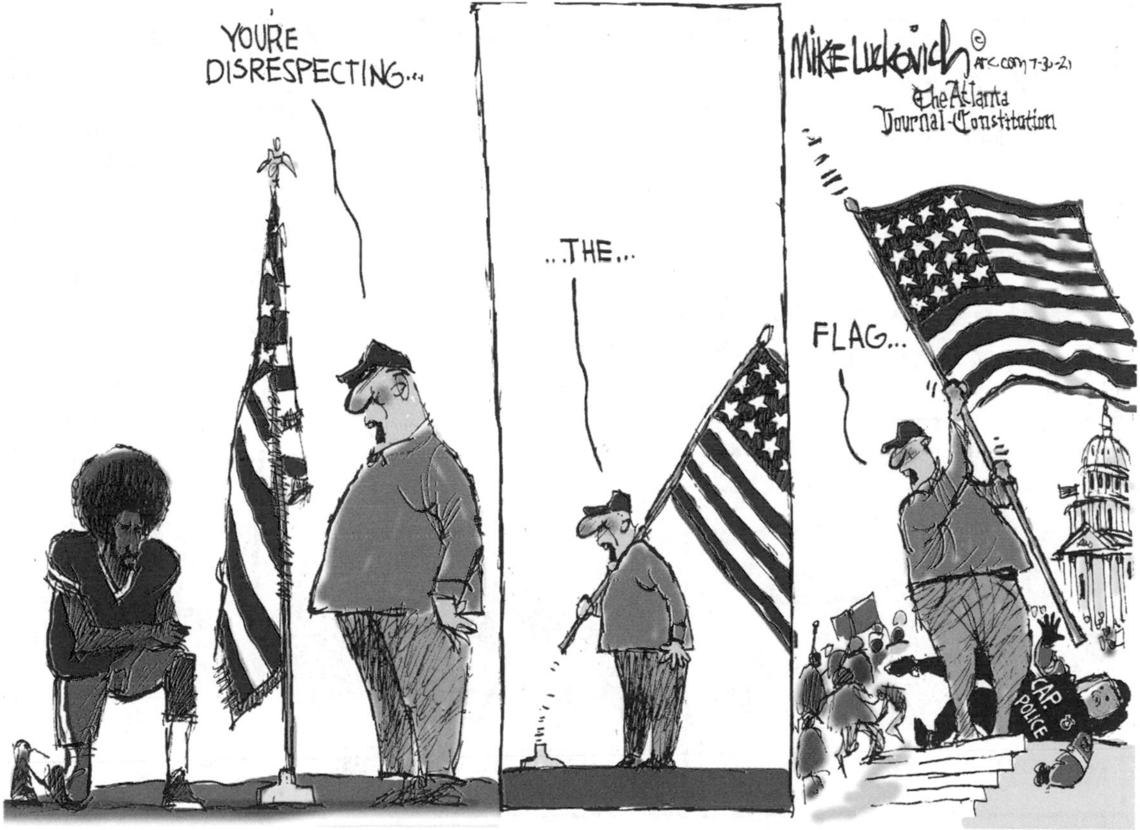
YOU'RE DISRESPECTING...
...THE...
FLAG...
MIKE LUCKOVICH © AJC.COM 7-30-21
The Atlanta Journal-Constitution
CAP. POLICE

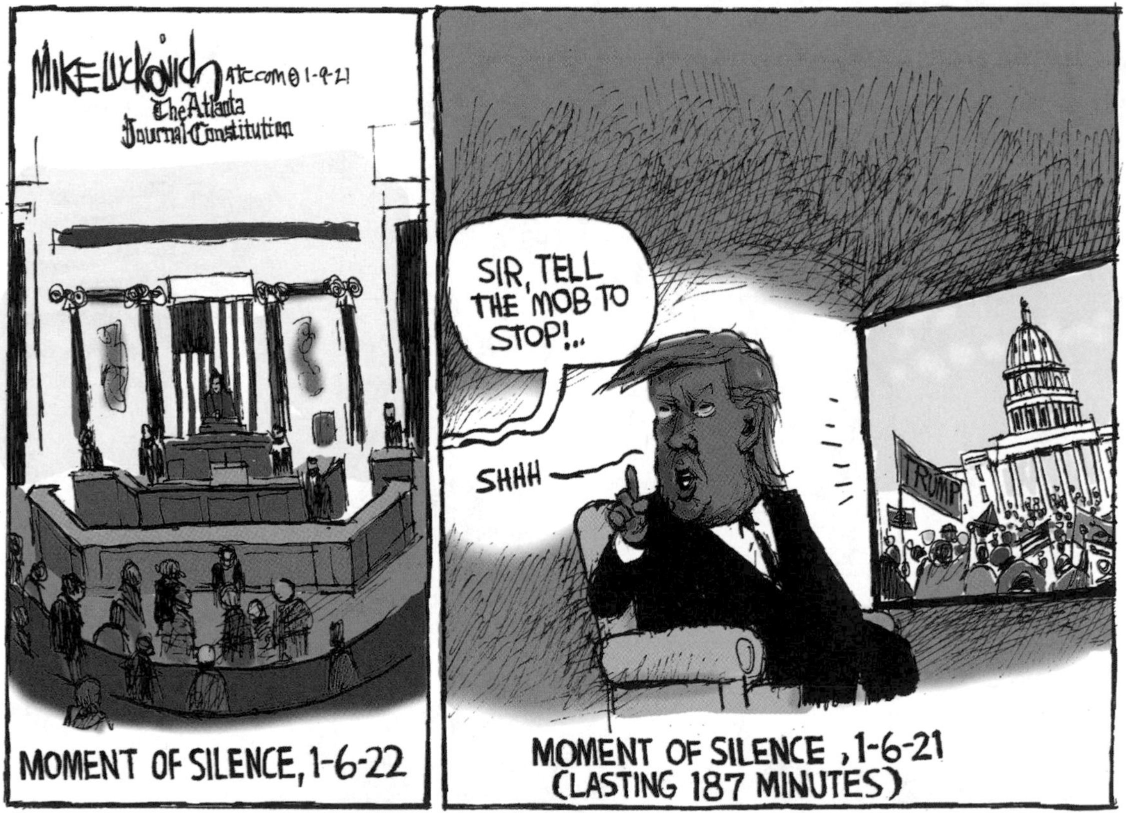
MIKE LUCKOVICH
The Atlanta Journal-Constitution
MOMENT OF SILENCE, 1-6-22
SIR, TELL THE MOB TO STOP!..
SHHH
TRUMP
MOMENT OF SILENCE ,1-6-21
(LASTING 187 MINUTES)

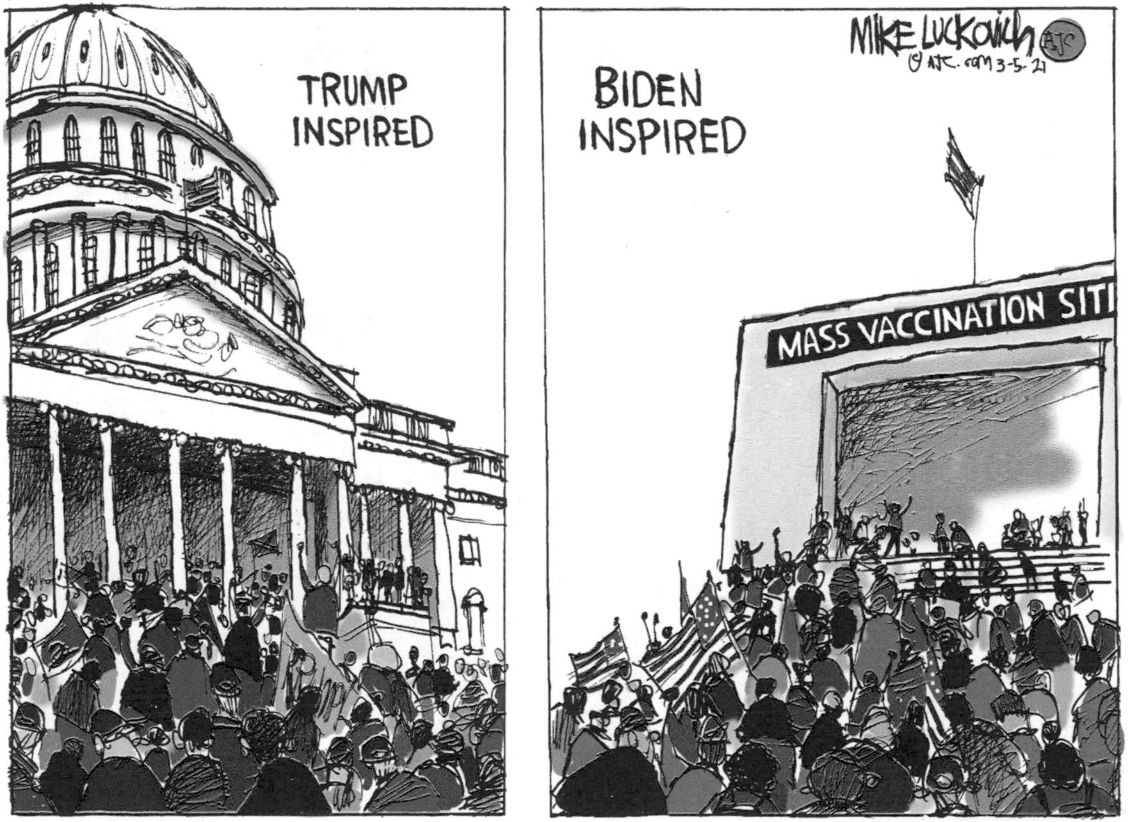
TRUMP
INSPIRED
BIDEN
INSPIRED
MIKE LUCKOVICH
AJC
© AJC.com 3-5-21
MASS VACCINATION SIT

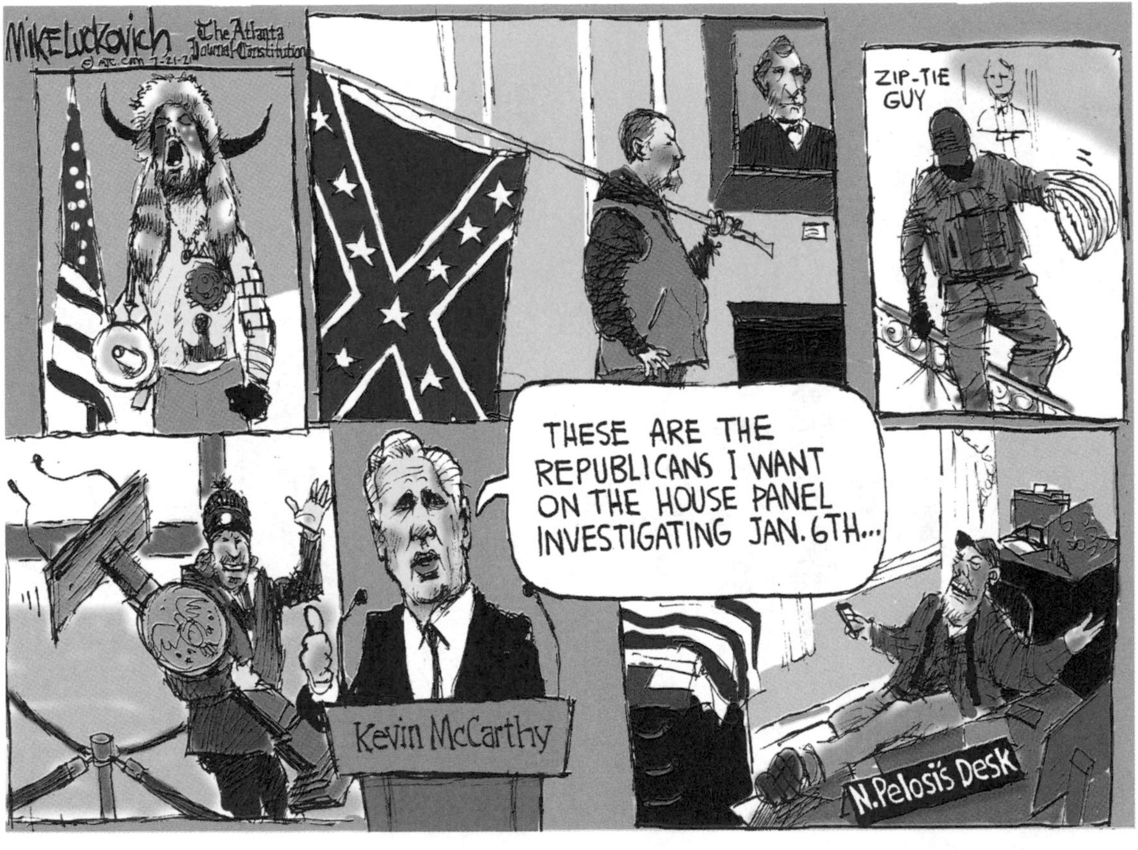
MIKE LUCKOVICH
The Atlanta Journal-Constitution
ZIP-TIE GUY
THESE ARE THE REPUBLICANS I WANT ON THE HOUSE PANEL INVESTIGATING JAN. 6TH...
Kevin McCarthy
N. Pelosi's Desk

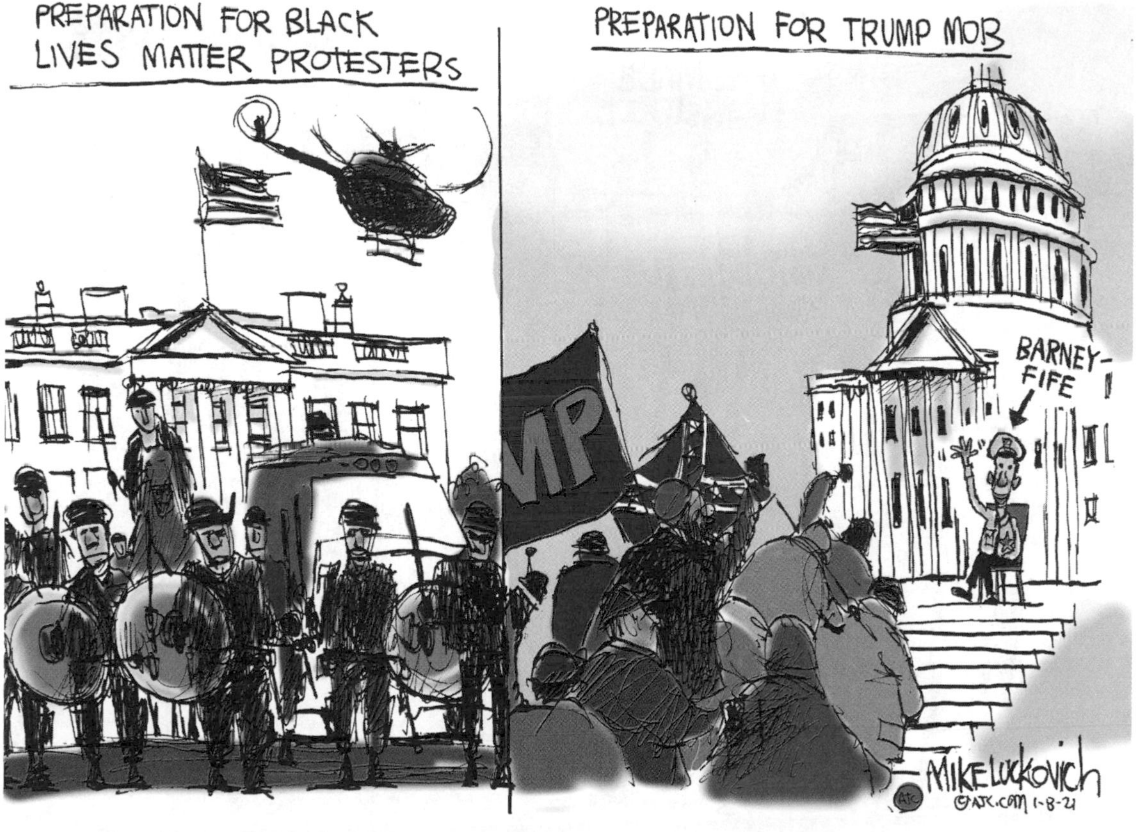
PREPARATION FOR BLACK LIVES MATTER PROTESTERS
PREPARATION FOR TRUMP MOB
MP
BARNEY-FIFE
MIKELUCKOVICH
©AJC.com 1-8-21

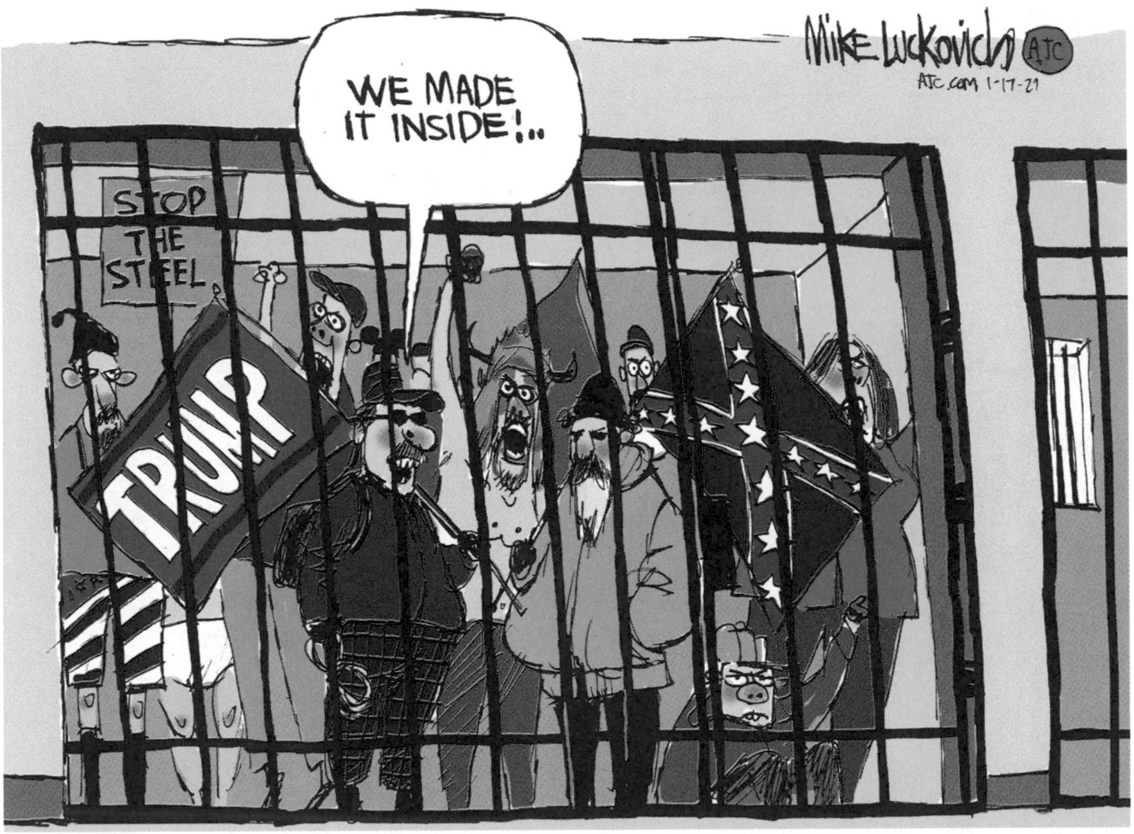
WE MADE IT INSIDE!..
STOP THE STEEL
TRUMP
Mike Luckovich
AJC
AJC.com 1-17-21

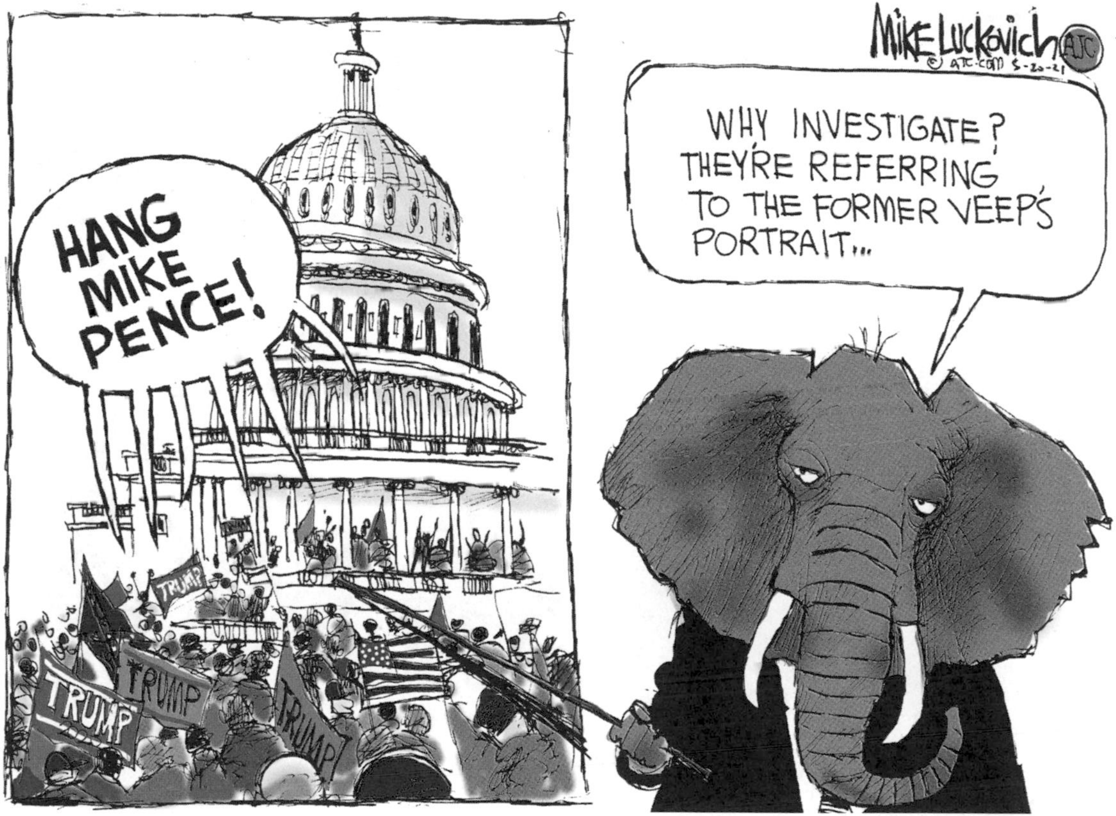
MIKE LUCKOVICH
© AJC.com 5-20-21
HANG MIKE PENCE!
TRUMP
TRUMP
TRUMP
TRUMP
TRUMP
WHY INVESTIGATE? THEY'RE REFERRING TO THE FORMER VEEP'S PORTRAIT...

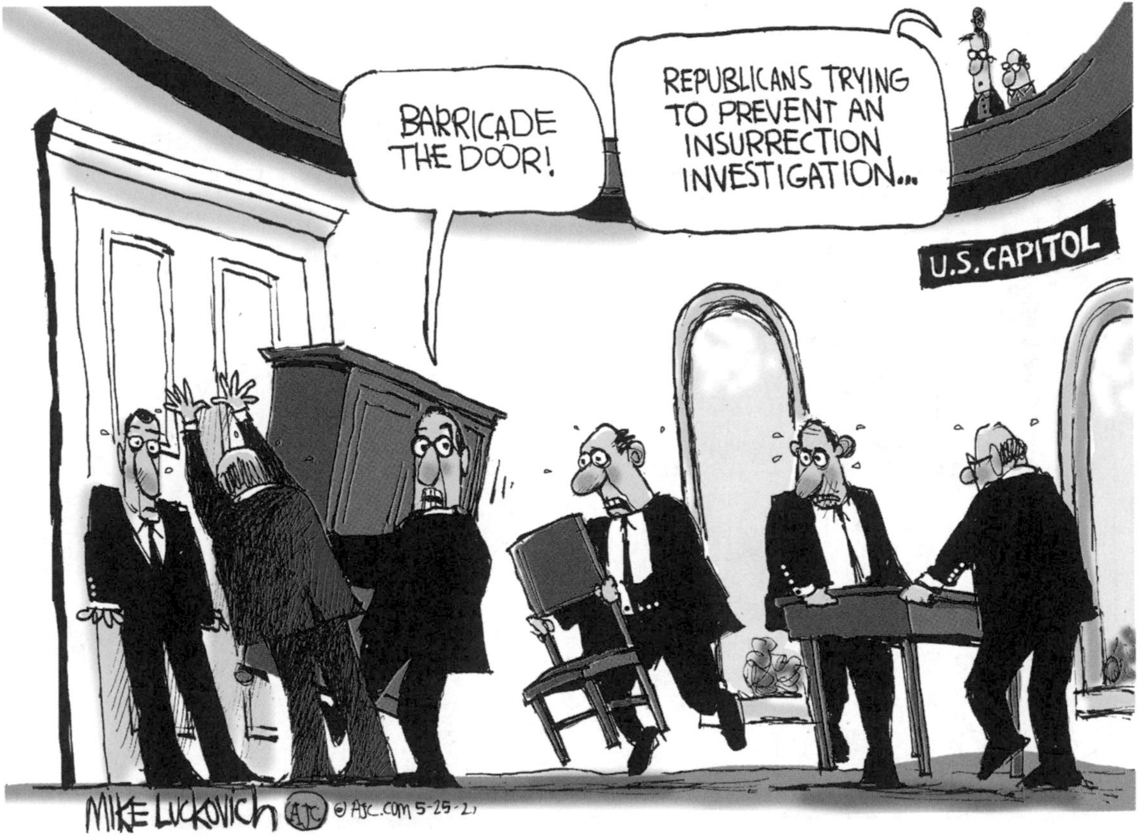
BARRICADE THE DOOR!
REPUBLICANS TRYING TO PREVENT AN INSURRECTION INVESTIGATION...
U.S. CAPITOL
MIKE LUCKOVICH
AJC
© AJC.com 5-25-21

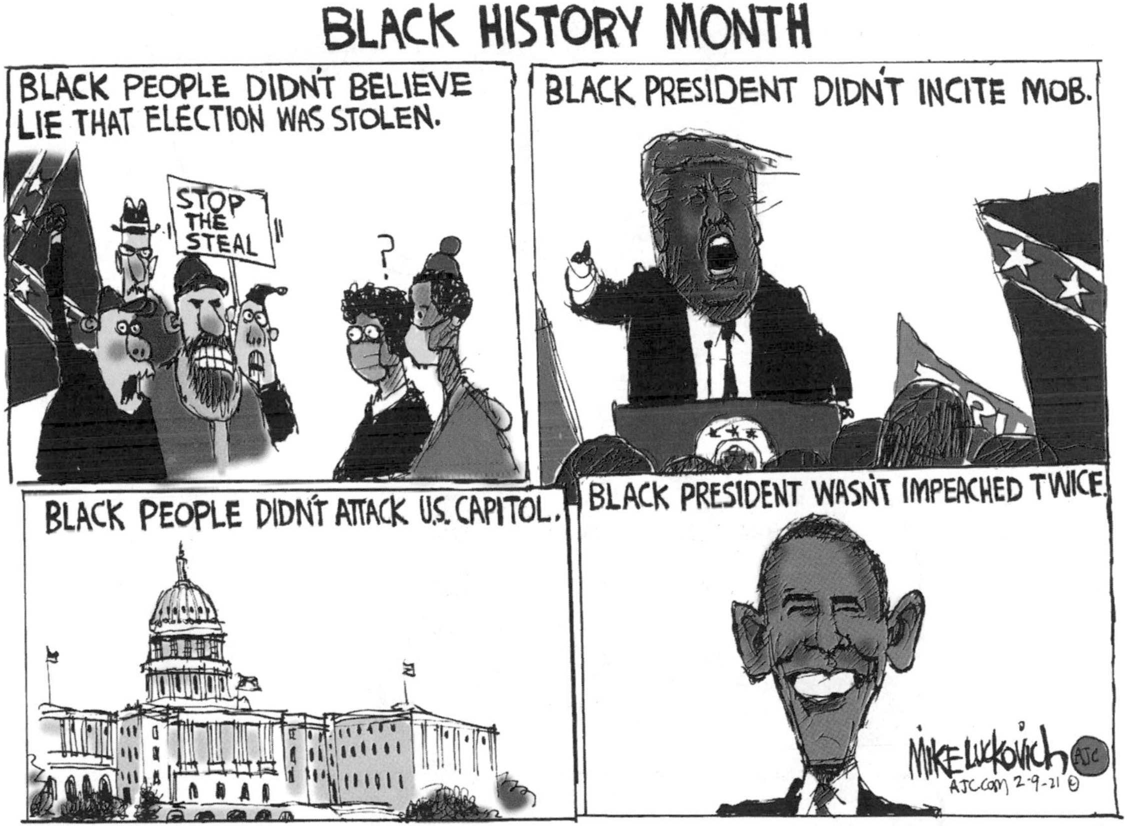
BLACK HISTORY MONTH
BLACK PEOPLE DIDN'T BELIEVE LIE THAT ELECTION WAS STOLEN.
STOP THE STEAL
?
BLACK PRESIDENT DIDN'T INCITE MOB.
BLACK PEOPLE DIDN'T ATTACK U.S. CAPITOL.
BLACK PRESIDENT WASN'T IMPEACHED TWICE.
MIKE LUCKOVICH
AJC
AJC.com 2-9-21 ©

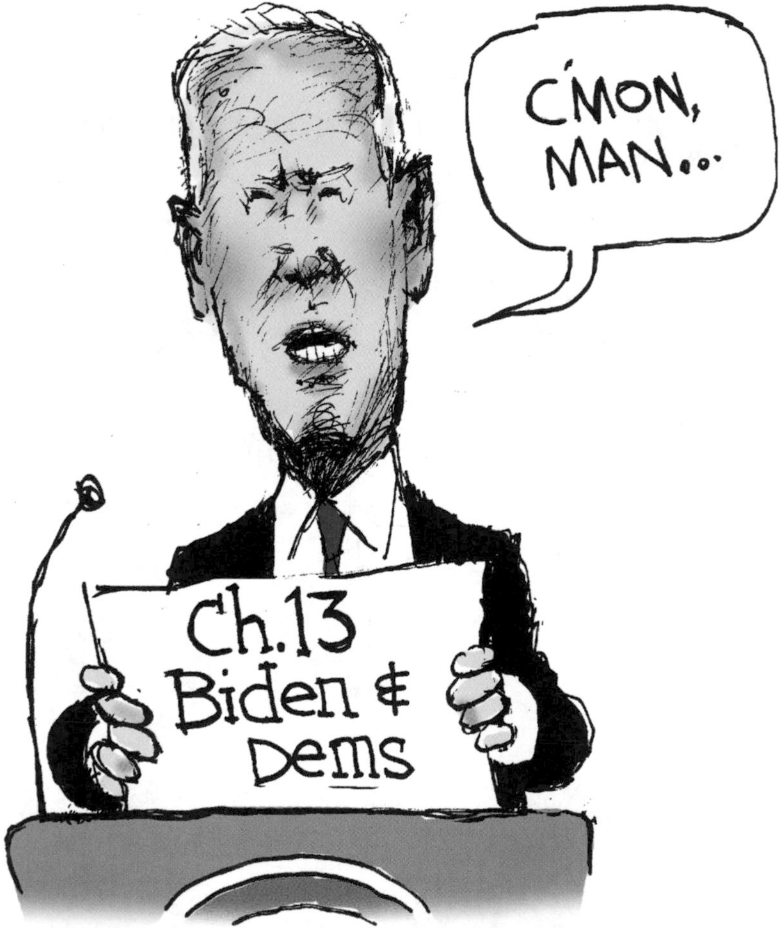
C'MON, MAN...
Ch.13
Biden &
Dems

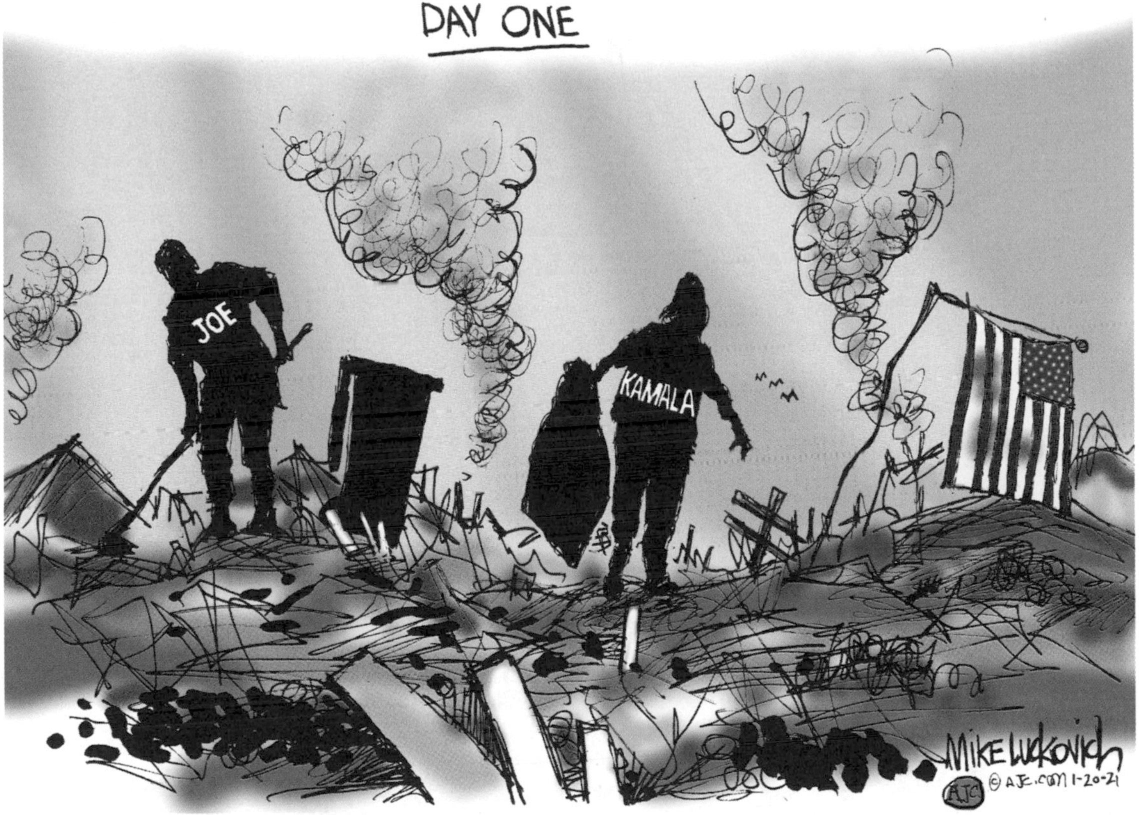
DAY ONE
JOE
KAMALA
MIKE LUCKOVICH
AJC
© AJC.COM 1-20-21

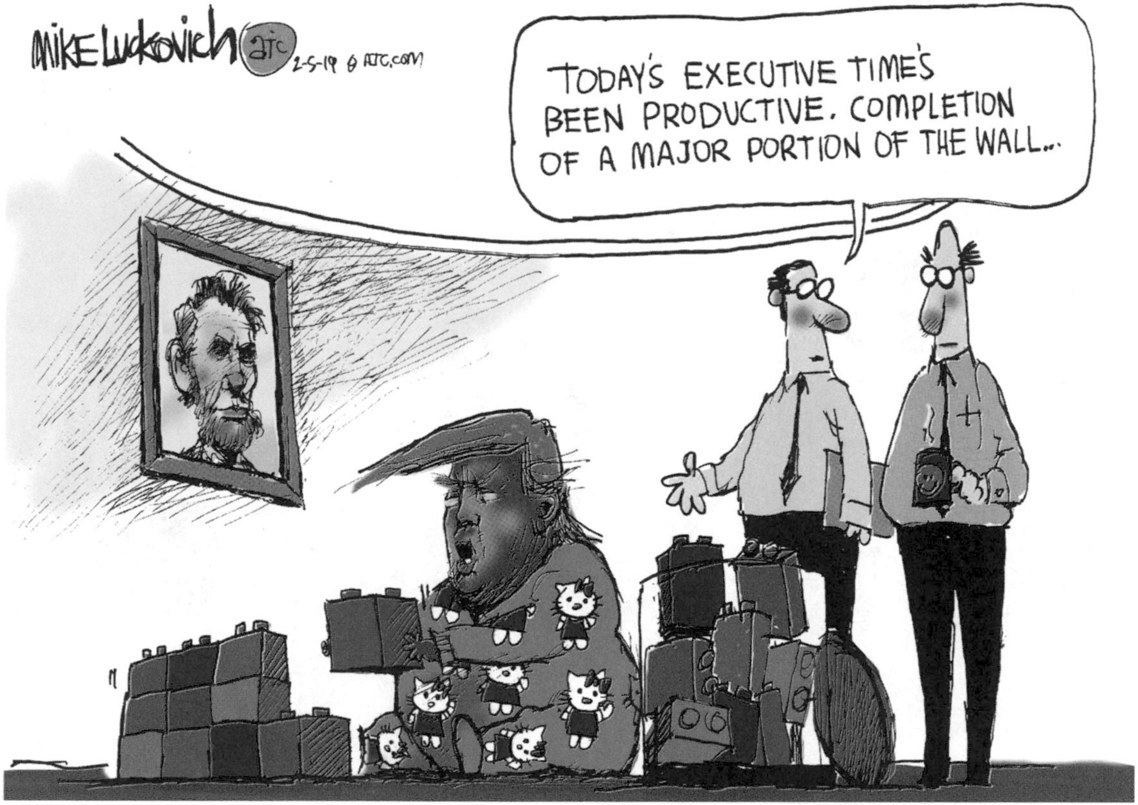
MIKE LUCKOVICH ajc 2-5-19 © AJC.COM
TODAY'S EXECUTIVE TIME'S BEEN PRODUCTIVE. COMPLETION OF A MAJOR PORTION OF THE WALL...

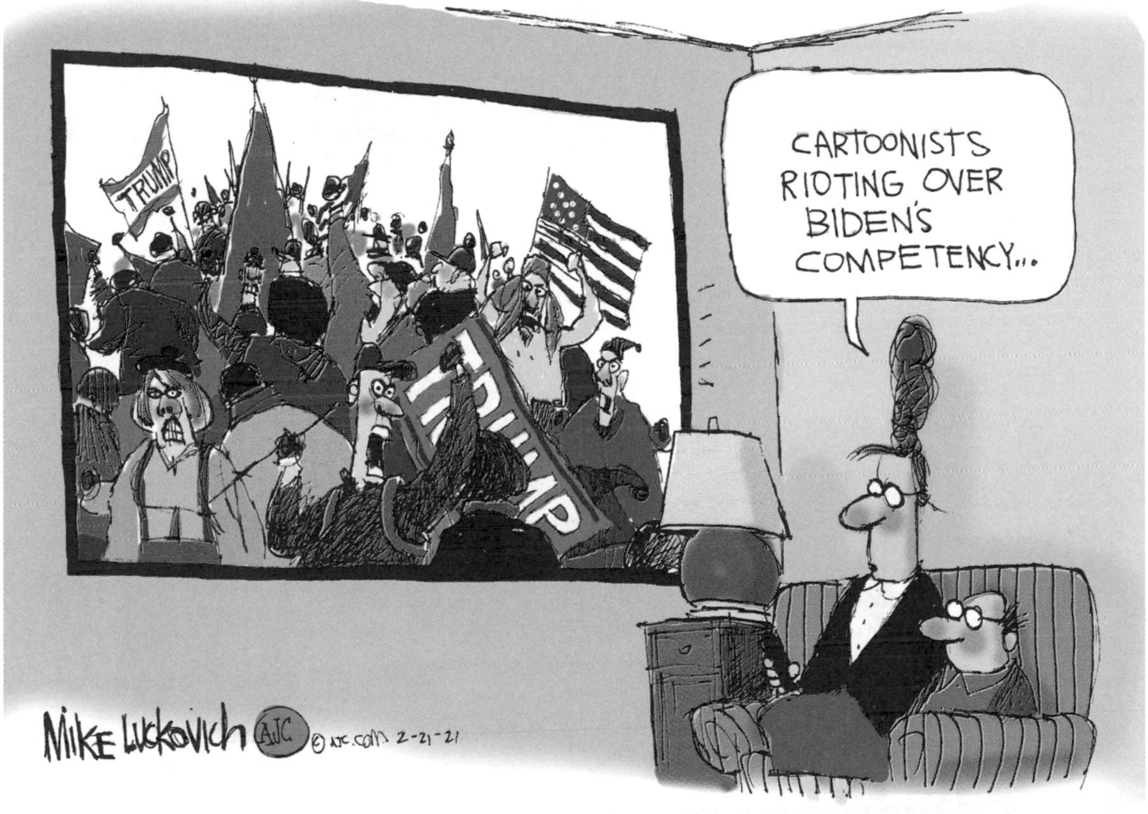
TRUMP
TRUMP
CARTOONISTS RIOTING OVER BIDEN'S COMPETENCY...
MIKE LUCKOVICH
AJC
© ajc.com 2-21-21

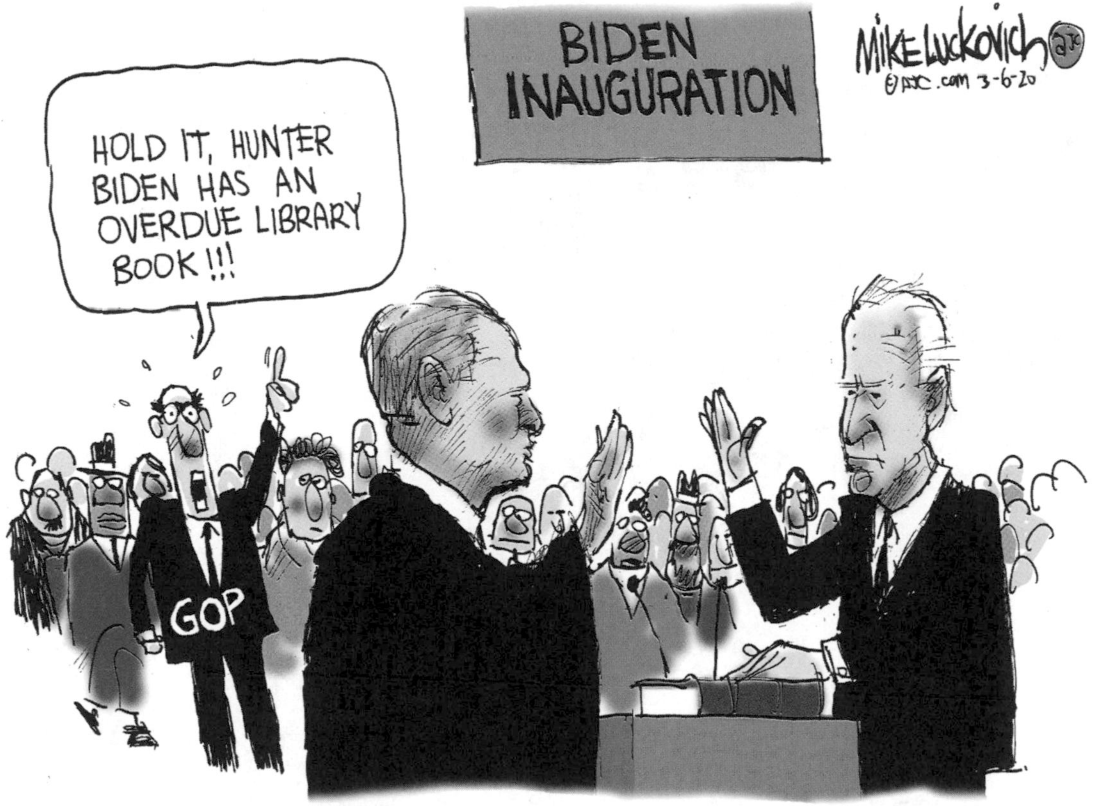
BIDEN INAUGURATION
MIKE LUCKOVICH
©AJC.com 3-6-20
HOLD IT, HUNTER BIDEN HAS AN OVERDUE LIBRARY BOOK!!!
GOP

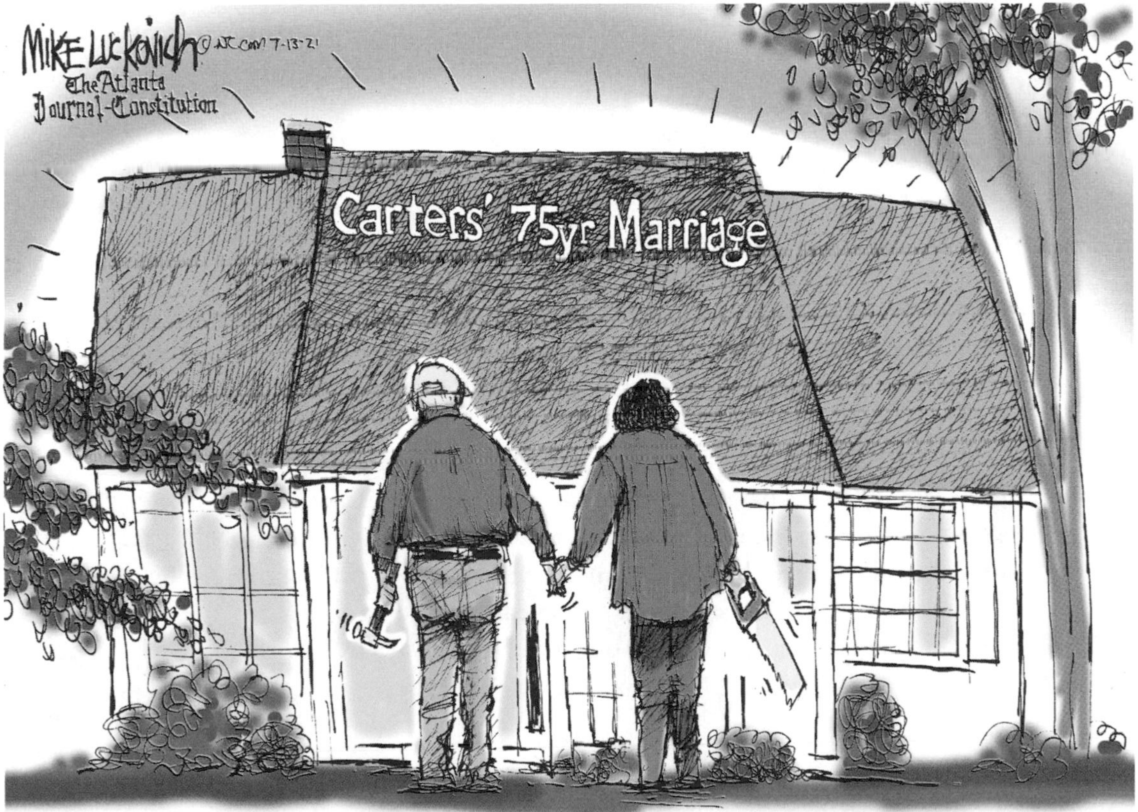
MIKE LUCKOVICH
©AJC.COM 7-13-21
The Atlanta
Journal-Constitution
Carters' 75yr Marriage

In the early evening, I was drawing my cartoon for the next day's paper when I learned Jimmy Carter had been diagnosed and was being treated for brain cancer. It was close to my deadline, but I asked my editor if I could do something on the former U.S. president instead. He agreed but told me to draw fast, so I hurriedly came up with an idea and just as quickly drew it. A day or two later, someone from Plains, Georgia — Jimmy Carter's hometown and where he's always lived — contacted me and asked if they could make actual campaign signs like the one in my cartoon. A few days later, after his treatment at Emory Hospital in Atlanta, Jimmy Carter and his wife, Rosalynn, were driven back to his home in Plains. As the SUV pulled onto the main street, the Carters were greeted with five hundred of those specially made campaign signs lining the road. President Carter got out of the car and took a picture of the signs, which he sent to me along with a note, which I'll always treasure.

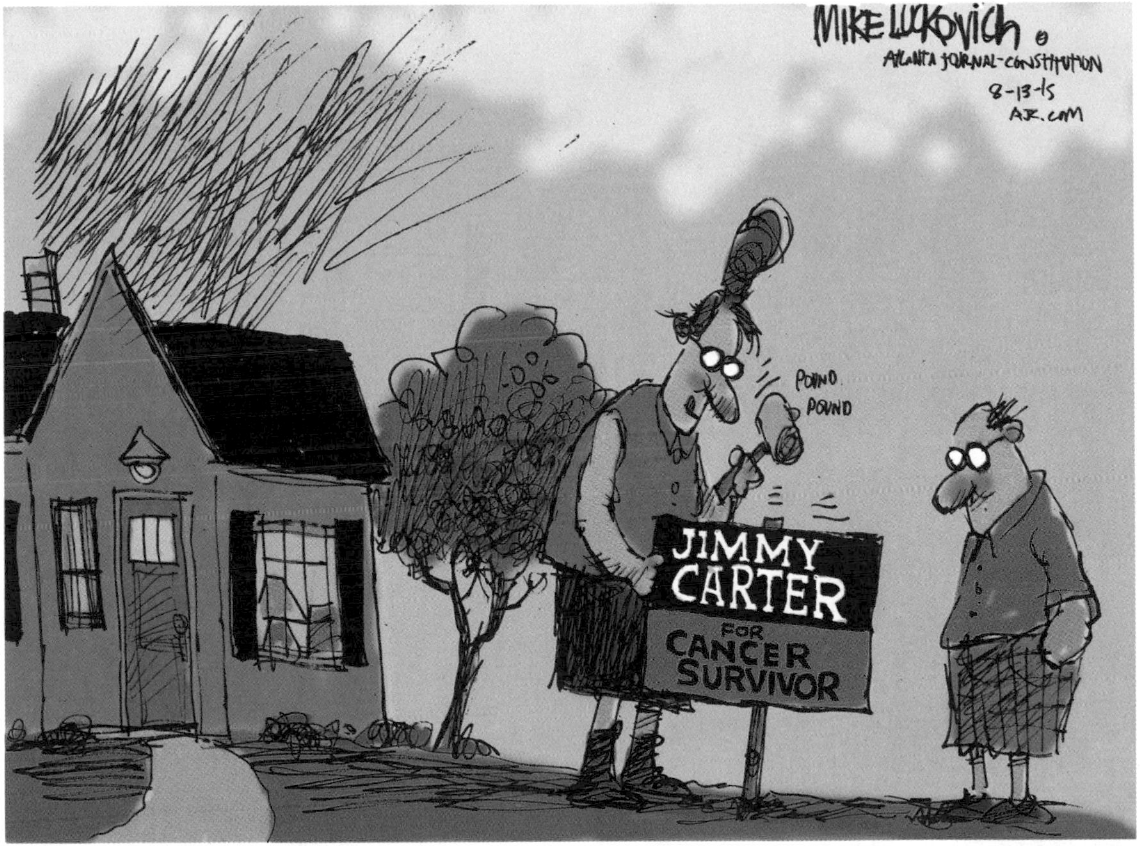
MIKE LUCKOVICH
ATLANTA JOURNAL-CONSTITUTION
8-13-15
AJC.COM
POUND
POUND
JIMMY CARTER
FOR
CANCER SURVIVOR

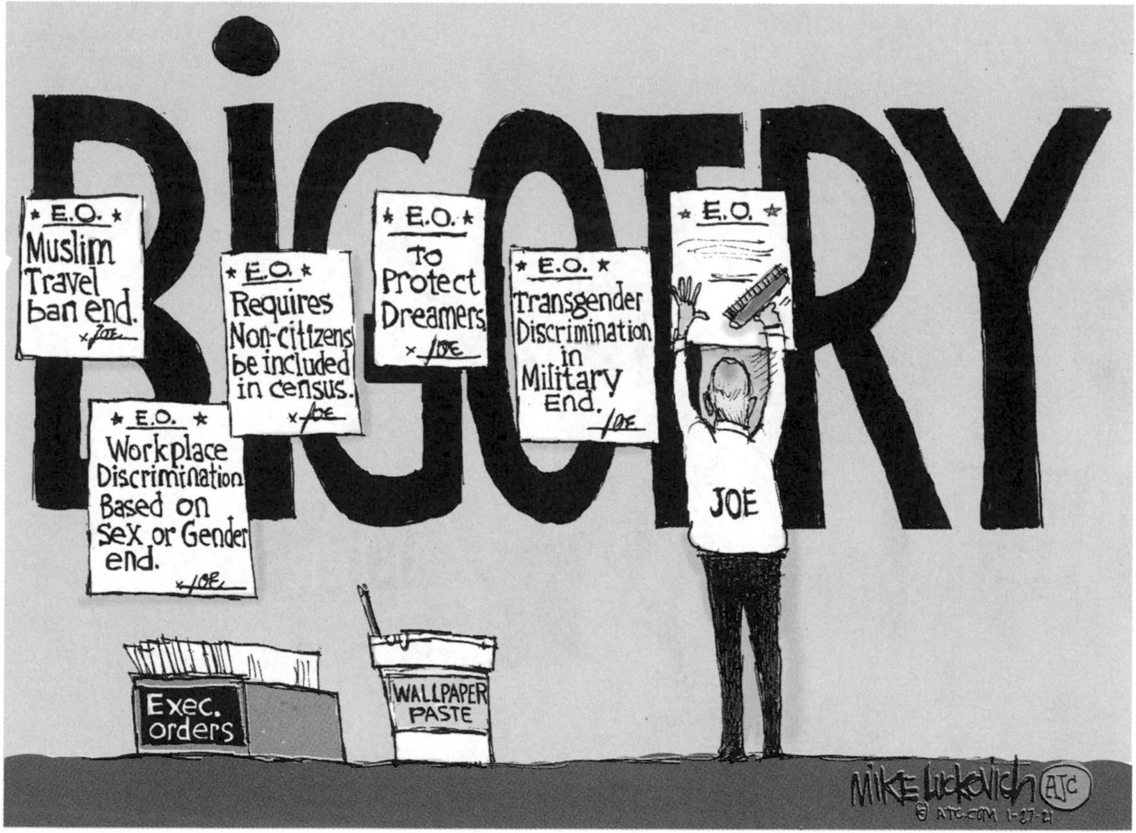
BIGOTRY
E.O.
Muslim Travel ban end.
x JOE
E.O.
Requires Non-citizens be included in census.
x JOE
E.O.
To Protect Dreamers
x JOE
E.O.
Transgender Discrimination in Military End.
JOE
E.O.
E.O.
Workplace Discrimination Based on Sex or Gender end.
x JOE
JOE
Exec. orders
WALLPAPER PASTE
MIKE LUCKOVICH AJC
© AJC.COM 1-27-21

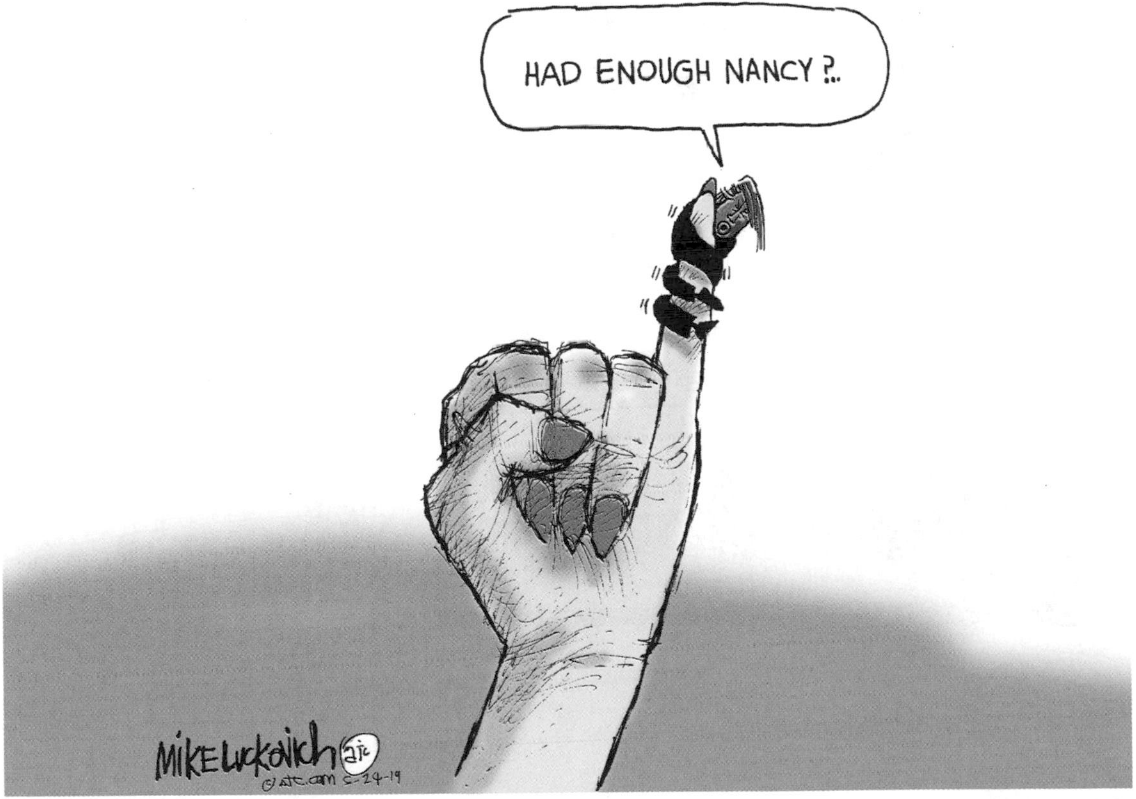
HAD ENOUGH NANCY ?..
MIKE LUCKOVICH
©ajc.com 5-24-19

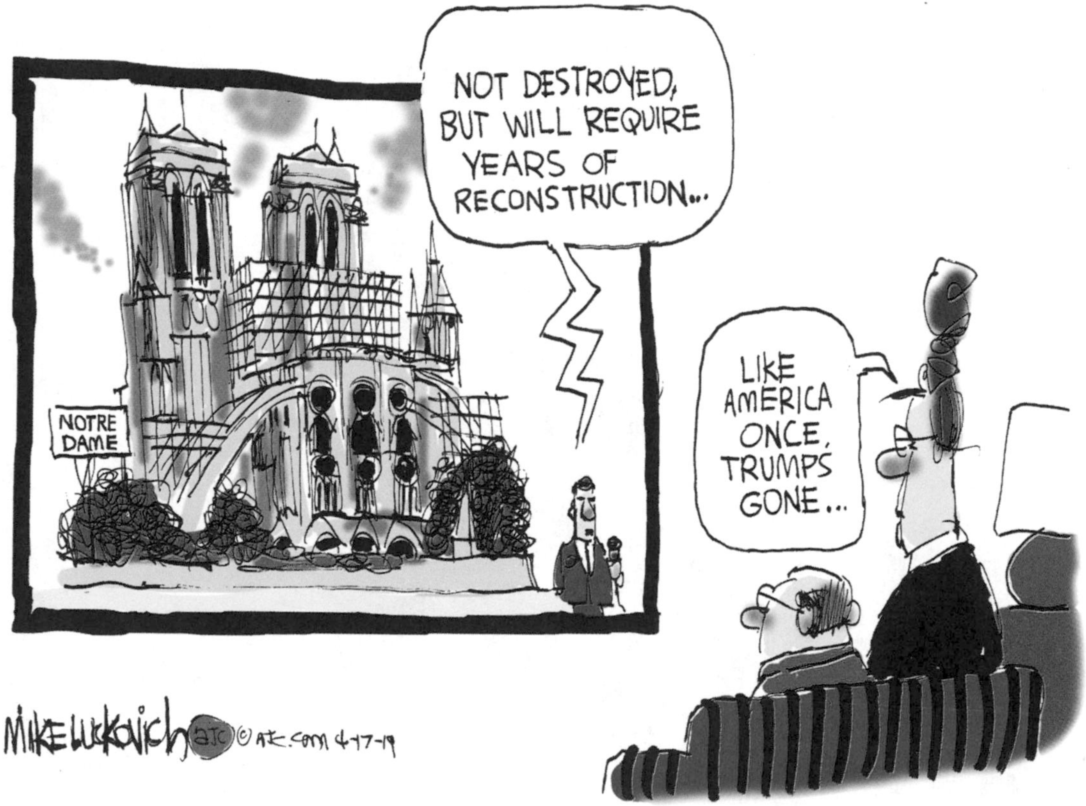
NOTRE DAME
NOT DESTROYED, BUT WILL REQUIRE YEARS OF RECONSTRUCTION...
LIKE AMERICA ONCE, TRUMPS GONE...
MIKE LUCKOVICH AJC ©AJC.com 4-17-19

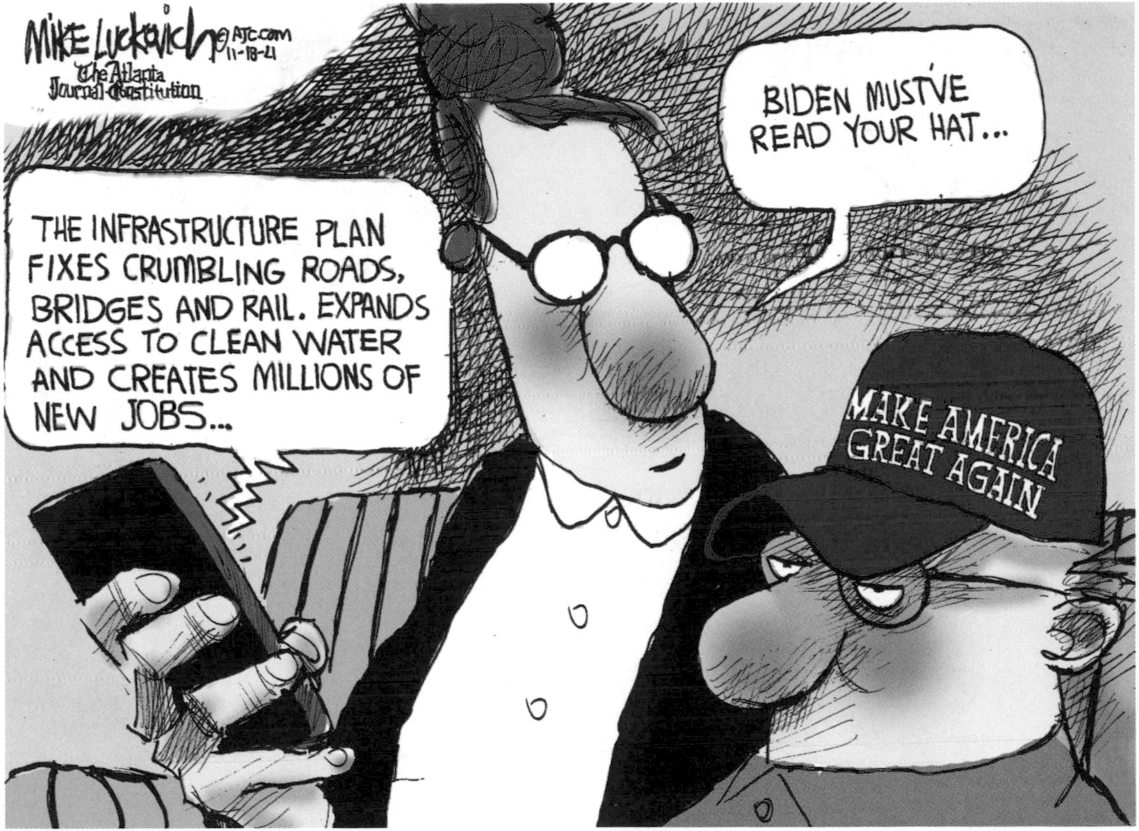
MIKE LUCKOVICH ©AJC.com 11-18-21
The Atlanta Journal-Constitution
THE INFRASTRUCTURE PLAN FIXES CRUMBLING ROADS, BRIDGES AND RAIL. EXPANDS ACCESS TO CLEAN WATER AND CREATES MILLIONS OF NEW JOBS...
BIDEN MUST'VE READ YOUR HAT...
MAKE AMERICA GREAT AGAIN

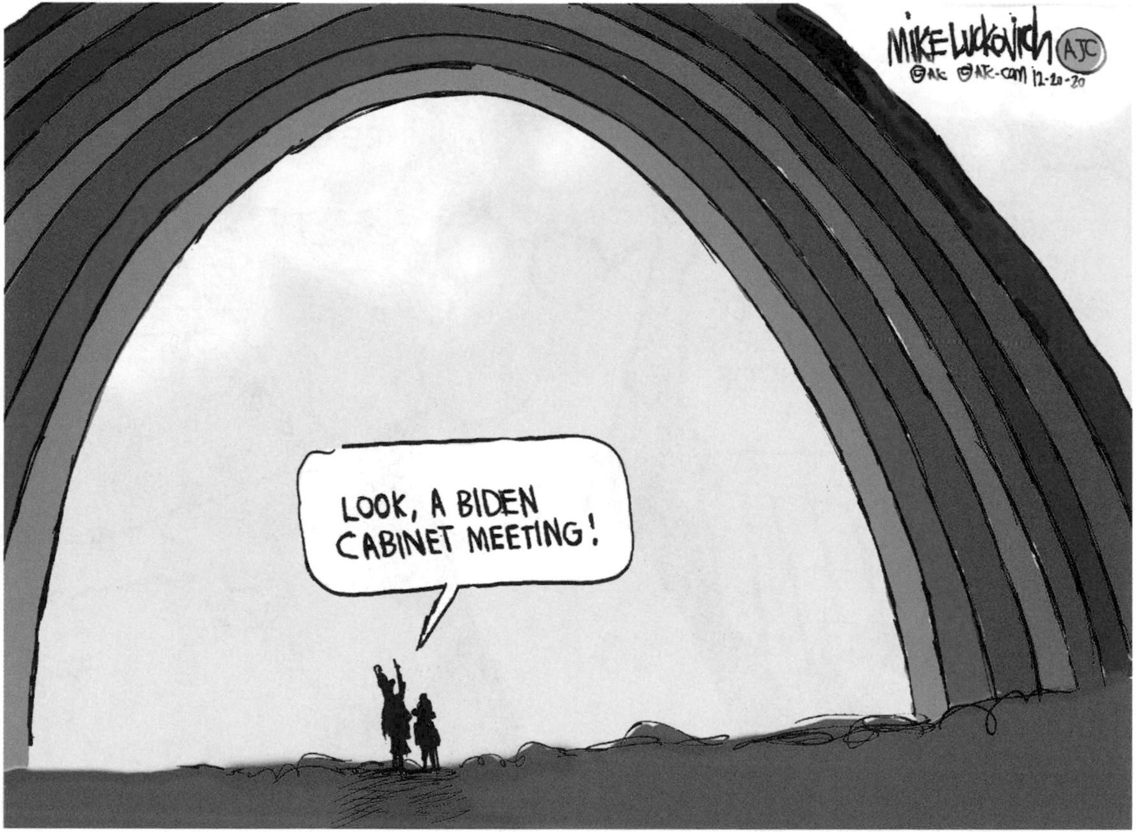
MIKE LUCKOVICH AJC
©AJC ©AJC.com 12-20-20
LOOK, A BIDEN CABINET MEETING!

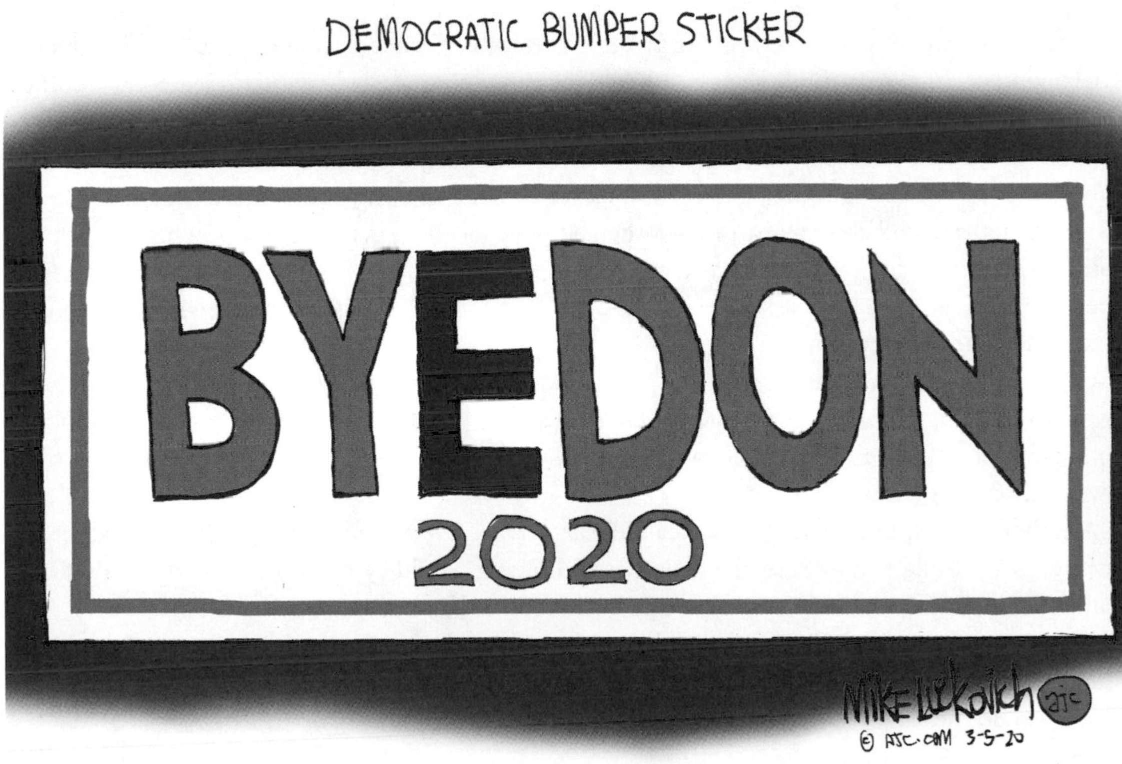
DEMOCRATIC BUMPER STICKER
BYEDON
2020
MIKE LUCKOVICH
ajc
© AJC.COM 3-5-20

I was fortunate to know John Lewis. As a young cartoonist, I ended up seated next to him at some official kind of dinner. During the meal, he told me about how as a kid trying to overcome a stutter, he'd go into the chicken coop in his rural Alabama backyard and preach to the chickens. When he finished the story, I got a pen and paper and drew the scene, putting his adult head on a little kid's body in a coop preaching to his feathered flock. I gave him the drawing, and he liked it. Over the years, our paths would cross many times. When he'd see me, he'd get a big smile on his face. I loved that. It was always fun drawing him. One cartoon was of him as Moses, saying, "Let my people vote." A few years ago, a friend sent me photos of the congressman next to the drawing in his office. I had no idea he had put it up.

One day, hard at work drawing at my paper, the *Atlanta Journal-Constitution*, a package arrived for me from Congressman Lewis. It was an American flag that had flown over the U.S. Capitol. He sent me this out of the blue. That's how he was. He was a heroic national icon and, at the same time, a sweet, thoughtful, humble person.

Another cartoon I drew of him was called *The Bridge*. Every time Jon Ossoff appeared on TV for interviews while running for the Senate, the drawing would be onscreen directly behind him. Hundreds of people emailed me to get signed prints. That had never happened before.

I miss Representative Lewis and wish he was here to lead us in the battle against the Republican assault on democracy. Hopefully, his example to never stop fighting and never give up will inspire all of us to do the same.

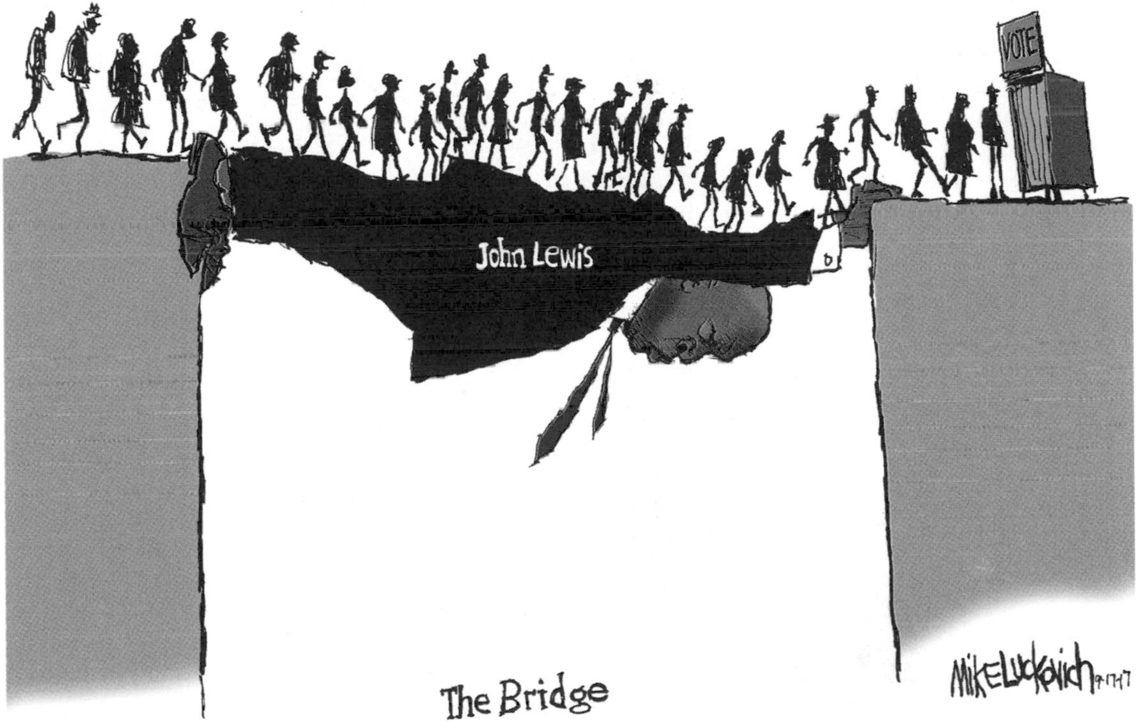
VOTE
John Lewis
The Bridge
MIKE LUCKOVICH

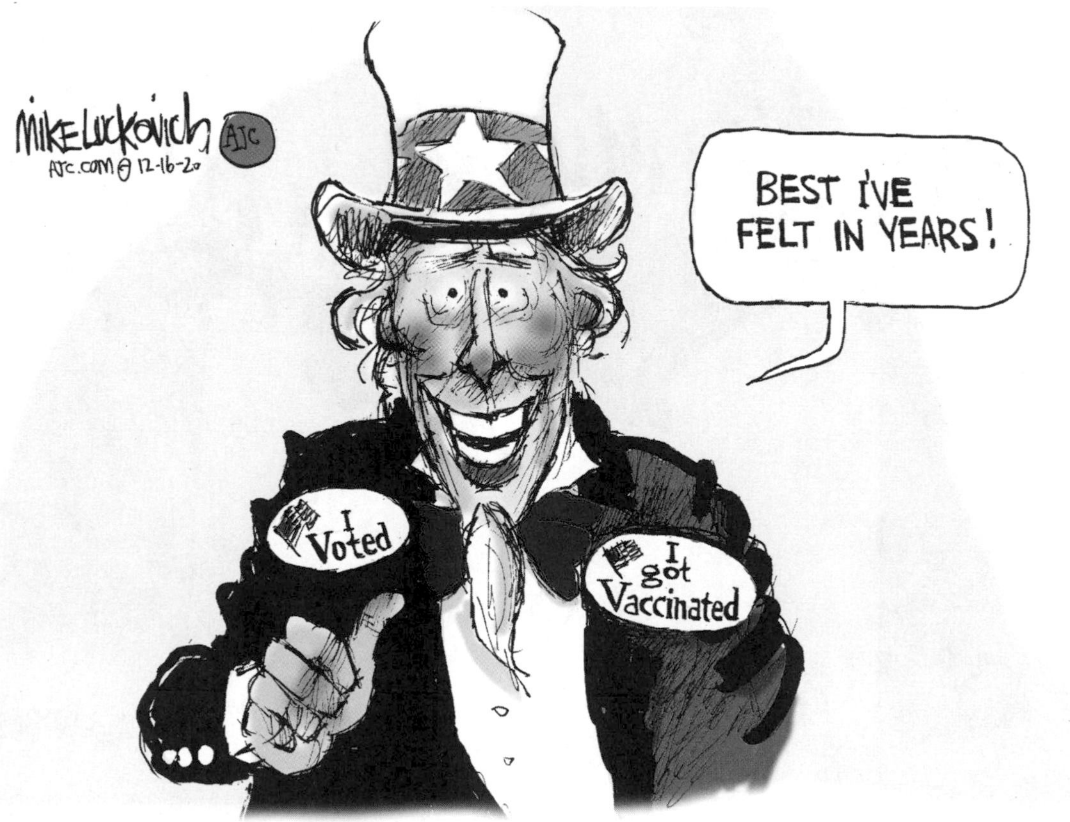
MIKE LUCKOVICH
AJC
AJC.COM © 12-16-20
BEST I'VE FELT IN YEARS!
I Voted
I got Vaccinated

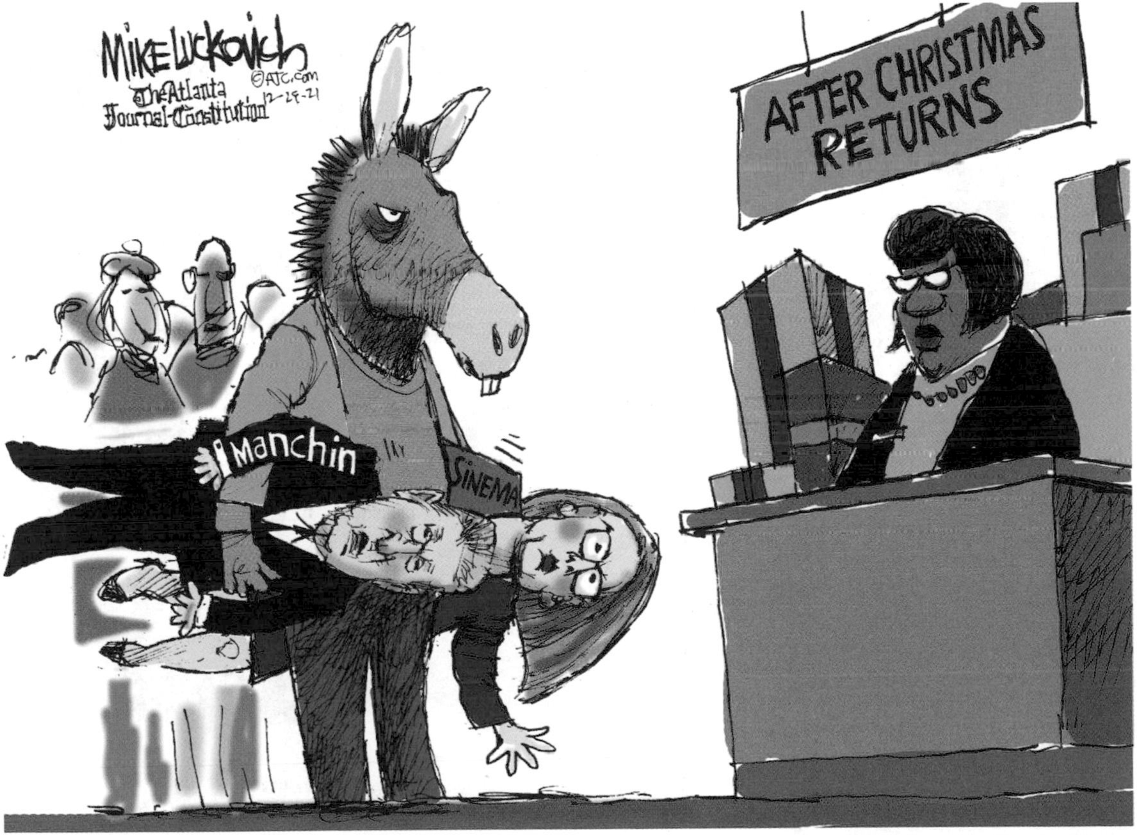
MIKE LUCKOVICH
©AJC.com
The Atlanta Journal-Constitution
12-29-21
AFTER CHRISTMAS RETURNS
Manchin
SINEMA

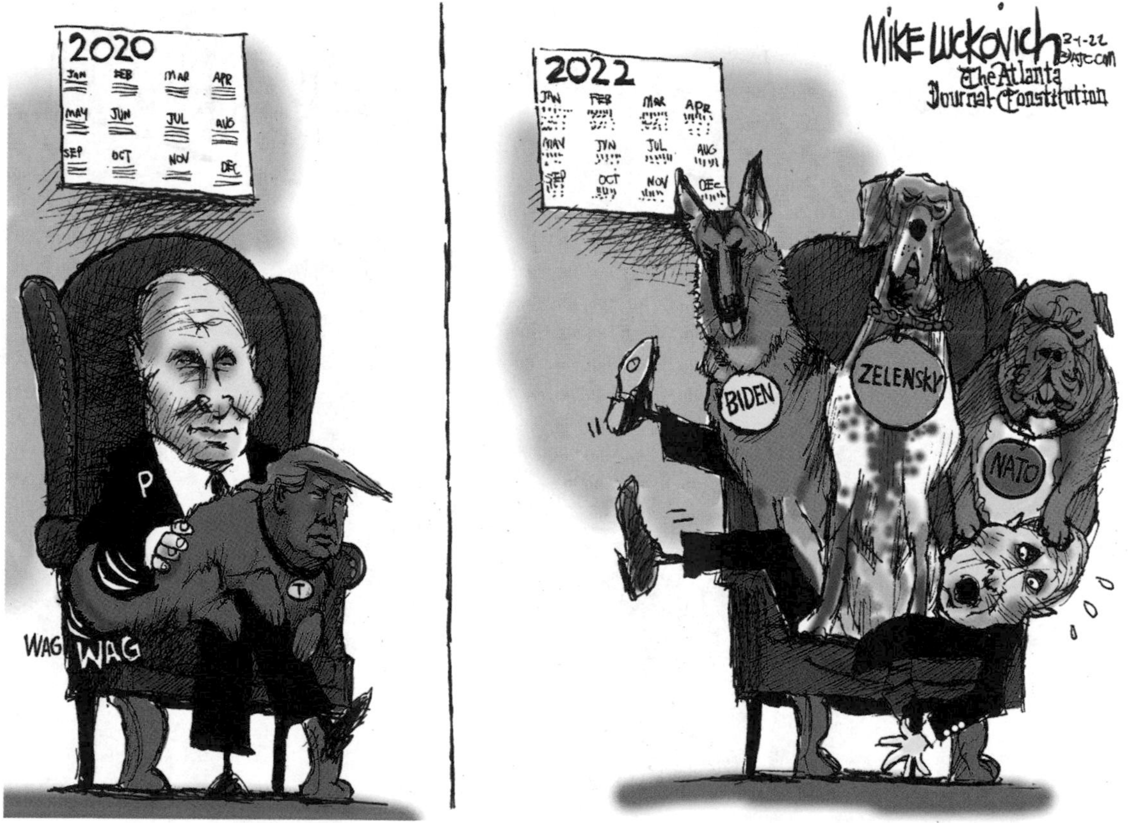
2020
JAN FEB MAR APR
MAY JUN JUL AUG
SEP OCT NOV DEC
P
T
WAG
WAG
2022
JAN FEB MAR APR
MAY JUN JUL AUG
SEP OCT NOV DEC
MIKE LUCKOVICH
The Atlanta Journal-Constitution
BIDEN
ZELENSKY
NATO

Country is worse off due to Luckovich Trump-bashing

I want to thank Mike Luckovich for four-plus years of bashing President Trump. Thanks to people like Mike, we have the highest inflation in over 40 years (remember Jimmy Carter). We have hundreds of thousands of new servants to clean our toilets, cut our lawns, take school seats away from our children and jobs away from actual citizens. Thanks, Mike, for having helped raise gas prices so high that some people need to choose between getting to work or food.

Thanks to people like Mike, we are seconds away from doomsday. Yet without Mike, we won't have the dumbest vice president ever, nor a potential new Supreme Court associate justice based solely on color, not qualifications. So, Mike, please keep bashing President Trump; it keeps ill-informed people like you from understanding the real problems facing America and the world.

Maybe Mike should have a seat on "The View."

[redacted]

…r must be no longer than 165 words and must
…umber for verification. Letters will be edited
…lished in both print an…

This letter to the editor appeared in my newspaper, the *Atlanta Journal-Constituion* — evidence of the destructive impact that I've inflicted with my pen. If not for my cartoons, America would be a utopia. For that, I am deeply sorry.

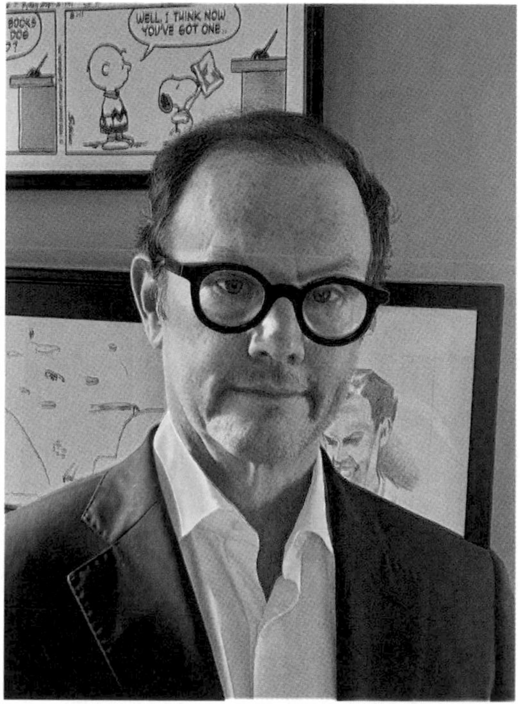
WELL, I THINK NOW YOU'VE GOT ONE.

Mike Luckovich is a Seattle native and has worked for the *Atlanta Journal-Constitution* since 1989. His cartoons are reprinted in newspapers across the country. He won Pulitzer Prizes in 1995 and 2006 for his editorial cartoons and the 2006 Reuben Award, presented by the National Cartoonist Society, for Cartoonist of the Year. His previous books include *Four More Wars!* and *A Very Stable Genius*.

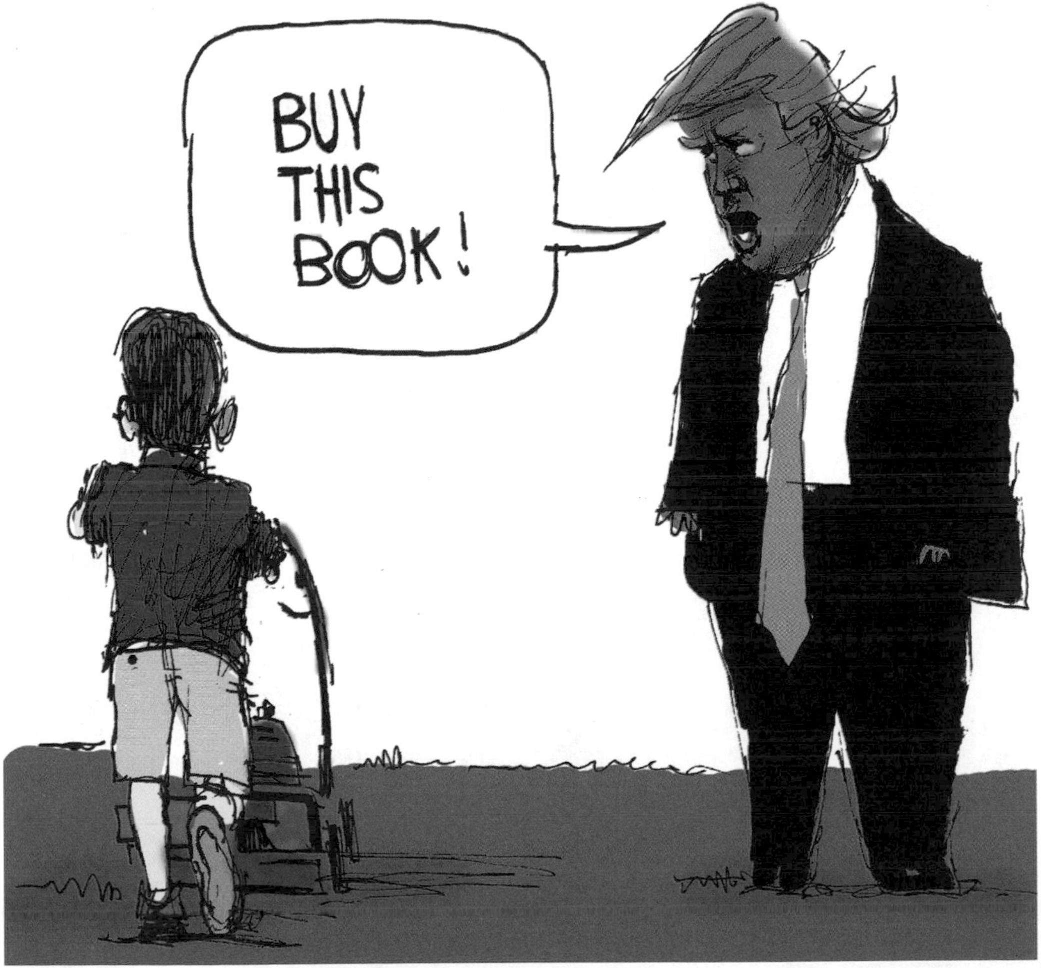
BUY THIS BOOK!

At ECW Press, we want you to enjoy our books in whatever format you like. If you've bought a print copy just send an email to ebook@ecwpress.com and include:

Get the ebook free!*
*proof of purchase required

- the book title
- the name of the store where you purchased it
- a screenshot or picture of your order/receipt number and your name
- your preference of file type: PDF (for desktop reading), ePub (for a phone/tablet, Kobo, or Nook), mobi (for Kindle)

A real person will respond to your email with your ebook attached. Please note this offer is only for copies bought for personal use and does not apply to school or library copies.

Thank you for supporting an independently owned publisher with your purchase!